101 More

Favorite

Play Therapy

Techniques

CHILD THERAPY SERIES

101 More Favorite Play Therapy Techniques

Edited by

Heidi Gerard Kaduson, Ph.D.
Charles E. Schaefer, Ph.D.

JASON ARONSON INC.
Northvale, New Jersey
London

This book was set in 10 pt. Palatino by Alabama Book Composition of Deatsville, AL, and printed and bound by Book-mart Press, Inc. of North Bergen, NJ.

Library of Congress Cataloging-in-Publication Data

Kaduson, Heidi.
  101 more favorite play therapy techniques / Heidi Gerard Kaduson, Charles E. Schaefer.
    p. cm.
  ISBN 0-7657-0299-1
    1. Play therapy. I. Title: One hundred and one more favorite play therapy
techniques. II. Title: One hundred and one more favorite play therapy techniques.
III. Schaefer, Charles E. IV. Title.

RJ505.P6 K25 2000
618.92'891653—dc21

                                                    00-56940

Printed in the United States of America on acid-free paper. For information and catalog write to Jason Aronson Inc., 230 Livingston Street, Northvale, NJ 07647-1731. Or visit our website: www.aronson.com

Dedicated to
all the children
who inspire us

CONTENTS

PREFACE

101 Favorite Play Therapy Techniques, published in 1997, has been considered a wonderful resource for practitioners, teachers, and students involved in conducting play therapy. *101 More Favorite Play Therapy Techniques* once again brings together new play therapy techniques by therapists across the world. We have invited leading authorities in play therapy to write either their favorite original technique or one that involves an innovative modification of a well-known procedure.

We have separated the techniques into seven categories for easy reference. Each author has also included a description and/or application of the technique to illustrate how the therapist used it in practice. The sections follow a grouping similar to the first volume: Storytelling Techniques, which illustrate the use of different methods to enhance verbalizations in children; Expressive Arts Techniques, which include the various mediums used in art to help children cope with psychological difficulties; Game Play Techniques, which use games to help children express themselves in a nonthreatening playful environment; Puppet Play Techniques, which help in the expression of conflicting emotions; Toy and Play Object Techniques, which illustrate the use of various toys and objects in playroom and how they can be useful in therapeutic play; Group Play Techniques, which include methods and play techniques to use in group settings; and Other Techniques, which are a group of miscellaneous techniques that are useful in many settings.

Psychiatrists, psychologists, social workers, nurses, child life specialists, therapeutic recreation specialists, teachers, and counselors at all levels of training and experience will find *101 More Favorite Play Therapy Techniques* very informative and clinically useful.

Heidi Gerard Kaduson
Charles E. Schaefer

CONTRIBUTORS

Debra Atchison, Ph.D., LPC, LMFT, RPT-S, Atchison Counseling Services, Montclair Road #151, Birmingham, AL 35210

Jeanine Austin, MSW, LCSW, 14 Cripple Creek Road, Howell, NJ 07731

Mark Berkowitz, MSW, RSW, CPT, Berkowitz Therapies Inc., 111 Pulford Avenue, Winnipeg, Manitoba, Canada R3L 1X8

Bernadette H. Beyer, MA, RPT-S, 20811 Kelly Road, Suite 103, Eastpointe, MI 48021

Terry Boyle, MA, Center for Child and Family Therapy, 7500 Old Military Road NE, Suite 103, Bremerton, WA 98311

Carol A. Brennan, Ph.D., The Phoenix Group, 3810 Osuna Road NE, Suite 2, Albuquerque, NM 87109

James M. Briesmeister, Ph.D., 54808 Alexis Court, Shelby Township, MI 48316

Richard Bromfield, Ph.D., 107 School Street, South Hamilton, MA 01982

Neil Cabe, LSW, LPCC, Act 1 Inc., 144 North Scranton Street, Ravenna OH 44266

Donna Cangelosi, Ph.D., RPT-S, 51 Upper Montclair Plaza, Suite 21, Upper Montclair, NJ 07043

Lois Carey, MSW, BCD, RPT-S, 254 South Boulevard, Upper Grandview, NY 10960

Jay Cerio, Ph.D., Professor of School Psychology, Alfred University, Saxon Drive, Alfred, NY 14802-1206

Jo Ann L. Cook, Ph.D., 1316 Palmetto Avenue, Winter Park, FL 32789

David A. Crenshaw, Ph.D., ABPP, 22 Mill Street, Rhinebeck, NY 12572

Joan Doherty, MA, NCC, Center for Integrative Psychotherapy, 1251 South Cedar Crest Boulevard, Suite 211-D, Allentown, PA 18102

Mary Ann Drake, Ph.D., RPT-S, and **David Drake,** MS, MFT, RPT-S, College Park Center, 1549 Coleman Avenue, Macon, GA 31201

Athena A. Drewes, PsyD, RPT-S, The Astor Home for Children, Residential Treatment Center, P.O. Box 5005, Rhinebeck, NY 12572

Marijane Fall, University of Southern Maine, 400 Bailey Hall, Gorham, ME 04038

Gregory Ford, BA, Center for Loss and Healing, 4880-A MacArthur Boulevard NW, Washington, DC 20007-1557

Sandra Foster, MA, 101 Worthington Street East, Suite 225, North Bay, Ontario P1B1G5

Diane E. Frey, Ph.D., RPT-S, Wright State University, 3640 Colonel Glenn Highway, Dayton, OH 45435-0001

Loretta Gallo-Lopez, Ph.D., Psychological Management Group, 15436 North Florida Avenue, Suite 102, Tampa, FL 33613

Brien D. Gilroy, LCSW, CACD, CEAP, 1926 Inverness Drive, Scotch Plains, NJ 07076

Hilda R. Glazer, Ed.D., Walden University, 155 Fifth Avenue South, Suite 200, Minneapolis, MN 55401

Herbert Goetze, Ph.D., Universitat Potsdam, Postfach 60 15 53, 14415 Potsdam, Germany

Paris Goodyear-Brown, LCSW, RPT, 121 McCall Street, Nashville, TN 37211

Tamra Greenberg, Ph.D., Center for Traumatic Stress in Children and Adolescents, Allegheny General Hospital, 4 Allegheny Center, 8th Floor, Pittsburgh, PA 15212

Douglas J. Griffin, MA, Wright State University, 3640 Colonel Glenn Highway, Dayton, OH 45435-0001

Mary L. Hammond-Newman, MA, LPC, The Heart Center Inc., 1578 Commercial Street SE, Salem, OR 97302

Judith Hart, LCSW, RPT, 18 Delaware Drive, East Brunswick, NJ 08816

Steve Harvey, Ph.D., ADTR, RDT, PRT/S, Naval Hospital, Sicily Italy, PSC 824 Box 507, FPO AE 09623

Deborah Armstrong Hickey, Ph.D., MFT, RPT-S, 230 Arabella Way, Oceanside, CA 92057

Linda B. Hunter, PhD., Director of Child and Family Services, 2773 South Ocean Boulevard #502, Palm Beach, FL 33480

William Walter Jenkins, Ph. D., 15233 North 62nd Place, Scottsdale, AZ 85254

Heidi Gerard Kaduson, Ph.D., RPT-S, Hights Professional Center, 951 Route 33, Monroe Township, NJ 08831

Michael Kantrowitz, Psy.D., Chrysalis Counseling Center, 30101 Town Center Drive, Suite 110, Laguna Niguel, CA 92677

Mary Margaret Kelly, Ph.D., Millersville University, P.O. Box 1002, Millersville, PA 17551-0302

Sally Kondziolka, P.O. Box 1593, Durango, CO 81302

Theresa A. Kruczek, Ph.D., Ball State University, Teachers College, Muncie, IN 47306-0585

Cynthia A. Langevin, Ph.D., RPT-S, 40 Pride Farm Road, Falmouth, ME 04105

Celia Linden, CSW-R, RPT-S, 395 Prospect Road, Chester, NY 10918

Sophie L. Lovinger, Ph.D., ABPP, 4 Carriage Lane, Charleston, SC 29407

Liana Lowenstein, MSW, CSW, 7 Broadway Avenue, Suite 601, Toronto, Ontario M4P 3C5

Berrell Mallery, Ph.D., 89 Bleecker Street, 3F, New York, NY 10012

Donna Marcum, Storyteller, Mount Carmel Hospice Evergreen Center, Columbus, OH 43215

Jamshid A. Marvasti, M.D., 63 East Center Street, Manchester, CT 06040

Victoria McGuinness, MA, LPC, CACIII, RPT-S, CPT-S, A Children's Therapy Place, PC, 31 North Tejon Street, Suite 200, Colorado Springs, CO 80903

Joyce Meagher, LPC, 10400 Eaton Place, Suite 110, Fairfax, VA 22030

Joyce C. Mills, Ph.D., P.O. Box 1030, Kekaha, Kauai Hawaii 96752

Myrna Minnis, Myrin Enterprises, P.O. Box 6211, Leawood, KA 66206

Dolores A. Mortimer, LMHC, RPT, 3137 Las Olas Drive, Dunedin, FL 34698

Emily Nickerson, CISW, RPT-S, 1620 East Entrada Once, Tuscon, AZ 85718

A. J. Palumbo, Ph.D., LICSW, CPTS, 18 Graham Street, Wareham, ME 02571

Harvey Payne, Psy.D., Greencastle Family Practice, 50 Eastern Avenue, Greencastle, PA 17225

Mary Anne Peabody, 47 Merrymeeting Road, Brunswick, ME 04011

Linda Perlis, LLB, MSW, CSW, The Coachhouse Clinic, 183 St. Clair Avenue West, Toronto, Ontario M4V 1P7

Roger D. Phillips, Ph.D., Research Director, Pinebrook Services for Children and Youth, 402 North Fulton Street, Allentown, PA 18102

Dee Ray, Ph.D., LPC, NCC, RPT-S, Dept. of Counseling, Texas A&M University, P.O. Box 3011, Commerce, TX 75429

Virginia Ryan, Ph.D., P-CPT, BAPT, 130 Victoria Avenue, Hull HU53DT, England

Charles E. Schaefer, Ph.D., RPT-S, Fairleigh Dickinson University, Center for Psychological Services, 139 Temple Avenue, Hackensack, NJ 07601

Janet Logan Schieffer, Ph.D., Assistant Professor of Counseling and Psychology in Education, University of South Dakota, 414 East Clark Street, Vermillion, SD 57069-2390

Nancy M. Schultz, 7311 Wildwood Drive, Takoma Park, MD 20912

Carla Sharp, Clinical Specialist in Child Psychiatric Nursing, 457 Iliwahi Loop, Kailua, Hawaii 96734

Cynthia Caparosa Sniscak, Good Hope Psychotherapists, 1035 Mumma Road, Wormleysburg, PA 17043

John Sommers-Flanagan, Ph.D., **and Rita Sommers-Flanagan,** Ph.D., 4100 Duncan Drive, Missoula, MT 59802

Douglas G. Sprague, California State University, Hayward, 25800 Carlos Bee Boulevard, Hayward, CA 94542-3076

Ellen M. Stickney, LISW, RPT-S, Child, Adolescent & Family Center, 1835 Miracle Mile Road, Springfield, OH 45501

Frances L. Strick, LPC, RPT-S, Camelot Counseling PC, 3542 Independence Drive, Birmingham, AL 35209

Erika L. Surkin, M.Ed., 363 Valleybrook Road, Chester Heights, PA 19017

Lois Theall, MA, LPC, Professional Counseling, P.O. Box 876, Youngsville, LA 70592

Barbara A. Turner, Ph.D., MFT, Waterfall Towers, Suite 208B, 2455 Bennett Valley Road, Santa Rosa, CA 95404

Mary Ann Valentino, Ph.D., 132 East North Avenue, Reedley, CA 93654-2533

Risë VanFleet, Ph.D., RPT-S, Family Enhancement & Play Therapy Center, P.O. Box 613, Boiling Springs, PA 17007

Deborah B. Vilas, MS, CCLS, Child Life Specialist, 7 East 88th Street, 4B, New York, NY 10128

Dotti Ward-Wimmer, RN, MA, RPT-S, Center for Loss and Healing, 4880-A MacArthur Boulevard NW, Washington, DC 20007-1557

Nancy Boyd Webb, Ph.D., RPT-S, Fordham University Graduate School of Social Work, 252 Hunter Avenue, Sleepy Hollow, NY 10591

Otto Weininger, Ph.D., C.Psych., Ontario Institute for Studies in Education, 252 Bloor Street West, Toronto, Ontario M5S1V6

Carol Whited, MA, LPC, RPT-S, 1330 Flannagan Street, Coos Bay, OR 97420

Marcie Fields Yeager, LCSW, RPT-S, Yeager & Yeager, 219 West Brentwood Boulevard, Lafayette, LA 70506

Section One

Storytelling Techniques

1

Garbage Bag Technique

Heidi Gerard Kaduson

INTRODUCTION

Children hold in a lot of their problems instead of communicating them to adults or even to other friends. Whether children are too frightened to reveal their problems or not consciously aware of what is bothering them, they feel bottled up with these feelings and have difficulty communicating and releasing their emotions. Several times parents might ask their children what the problem is, and many times the answer will be "nothing" or "I don't know." The garbage bag technique was developed to help children release problems they are holding on to and then to follow up with playing out those problems in order to find some resolution or solution.

RATIONALE

It is very therapeutic for children to focus on their problems and find solutions to those problems to help them cope with everyday issues in their life. With the implementation of the garbage bag technique, children write down things that bother them (at home and at school) and then focus on playing out the solutions to those problems. This empowers the children to feel more in control of their lives and be more responsible to themselves. Communication is very difficult for children to do through words. However, through the therapeutic power of play, children are able to see how to "tell" what their problems are and how to "fix" them so that they can be relieved of the pressure that holding in these problems could cause.

DESCRIPTION

Materials Needed

    Two brown sandwich bags

    Colored pencils or markers

    Twelve strips of paper to write problems on

Process

The therapist introduces the technique by giving the child the paper bag to draw anything the child wants to draw on it. The therapist also draws on his/her own bag. While the drawing is taking place, the therapist talks about "garbage" in the following manner:

> You know what garbage is? It's that stuff you put in the garbage can when you are done with it. It's stuff that turns green in the back of the refrigerator when it's been left there too long. You know how things grow on top of it and it looks all yucky?

The therapist continues to do descriptors of garbage until the child hooks on to the image and is going along with the comments of the therapist. Once that is accomplished, the therapist continues:

> Well, what if all the garbage we threw out in the garbage cans was never picked up? What if weeks and weeks and months and months of garbage were left in your home? Then there wouldn't be any place to walk or sit, and we would have to carry our

garbage around wherever we went. We'd have to take it to school, to birthday parties, to bed with us, and we would never get rid of the garbage. Well, we keep garbage inside of ourselves as well. Things that bother us. Things that we can't stop thinking about. Stuff like that. So, let's finish drawing on our bag, and then I will give you six pieces of paper so that we can each write down six pieces of our own personal garbage and put them in our garbage bags. Let's start with something from home. Something that really bothers you that you can write on your piece of paper.

The therapist writes down a problem that s/he knows the child is having and says what is being written. This will guide the child on how to start putting his/her own "garbage" down on paper as well. After three problems have been written about by the child, the therapist guides the child to write things about school.

Now that we each have three pieces of garbage from home, let's write three pieces of garbage that we might feel at school.

Once again the therapist starts writing one and leads the child to do the same.

Now we'll close up these garbage bags and leave them closed until next time. Then you can pick from either garbage bag, and we will play out what we could do about that garbage.

The therapist puts the bags away. The next session starts with the child picking out one piece of garbage to play out in miniatures or in role play. The therapist should be prepared to play out any of the items written in the previous session. If there aren't the appropriate miniature toys to play out the "garbage," then the therapist should provide the child with clay so that s/he can make whatever is necessary to bring the play session as close to reality as the child chooses. Many times the child will come up with a solution to the problem or "garbage," but sometimes the therapist will have to be more directive and intervene with some suggestions for the miniatures or in role play. The therapist should not directly relate the problem to the child once the play begins. Keeping everything in the third person is important to allow the child to have enough distance from the problem to help solve it.

APPLICATION

The garbage bag technique can be used with children ages 4 through 16. It can be used with clients who have trouble verbalizing their problems in talk therapy. By allowing the "garbage" to be written down, the children can externalize their problems and relieve the pressure inherent in holding on to problems.

Samantha was a 6-year-old girl referred for treatment of anxiety. She had difficulty falling asleep at night, and she was extremely shy in school, which resulted in her not participating in class. Her parents and teachers were concerned about her behavior, as she was chewing on her clothing, biting her nails incessantly, and withdrawing from friendships. Samantha could never communicate to her parents or teachers what was bothering her. When she entered therapy, she was very reserved and self-conscious. The garbage bag technique was introduced, and she immediately understood the "garbage" metaphor. When she was asked what she would do if she had to walk around with her garbage every day, she commented that she would look like the Hunchback of Notre Dame. As the therapist started to print out "garbage" by writing, "I hate when I'm called on in class," Samantha followed with "I feel stupid when I don't know the answers." Two other school-based issues were reported and written by Samantha: "I don't like working in groups," and "My friends think they are smarter than me." When the therapist initiated home issues by writing "I can't fall asleep at night," Samantha reported, "I hate having bad dreams." The two other issues for Samantha were "I hate when my parents fight" and "My sister is always getting more attention than me."

The following session, Samantha picked out a piece of her garbage from her own bag. She had the therapist read it. "I feel stupid when I don't know the answers." The play began with Playmobile's school. She set up everything just the way her class was set up. She played the role of the students and gave the role of the teacher to the therapist. In her play it was clear that she felt that other students were smarter than she, and the teacher had to modify the students' behavior. With some cognitive restructuring, Samantha was able to play out a resolution to the problem by stating that her doll was smart at a lot of things, and not knowing the answer was not being stupid.

During the rest of the therapy, a problem a week was played out, and in most instances Samantha was able to solve her own problems. She began to improve behaviorally, joining in class situations, asking for play dates, and showing more assertive behavior.

2

TV Show Storyboard

Loretta Gallo-Lopez

INTRODUCTION

Most children are resistant to openly discussing and revealing their feelings about disturbing issues or events. Children who have experienced trauma are especially cautious and guarded in therapy, often finding it difficult to trust adults. However, these children have been found to respond positively to play and expressive therapy techniques. The TV show storyboard technique, which I present to children as "The _____ Show" (child fills in the blank), provides traumatized children with a fun, nonthreatening way to explore significant issues.

RATIONALE

By utilizing strategies that provide emotional distance as well as structure, the threatening nature of traumatic events can be reduced. The TV show storyboard offers children and adolescents a safe vehicle for confronting these issues. Children connect easily to the TV show theme, and older children and young adolescents tend to see this activity as more age appropriate, and they therefore offer less resistance.

8

DESCRIPTION

Prior to the session, the therapist prepares the storyboards. The boards can be computer generated or drawn by hand. Blank forms can be photocopied to provide a ready supply. To create the original, fold a sheet of white, 8½ × 11" paper in half horizontally and then into three columns vertically, creating six equal squares. In each square draw a simple TV set (a square with small circles along the bottom and a "V" to represent an antenna on the top).

At the start of the session the therapist provides the child with several storyboard sheets, pencils, and markers. The therapist explains to the child that they will be creating the story for a pretend TV show, using words and pictures on the storyboard. Next, the therapist asks the child to pick a title for the show by filling in the blank in "The _____ Show." Most children enjoy naming the show after themselves, for example, "The Emily Show" or "The Nick Show." Other children might want to make up a purely fictional title. The title should be written in the first TV with a drawing to accompany it. After the show is titled, story development begins. The therapist may need to guide the activity if the child is doing it for the first time. In the second TV, the therapist can help to introduce the show to follow by writing something like "Hello, ladies and gentlemen! Welcome to the Emily Show. In today's episode . . ." The child should then fill in the blank. Some children will be able to create stories on their own from this point, with the therapist having to offer little more than "And what happens next?" or "How will the story end?" Other children may need the therapist to help the process along by providing a story idea such as, "Let's make up a story about a bully." With children or adolescents who have difficulty with reading or writing, the therapist should offer to write in the words so the child does not experience anxiety related to that aspect of the activity. Children who are especially resistant or hesitant might respond well to a fill-in-the-blank type of story, in which the therapist develops the story line based on issues or concerns of the child. She begins the sentence in each TV and asks the child to fill in the blank. An example follows:

The child is an 11-year-old who is bullied and fearful in his first year of middle school.

TV 1: The <u>Andy</u> Show.

TV 2: Welcome, ladies and gentlemen to the Andy Show! In tonight's episode, Andy takes a trip to a distant, unknown planet and meets <u>strange aliens bigger and stronger than him.</u>

TV 3: The aliens steal Andy's <u>bravery</u> and Andy feels really <u>miserable.</u>

TV 4: Andy wishes he could <u>destroy</u> the aliens but <u>he's too scared.</u>

TV 5: So in a loud voice he tells the aliens <u>"Go away and leave me alone!!"</u>

TV 6: Finally <u>some of the aliens start to be friendly to him and send the bad aliens away to another planet.</u>

TV 7: Join us next week when <u>Andy battles the king of the apes.</u>

When the story is complete the therapist may want to provide interpretations for the child or might focus instead on the child's emotional response to the story. The stories can also be used as the basis for role playing and can involve audio- or videotaping.

APPLICATION

I have found the TV show storyboard technique to be effective with both younger children and adolescents. Adolescents are more willing to engage in this type of activity than in some other play therapy techniques that they might perceive to be too babyish. Both young and older children seem to quickly connect to the TV theme. Although "The _____ Show" is a fun and helpful technique for most children, it is especially valuable for those children who have experienced some form of trauma or are particularly resistant in treatment. It provides the emotional distance necessary for comfort to increase and trust to be established, while providing a somewhat structured, boundaried format to enhance feelings of safety and security.

3

Candie Canary's New Home: A Bibliotherapeutic Intervention for Children in Group Home, Residential Treatment, and Shelter

Jeanine Austin

INTRODUCTION

I developed this technique because I found gaps in the play therapy literature regarding children in group home, residential treatment, and shelter settings—an often overlooked population. Certainly, fewer children are in these types of settings than in the foster care system. Because the issues in foster care settings are so different from group, shelter, and residential treatment issues, this technique addresses the specific characteristics of these settings, even though many children in these settings have previously been in several foster care settings. These children are often the most traumatized of all children, resulting in the need for specialized care. Clinical directors, therapists, and child care workers from these settings often find themselves overwhelmed by the myriad therapeutic and case management needs of these children. This technique provides the opportunity to be proactive in reaching out to these children.

RATIONALE

Bibliotherapeutic techniques such as this one (see Resource) are nonthreatening interventions that can provide a coping model for the child. They can help the child feel less alone and isolated, as the child can identify with a character's similar struggle and ultimate mastery over challenging or traumatizing events and circumstances. Because of the educational component of "Candie Canary's New Home," the child is helped to acclimate to his or her environment. Questions are answered, and latent fears may be addressed and extinguished. Because of complex multidimensional features of congregate care, children may become less overwhelmed and less traumatized in dealing with their current situation. This technique can be utilized in a one-on-one situation with a caring adult or in group therapy, particularly in the beginning "forming" stage of a group when trust is not yet developed and direct discussion with group participants may be too threatening. This technique can also introduce situational events to an individual or group without the facilitator having to do it in a direct manner, which may provide a certain comfort level to the child. Storybooks with interesting characters such as "Candie Canary" may be a springboard into other therapeutic interventions such as dramatic play, art therapy, puppet play, and sand tray play. This technique can be used to hone a skill, create a play vignette, or master a situation.

A journal with questions surrounding acclimation provided in the back of the storybook can be used to address issues to a group of resident children or with individual resident children. Written, verbal, or art picture responses from children can be useful in creating a treatment plan.

DESCRIPTION

Candie Canary's New Home is a book specifically designed for children of developmental ages 4 or 5 to 11 to address and provide a coping and acclimation model for the very unique issues children face in group home settings. Candie Canary, the story's heroine, is dealt many of the challenges that are specific to group home, residential treatment, and shelter settings.

Some of the challenges and concepts Candie Canary is introduced to that are specific to her new home are leaving her foster care setting with her social worker, Shelley Stork, for a very different kind of home; feeling bad because she thought she "failed" her foster home; leaving a home with other canaries (foster or biological home) to be with other types of animals (group, shelter, or residential treating setting); being introduced to many care animals and peer animals of a different type that she has negative preconceived notions about (dealing with ethnic differences, different personalities, and her own biases); being whisked off to the nurse for medical care upon arrival; being introduced to shift changes (three shifts of animal caregivers); being introduced to the idea of recreational activities and the recreation coordinator; being introduced to the concept of time-out/away; developing conflict resolution skills and learning about behavioral expectations; doing chores; being introduced to unfamiliar food; dealing with another animal's transition to a new setting; dealing with a bed-wetting incident and other nighttime issues; learning about the token economy system and token store; dealing with bath time; adjusting to a roommate; being introduced to court issues and legal personnel; adapting to a new school setting; being teased; meeting a therapist; and going to play therapy.

The journal section of the book can be utilized to address specific issues related to the setting in an individual or group session. The play therapist should help the child keep the book safe and private.

APPLICATION

Candie Canary's New Home can be read to or with children who are acclimating to a group home, shelter, or residential treatment setting or who are currently residing in such a setting. Many clinicians are using the book in myriad creative ways. Some are reading a small section of the book to the child and using it to inform sand tray and dramatic play exercises. Others are using the topic area index to focus in a target area such as getting used to different foods, making puppets, writing poetry, and drawing pictures. The journal portion of the book can be used by having a child write down responses, draw pictures in response to questions, dictate responses, or by asking the journal's questions to spark discussion in group therapy.

For Use by a County Case Manager

The book can be read by the case manager to the child before and after transition. It may be utilized as transitional object. *Put the child's name on the book*. Areas of fear or confusion can be targeted by utilizing the topic area index (pages 62 and 63). Information can be relayed to the child's therapist to assist with creating a treatment plan.

For Use by a Therapist in Individual Work

The book can be used by a therapist to help prepare the child for the new setting he is moving to. Areas of fear or confusion can be targeted by utilizing the topic area index. The book can then be used immediately upon the child's arrival at the new setting. The child can read it to the therapist or the therapist can read it to the child. Asking questions such as "Is that how you feel?" and "Did that happen to you?" may be appropriate when the child is ready.

The book can also be given to a child who is already residing in a congregate care setting because it provides a coping model and a story line that children can identify with, demonstrating to them that they are not alone and they are not bad. *Candie Canary's New Home* is a legitimate bibliotherapeutic intervention to identify by name on the child's treatment plan. It provides (1) a coping model, (2) a social interaction model, (3) a conflict resolution model, (4) a model of a milieu that can help the child become familiarized with expectations and norms, and (5) a first step in building the therapeutic relationship and basic trust (because the therapist demonstrates an understanding about the child's current situation).

The book helps the child to acclimate to new and somewhat complex concepts such as token economy systems, time-away, shift changes, admissions and terminations of other children, therapy, peer interaction expectations, tolerance of those from other cultures, and structuring of daily activities.

The journal section of the book can be completed over time in the weeks and months following admission, and can be an excellent indicator of how the child is progressing. For example, can the child identify any of his/her own treatment goals?

In many group home settings, it is very difficult for the child to have true ownership of anything. The book could prove to be an item of that nature. It might help if each child had his/her own, so that stealing would be less tempting, or the books could be kept safe by the therapists.

Target area pages could be copied and then colored by the child. Pictures could be reinforced with card stock, and popsicle sticks/tongue depressors or straws could be taped on the back to make a puppet. The puppet animal character can talk about fears or ask questions. Copied pictures or animal figurines or a similar type could be used for sand play.

Children can take on different roles, assuming each character. "What does it feel like to be Polly Platypus when she had time-away?" "What would you do if you were Sung Snake and your friend Angel Albatross moved away?" The child's dramatic play could also be audio- or videotaped (a signed release may be required).

For Use by the Therapist in Group Therapy

The book also works very well with groups of children. Since bibliotherapy is a very nonthreatening activity, the book is highly appropriate in the initial stages of group therapy work when interactive activities may be too threatening before trust between group members has formed. The journal section of the workbook can be used for discussion or debriefing following a relevant activity. This is an excellent indicator of how the group is progressing. Can the group name any positive aspects of the setting? *This information can be given to the executive, clinical, and program directors, if appropriate.*

Each child could assume the role of a character in the book. Allow each child to try on different types of characters. Have the children use the characters to devise different scripts. Change the outcome. What happens then? Make a situation more complex. What roles did the children gravitate to, and why? It's fun to have the children construct a set or be the director.

Copied pictures or animals figurines of similar type could be used for sand tray play. Put several sand trays together. What unfolds between characters? Consider taking Polaroid pictures of the trays to give to each child.

For Use by Clinical Directors

Rather than buying a welcoming gift for a transitioning child that could be pilfered or broken, a therapeutic book such as "Candie Canary's New Home" can help a child successfully acclimate to the new setting. The book can also be given to children who are already residing in the setting because it provides a coping model and provides a story line that children can identify with.

Consider asking a philanthropic group to donate books. In calculating the number of books needed, consider ordering both books for all children already in placement and for new children who will arrive in the future. Each therapist, nursing station, program, and clinical and executive director should also have copies, as should the board of directors, to help them better understand the treatment goals and challenges children face and the therapeutic milieu you are creating daily.

An excellent use of the book is to make copies available for training sessions with child care workers. The animals caregivers in the book provide an excellent model in terms of staff appropriateness, patience, and technique.

If readers have ideas for creative uses for the book, please contact Jeanine Austin at: www.geocities.com/Heartland/Pointe/8518/, jeanine austin@juno.com, or (732) 730-0270. Feedback is welcomed and appreciated.

Resource

Candie Canary's New Home: A Trilingual Book and Journal in English, Spanish and Vietnamese for Children Transitioning into or Residing in Residential Treatment, Shelter, or Group Home Settings (ISBN: 1-890961-04-3) by Jeanine Austin, BSW, MSW, LCSW, illustrations by Will Duke, Spanish translations by Yolie Munoz and Katty Romero, MSW, Vietnamese translations by Jackie Le, MA.

Book Ordering Information:
  Call: The Carol Cole Center (714) 536-0305
  Write: Carol Cole, LCSW, 20042 Beach Blvd., Suite 130, Huntington Beach, CA 92648. $15. Copy, CA res.+ state tax (15.+ copies 20% discount) s&h $5. Per individual order in US—MC/VISA

4

Knights and Dragons

Judith Hart

INTRODUCTION

A few years ago I found that several of the children I was working with had been referred because of social difficulties. They were teased and picked on by peers.These children felt like victims and could see no way that they could have a part in changing their situations. They would listen to my suggestions, and then "Yes, but . . ." me, explaining why these suggestions couldn't possibly work. They did well in social skills groups, where each member's behavior was under adult scrutiny, but they couldn't transfer skills to the outside world—the playground. I invented this game to play with these children, in the hope that it would inspire them to try new things, think optimistically, and problem solve on their own.

RATIONALE

This technique is empowering. It shows kids that if they take the time to think things through, they can find a way of coping with difficulties and handling others without having to physically fight. It teaches them that you don't have to be big or strong in order to come out a winner. Also, it has a fairy tale quality about it. Since almost every child is familiar with some fairy tales, they can relate to this game and feel comfortable with it. Each child's uniqueness is fostered, there is no right or wrong solution, and the child can take the game as far as his imagination permits.

DESCRIPTION

The therapist tells the child that they will be playing a game using imagination:

> We are both brave knights who have been sent on an important mission by the King. We must venture into a deep, dark forest, where we might meet dragons, or monsters, or have to overcome dangerous obstacles. We must rescue the princess. We get to give each other certain objects to help us. You give me what you think might help, and I give you what I think might help. We each get three things. We are allowed to trade with each other, or borrow from each other. Then we make up the monsters or obstacles for each other to overcome.

I usually give the child items such as a rope, a bottle of oil, a big black blanket, or an enchanted wand. The child at first often gives me a sword, a knife, an ax, a bludgeon. I model creative problem solving. For example, when confronted by a huge, metallic monster, which can't be pierced by a sword or knife, I suggest spilling a puddle of oil in his path, so that he slips and falls and can't get up. I will sometimes use one of the weapons a child has assigned to me and show a creative, nonviolent way to get over, under, or around a pitfall. For example, I might use a sword to cut branches and use them to construct a tower from which I can swing on a rope (borrowed from the child) over the bottomless well. This technique also encourages cooperation.

You can change and structure the game to suit the participant. For instance, if I were playing with a girl who is really into gender roles, I would change the knights to princesses or maidens, and have the mission be to rescue a puppy or a good fairy. As children play this game from session to session, they become more creative with the things they give me—in one instance an "invisibility cloak" and a wig.

One 8-year-old boy did especially well with this game. He had been born with a heart defect, and needed surgery to repair it when he was just a few weeks old. After surgery, he had a blood clot, which caused a stroke, and he was left with impaired vision and no peripheral vision. This condition made it very hard for him to participate in sports, since he was prone to be hit in the face, being unable to see the ball or another player coming at him from the side. When he first started coming to therapy, he was convinced his situation was hopeless and that kids just didn't like him. At first he resisted playing, preferring, he said, to "just talk about my problems." But I persisted, and finally he agreed to try. He began to enjoy the game, and after several sessions of playing, he decided to move the game to the sand tray, and act it out with small figures and animals, legos, and other objects. At school he began asking classmates to play with him at recess, suggesting imaginative games instead of sports, and he found friends willing to do this. His outlook became more positive and he stopped dwelling on his disability.

This game empowers kids who aren't athletic or physically powerful; it gives them the ability to conquer their own dragons in their head, and to know they have options.

APPLICATION

This technique may be applied in cases with children who are shy, withdrawn, pessimistic, and physically disabled. Children who are being bullied might especially be able to transfer what they learn from the game about coping skills to real life, and become more optimistic and confident.

One of the advantages of this game is that it requires no supplies. Also, it can be played anywhere. Therapists who need to travel to their clients, who move from one location to another, or who have limited space can use this game very effectively. The game can be expanded to whatever level the therapist wishes to take it—to the sand tray, for example. It can also be played on a very rudimentary homemade board, picking cards to choose the objects to use on the mission. It can be a physically active game, complete with dress-up costumes. The therapist can tailor the game to fit the client.

5

Take-Home Stories from the Playroom

Mary Margaret Kelly

INTRODUCTION

I learned this technique from a 6-year-old child with whom I had recently started therapy. She had just been placed in an emergency foster home following hospital treatment for injuries stemming from parental physical abuse. In a late-night phone call, her foster mother requested my assistance in helping the child to settle down and go to sleep in the new foster home. After some discussion the child indicated that what she needed was a bedtime story. Together we generated a "good-enough" story and shared the story with the foster mother who retold the story to encourage the child to get to sleep.

RATIONALE

Many children referred for therapy have a history of physical, sexual, or emotional trauma, or are attempting to cope with life circumstances that seem insurmountable. Storytelling is widely recognized as facilitating mastery of trauma, and it can be woven into a play therapy context by using play figures that are significant to the child. Frequently in play, children assign aspects of their own personality and situation onto certain play figures in the therapy room. In fact, much of play therapy involves the child telling the therapist various stories about these figures.

If a traumatized child is experiencing anxiety, sleep difficulties, and inability to comfort himself or find comfort in his environment, soothing "take-home" stories can be developed including the characters and scripts that unfold in the play session.

DESCRIPTION

This technique typically is used toward the end of the therapy session. After the child's play has wound down, the therapist might elect to ask the child if she would like to join the therapist in creating a story that the child could take home. Stories unfold in such a wide variety of ways that no standardized procedures are routinely applied. Nevertheless, the following guidelines consistently meet with considerable success:

1. The child selects which play character is central to the plot. He may be encouraged to indicate why he selected that particular character.

2. The child selects a theme for the story. The theme usually emanates from the character: "Let's make a story about that little dinosaur whose voice isn't loud enough"; "This story will be about the teddy bear who flew to Mars in this space ship."

3. The therapist tells a brief story about the character, elaborating on themes developed in the child's play. The therapist avoids chaotic or troubling themes that would not easily be resolved within the story. Continuing the themes in guideline 2, above, "A soft voice makes it really hard to be heard by others"; "On a trip to Mars the teddy bear might wonder what he will find there and he might feel a little homesick, too."

4. The therapist introduces resolution and hopefulness into the story by commenting on positive attributes of the characters and describing how these characteristics impact the characters'

environment: "The dinosaur discovered that if he sat straight up on his hind feet and took a deep breath, his voice became stronger"; "The teddy bear had very curious eyes and he learned all about the stars until he could use the stars to guide him to go whenever he wanted to go."

5. The therapist asks the child to think about what the character had within him to make the resolution of the story possible. The therapist and child can discuss the child's impressions of the story during the current as well as subsequent sessions. Later the therapist and child might identify qualities in the character that resemble some of the child's qualities: "That dinosaur had a strong back bone to sit up like that. Having a strong back bone means . . ."; "That teddy bear was just about the most curious teddy bear, just like me."

APPLICATION

This type of storytelling is helpful to children in time-limited therapy who have trouble soothing or consoling themselves due to inadequate family and social support, incapacitating trauma, or constitutional inability to tolerate anxiety. These stories can be adapted for use as a bedtime story, or a story the child shares with his family to stimulate communication. They can be used as growth-enhancing puzzle stories (e.g., the therapist says, "Next week I want you to tell me all your guesses about how the dinosaur got himself to stand up so tall"). They can also be used at termination to consolidate learning that transpired during therapy. Weekly stories might provide the child with the opportunity to continue the growth and healing process between visits to the playroom.

This technique is not appropriate in most long-term, nondirective play therapy because therapist generation of closure-producing stories about the child's play characters is likely to intrude and interfere with the child's spontaneous efforts at mastery.

6

Super Me!

Emily Nickerson

INTRODUCTION

This technique was developed as a way to facilitate the termination process for children between the ages of 4 and 9. Over a three- to four-week period, depending on the therapist's evaluation, the child and therapist assess the gains that have been made and set future goals by creating the child's own superhero. This can be introduced to the child as, "If you were going to make up a story about a superhero what would he/she be like? What kinds of superpowers would your hero have?"

RATIONALE

Concrete visualization and guided imagery aid a child in internalizing the new perception of gains made in therapy and awareness of the child's own strengths and future goals. The storytelling, using both the child and the enhanced image or superhero, encourages the process of creating a rich internal life, visualizing successes and growing self-confidence. The therapist encourages the child to continue using this technique on his/her own as this acts as a bridge between the therapist's work with the child and the child's own impetus to grow and change.

DESCRIPTION

The therapist has on hand outline drawings of male and female figures. Using outlines of animated paper dolls such as Disney figures works well. The body shapes are not obviously adult, which facilitates the child's identification with the hero when the child begins to draw and define the character visually.

Week 1

Therapist and child talk about qualities that the child would give to a superhero. This is a way for the therapist to introduce gains that the child has made and goals that he/she wants to set for the future. Also the therapist can assess the child's projection of needs and possible anxieties. There will be a great variety here according to personality and needs:

> "My hero can read a thousand books a day." (Use child's reading interest to encourage bibliotherapy on his/her own or with parent.)

> "My hero is very, very, very strong." (Talk about different kinds of strength and how child has grown as therapy progressed.)

> "My hero can be invisible." (Talk about reasons someone might not want to be seen.)

Week 2

Therapist and child begin to plan the wardrobe and equipment that the superhero will have. At this point when the child declares the hero will have a certain type of weapon or defense mechanism, the therapist can bring up the child's skills that solve the same or similar problems. The child chooses his/her favorite colors for the hero's costume and with help from the therapist picks a name for his superperson. It is a good idea to incorporate some form of the child's name or some aspect of the child in the hero's name. At the beginning of therapy I use a name book to give the child the meaning of his/her name. In the case where the child has an invented name or very unusual one, then the child chooses the meaning for the name. At this point the child goes back to this meaning and with guidance from the therapist names his/her superhero.

Week 3

The therapist brings several copies of the outline figure as well as washable markers, glue stick, glitter, feathers, buttons, and whatever the past discussions suggest as possible enhancement of the figure. Using whatever materials are at hand, the child creates his/her superhero, and titles the drawing with the name chosen. The therapist then makes up a story about the child and the superhero solving an appropriate problem together. These activities can be done in one or two sessions, according to the therapist's discretion. At the end of the last session the child is allowed to take the drawing home.

APPLICATION

This activity provides an opportunity for the child and therapist to focus on both gains and goals in a metaphorical manner. The use of the child's own hero figure works as a transition object for the child when terminating therapy. The child has assessed his/her progress and skills and has a metaphor of this for support as the child leaves therapy. In this way a sense of the therapist and the process supports continued progress.

The parent can be incorporated into this project by explaining to the parent how the hero figure will help the child. It is important that the parent understand that this hero figure may not be used for future discipline or punishment but only to assist the child in problem solving as the need arises.

This process is in itself a ritual of closing. The story the therapist tells (the child can add to this or make up one individually if desired) and the completed superhero figure represent the therapy experience and allow the child to leave therapy with a tangible reminder of accomplishments.

7

Metaphorical Stories

Herbert Goetze

INTRODUCTION

This technique uses metaphorical stories embedded in play therapy. Mills and Crowley (1986) and Lankton and Lankton (1979) discuss the historical background and rationale for using metaphorical stories in play therapy.

RATIONALE

Psychodynamic therapies stress the importance of the unconscious. Symptoms are seen as external manifestations of internal disturbances that usually cannot be reached by conscious efforts. In the Freudian context, clients are led back to traumatic incidents in early childhood for the purpose of bringing those experiences into the conscious mind. In cognitive terms the client is helped to gain new interpretations of those events. C.G. Jung contributed his idea of the collective unconscious and the (inherited) archetype (e.g., animus). Another theoretical approach is hypnotherapy, founded by Milton Erickson. In Erickson's view, symptoms are expressions of the unconscious. The difference between Erickson's and the more traditional psychodynamic views is that symptoms are seen not only in their diagnostical function but also as part of a solution to the problem. Thus, the unconscious expresses blockades, symbolically or metaphorically, to the outer world by presenting symptoms. At the same time, the client's inner resources and potential become apparent. Thus, symptoms become manifestations of an untold story. It is the task of the therapist to facilitate exposing the client's story. Fairy tales are excellent tools, in working with children, for expressing and resolving fundamental conflicts. Themes of despair, danger, and threat are depicted in an imaginary way to lead to a positive outcome. It is also possible to make up stories to facilitate the child's spontaneous problem-solving processes.

What a child talks about in therapy and how he plays seem to be metaphors for the problems that require therapy. Metaphors have been used in play therapy from the beginning of Melanie Klein's and Anna Freud's work. Virginia Axline's (1947) idea of recognizing and reflecting the child's feelings gains new meaning by including metaphors in play therapy. While client-centered therapy focuses on the reflection of the client's here-and-now expressions, which are put into language, the inclusion of metaphors raises therapeutic exchanges to a different level. The therapist tells metaphorical stories, which are constructed to be analogous to the child's problem. In this way it is easier for the child to gain a deeper understanding of his problem than in the simple reflection technique. Often an understanding is reached that could not be achieved by the reflection of feelings, because reflections would not fit the child's thinking and language abilities.

One major concern in play therapy is to encounter the child in his world. If metaphors are included in play therapy, this concern is met in a very special way. In explaining the effectiveness of therapeutic metaphors (Mills and Crowley 1986), one can turn to both a conscious and an unconscious level. The conscious level is the text sequence, which affects the superficial course of the story; an unhappy protagonist experiencing or suffering conflicts is introduced. More characters enter the stage with whom he is in either friendly or hostile contact. The protagonist experiences life and eventually enters a dramatic problem situation that threatens him. By activating all available powers and potentials, he will solve this problem. He sees himself in a different and more favorable light, recognizing his new abilities, and is socially awarded by his peers.

The unconscious level may be working spontaneously while the child listens to the textual level and scans the story for personal hidden meanings. Unconscious processes are supported by suggestions that are interspersed in the text, a practice commonly used in hypnotherapy. Such suggestive remarks are directed toward the child in a somewhat hidden way. They are merely slipped into the thoughts of the characters (e.g., "Then he was reminded of something he had learned earlier . . ."). By way of voice change in such text sections, the suggestive effect is deepened.

DESCRIPTION

While Gordon (1978) differentiates three steps for the construction of metaphorical stories—(1) collection of information, (2) formation of a metaphor, and (3) conversion into a linguistic mode—Mills and Crowley (1986) have developed six steps:

1. *Presentation of a protagonist and a metaphorical conflict*: A protagonist, for example, an animal, experiences conditions of conflict that are similar to those of the client. The protagonist lives through typical conflict stages. If, for example, the problem deals with social exclusion, some typical situations are outlined in which the protagonist is laughed at, rejected, and isolated. The protagonist's existential dilemma is described concisely and with simple words.

2. *Appearance of other characters*: New participants who act as friends or opponents appear in the unfolding story, and they get in closer touch with the protagonist. Psychologically, the description and the activation of the client's unconscious processes and inner resources are dealt with in this second step. Such processes are personified and thus made conscious to the client on a surface level. Exaggerations are used as linguistic means.

3. *Acquisition of abilities and the making of learner experiences (parallel learning situations)*: The protagonist copes with everyday life situations. He learns skills that will be extremely useful to him later. Psychologically, development with its slowly unfolding personal potentials is described.

4. *Metaphorical crisis*: The protagonist lives through and survives one of several situations or life crises. He overcomes the crisis by using the skills he has learned before (step 3). Psychologically, the process of discovery and the use of one's own potential becomes important. The client is made aware of how to overcome a crisis by the means available to him.

5. *New identification*: After getting over a major crisis, the protagonist reaches his higher goal. His journey has a happy ending. Since he has overcome the crisis, he finds a new identity for himself. Psychologically, this step deals with the everlasting human issue of how to overcome an existential crisis and how to have a successful transition to a higher self.

6. *Celebrations*: The characters of the story celebrate the protagonist's success. Psychologically, the newly gained positive self-esteem is reinforced by others.

Everyday life events of the child form the raw material of the story. On the textual level, the analogue circumstances to life and to the problem of the child are to be built up. Analogue incidents, relationships, and developments are constructed that lead to the understanding that the previous solutions of problems won't help the protagonist (and the child) any further. To construct fitting analogue conditions in the story, a diagnostic clarification of the actual experiences, strains, and circumstances has to be made. The basic metaphor finally chosen, for example, a bird's nest, a pirate ship, a space ship, the zoo, depends on the diagnostic data. If a child has a favorite animal, for example, a penguin, the story could involve a family of penguins. But if the child has fears of flying or swimming, the metaphor of a space ship or a school of fish should not be used. Hobbies, journeys, friends, memories, and other positive experiences are sources that can be explored by the child. These personal recollections offer useful background for a story that evokes the child's inner resources.

The linguistic transformation facilitates the spontaneous search of the child for a personal meaning the story might contain for him. A few linguistic factors have proven to be helpful:

- Using nonspecific, vague language: This principle makes it easy for the child to transform story events to his situation; a detailed description of unimportant specific details (who, how, what, where, when) may prevent an identification with persons and actions.

- Describing actions in a spare, simple, and lively way.

- Using descriptive terms: For example, instead of "He trusted him," saying, "He put great faith in him."

- Including sensual experiences: The story should contain visual, aural, and kinesthetic experiences of the protagonist to make subconscious processes therapeutically effective. Let's look at a sentence of a text that doesn't contain sensual experiences: "He threw the ball into the street, where it caused damage, and he was afraid of the consequences." The corresponding excerpt with the inclusion of sensual experience would be different: "He threw the ball with great strength into the air (kinesthetic); he saw it flying in a curve (visual); he heard it swoosh in the air; then he heard it land with a thud on the ground (aural); he ran to that spot (kinesthetic); he glanced (visual) at the ball that was now lying in the gutter, although it had smashed a headlight on a car (kinesthetic), and he could already hear (aural) the balling out he would get; in fact, he could see (visual) his father already coming toward him."

APPLICATION

For nearly all play therapy cases and conflicts, metaphorical stories can be applied. There are several references in the literature that prove this is not mere speculation but empirically provable. Although the field of metaphors does not stand up to empirical research methodology, with its rigorous criteria and experimental rules to prove effectiveness, some encouraging results have been found (Mills and Crowley 1986). Some reports show that metaphorical stories have been successfully used for the following problems: child abuse, enuresis, hospitalization, minimal brain damage, attention-deficit/hyperactivity disorder, phobias, sleep problems, sexual abuse, neglect, and low self-esteem. Alexandra J. Rogers (1982) used metaphors in treating bed-wetters.

I used metaphorical stories with institutionalized 8-year-old Ronny, about whom it was impossible to get diagnostic information. By his playing out scenes with two dinosaurs, I suspected he was sexually harassed by his older brother, who used to live in the same institution. My goal during this initial therapy phase was to show Ronny that this is a safe environment for him to open up in. Here is the story I made up for him (which was originally accompanied by pictures showing six scenes).

The Story of Tommy and Timmy

This story happened a long time ago when dinosaurs populated the earth. There was a dinosaur named Tommy. He was a bright, handsome dinosaur. He loved to dance around, to sing, to jump, and to play. At times, he was also a little sad because years ago he had lost his parents during an earthquake. This sadness did not last long because he was not alone. People who lived around him liked him very much. One of them loved him dearly and this was his older brother Timmy. Tommy and Timmy lived together in a cavern, ate together from the trees, and played together. Tommy, the handsome, brave dinosaur, felt very close to Timmy.

But you know how brothers are. Often things did not go well between them. Tommy and Timmy would quarrel, fight, and spit at each other. Every time a battle occurred, they would turn into dragon dinosaurs with roaring, smoke blowing, spitting, and terrible fighting. Tommy was smaller, and that's why Timmy was able to put him down. Poor Tommy! It is not a nice feeling to be put down, to be defeated, when you cannot move and you have to obey and do whatever the other one orders. Tommy's feelings were hurt. When Timmy put Tommy down, Timmy would act even more crazy. Tommy was so ashamed. Timmy then told him: "If you ever tell other people that I beat you, I'll kill you." This made Tommy even more anxious. And he thought: "I don't love Timmy anymore." After a while Timmy got off Tommy, and they made up peacefully.

But the same thing happened again and again, and poor Tommy became confused. Something went terribly wrong with Timmy, who acted harmfully and strangely toward Tommy. Timmy treated Tommy with no respect. At times Timmy was the ugly dinosaur, whom Tommy hated, but at other times he was a different Timmy—lovable, nice, the best brother you could imagine.

As Tommy grew older, he met a very old dinosaur who was friendly to him. This gray dinosaur was too old to jump and dance and fly, but nevertheless Tommy like him. They became friends, and Tommy could talk about everything he liked with the gray dinosaur. Tommy hesitated to talk about the awful secret of what happened with Timmy. However, the old dinosaur had a deep feeling for Tommy, and he knew that Tommy was hiding something terrible. One day the old dinosaur spoke to Tommy about when he was young, those days that had passed a long time ago, when the air had a smell that Tommy could not smell and the wind sang a song long forgotten. The old dinosaur told Tommy a secret, a terrible thing that happened to him when he was very young, even younger than Tommy was now. Tommy's eyes became larger and larger. He could not believe what he heard. He understood that this old dinosaur was treated like dirt by grown-ups when he was young. Immediately Tommy thought about his own secret, and his mouth opened and out came the truth about Timmy. "What did you do, when this happened to you?" Tommy asked the old dinosaur, for Tommy hoped that he could learn from the old dinosaur what to do. "Well," answered the old one, "I did do two things, which helped me a lot. One of those things was, I said to myself that this is not O.K., not O.K., not O.K. And I told them: 'This is not O.K.!! This is not O.K.!!' And Tommy, can you imagine what happened?" Tommy shook his head. "They continued to treat me badly, but it did not hurt as much. Then they wanted to shut me up. My 'This is not O.K.' had gotten on their nerves. After a while it stopped and it was all over." Tommy paid great attention to what the gray dinosaur had told him about the end of his worst secret.

A day passed, and Tommy and Timmy again began quarreling, fighting, spitting, and acting terribly toward each other. They turned into dragon dinosaurs, roaring, blowing smoke, spitting, and fighting, leading to the same end as before: Timmy put Tommy down—poor Tommy—with this awful feeling of being defeated, and, even worse, Timmy's cruel crazy acting, which made Tommy feel so confused and ashamed. But suddenly Tommy remembered the words of the gray dinosaur: "No, no, not O.K.!" And with a scream the world had never heard before, he shouted at Timmy "No, no, not O.K., not O.K.!" for a long time. A strange thing happened that Tommy never had expected: Timmy got off him, stared into the air with a pale face, and stuttered "I'm sorry." Tears fell down from Timmy's face. He felt sorry. "See," said the old dinosaur the next day, "see what power your thoughts and your words can have. I know that you are a young dinosaur who knows what is right and what is wrong and I tell you: You will be one of the great dinosaurs in our community if you do what your heart and mind are telling you." These words were spoken many years ago. The old dinosaur is long dead and nearly forgotten, but his words became true.

References

Axline, V. (1947). *Play Therapy*. Boston: Houghton Mifflin.

Gordon, D. (1978). *Therapeutic Metaphor*. Cupertino, CA: Meta.

Lankton, C. H., and Lankton, S. R. (1979). *Tales of Enchantment: Goal-Orientated Metaphors for Adults and Children in Therapy*. New York: Brunner/Mazel.

Mills, J. C., and Crowley, R. J. (1986). *Therapeutic Metaphors for Children and the Child Within*. New York: Brunner/Mazel.

Rogers, A. J. (1982). *Metaphors in the treatment of bedwetting*. Dissertation. Ann Arbor, MI.

8

The Little Leaf Transition Ritual

Jay Cerio

INTRODUCTION

Transition rituals are useful in situations in which the client leaves the playroom upset or overstimulated, continues play behavior in class or at home, or discusses therapy issues at inappropriate times or in inappropriate places. These situations indicate that the child has difficulties delineating the boundaries between the counseling situation and everyday life. That is, the client doesn't understand where and when the rules for behavior in play therapy stop and the rules for behavior outside of play therapy begin. A transition ritual is a way of creating a boundary by having a period of time that is neither play therapy nor everyday life, in which the child adjusts to the move back to the classroom or home. It is a type of planned time-out.

RATIONALE

The type of transition ritual that is used depends on the type of transition problem a client is exhibiting. For children who become overstimulated or have difficulty discontinuing with play, it helps to plan some type of quiet activity that will occur at the end of each session. Metaphorical stories are one type of transition strategy that is useful in these situations. This type of transition activity helps the child disengage from the play therapy situation.

"The Little Leaf" is a metaphorical story adapted for use with children from Gunnison's (1990) hypnocounseling approach. Gunnison conceptualizes hypnocounseling as a counseling approach that utilizes metaphors and induction techniques differently from how they are used in traditional hypnosis or hypnotherapy. Gunnison incorporates Erickson's induction techniques (Haley 1976) into hypnocounseling, giving clients complete control when such techniques are used. These techniques do not involve hypnosis or hypnotic trances. They are simply ways of "seeding the unconscious" (Whitaker and Bumberry 1988) in order to help clients utilize their own internal resources.

"The Little Leaf" is a relaxation story that is useful for helping children decrease feelings of anxiety or stress. It provides a concrete symbol, the leaf, on which the child can focus as the therapist tells the story. Clients can also learn to tell themselves the story as a strategy for calming themselves in real-life situations. Basically, it is very similar to bedtime stories that are used to relax children and lull them to sleep. For all these reasons, I have found this story to be useful with children who tend to get overstimulated in play therapy sessions.

DESCRIPTION

The delivery of the story requires that the counselor use voice modulation as a technique for inducing relaxation. The counselor uses a singsong type of intonation, alternating the tone from high to medium to low, and the volume from moderate to whispers. Emphasis is also placed on certain key words, which in the story, cited below, are capitalized. The rate of speech (pacing) is slow and deliberate, and needs to match the client's responses. For instance, if the client begins to breathe slowly, the counselor might state, "You might even find yourself breathing very SLOWLY and DEEPLY." For a more thorough description of this technique see Gunnison (1990). Here is the story, as told in the counselor's voice.

We're going to do something a little different today. Remember, we talked about how you tend to be too excited after your session, and then get in trouble in your room. Today we are going to take some time out now, so you will be CALM and RELAXED when you get back to your room. Ready?

I want you to get COMFORTABLE in your chair. You might CHOOSE to place your hands in your lap, or put your head down on the table, or NOT. (Pause)

I am going to tell you a story, and as you sit and LISTEN, you may CHOOSE to close your eyes, or not. (Pause)

Once upon a time there was a little leaf. He was a very happy little leaf who loved to hang out with his brother and sister leaves on a big maple tree in the woods. (Pause)

He especially enjoyed the FEELING of BLOWING GENTLY in the wind. (Pause) SWAYING back-and-forth and back-and-forth, until he was almost ASLEEP. (Pause)

He played like this through the spring and into summer, all the time just SWAYING in the BREEZE, until fall came. Well, you know what happens to leaves in fall, and as the weather became COOLER and COOLER, the little leaf's brothers and sisters let go of their perches on the tree, and FLOATED GENTLY to the ground. SWIRLING in the breeze they floated DOWN, DOWN, DOWN. (Pause)

The little leaf felt very lonely, and wanted to join his brothers and sisters. So, one WINDY day, he closed his eyes very tightly, loosened his grip, and JUMPED from the tree. And before he knew it, the wind had PICKED HIM UP and carried him UP, UP, UP into the COOL AIR. (Pause)

Then the little leaf began floating DOWN, DOWN, DOWN, floating in the breeze DOWN, DOWN, DOWN. (Pause)

And you may notice that your eyes are looking UP as if you can SEE the leaf floating. Or your eyes may be looking DOWN watching the leaf floating DOWN, DOWN, DOWN. (Pause)

And so the wind carried the leaf UP and then DOWN, GENTLY, GENTLY, GENTLY. (Pause) DOWN, DOWN, DOWN. And you may see the leaf FLOATING down. Or you may see nothing. (Pause)

Or you may FEEL as if you are FLOATING like the leaf. Or you may just feel COMFORTABLE and RELAXED. I don't know. It's your CHOICE. (Pause)

And the leaf floated DOWN and watched as he came closer and closer to the ground. SLOWLY and GENTLY floating in the AIR. (Pause)

DOWN (Pause), DOWN (Pause), DOWN (Pause) he went, SLOWLY approaching the ground. (Pause)

And then the leaf landed in a pile of leaves, like landing on a giant, SOFT, STUFFED, pillow. (Pause) So soft that he sank into the pillow for a few moments. (Pause)

And then he felt RELAXED (pause), and CONTENT (pause), and SAFE (pause), and almost SLEEPY. (Pause) Glad to be with his brothers and sisters again.

And you might even feel a little SLEEPY, now, or not. (Pause for a minute or so.)

And now, remaining RELAXED and CONTENT, you will begin to feel more alert as I count to three. One, your feet and legs are feeling more alert. (Pause) Two, your body is feeling more alert. (Pause) Three, your arms, neck, and head are feeling more alert. And as you sit there you will open your eyes and feel ALERT, RELAXED, and CONTENT.

Now when you return to class, you will continue to feel relaxed and alert. Go to your desk, sit down, and join the class.

APPLICATION

In addition to using "The Little Leaf" as a transition ritual, I have also found it to be useful as a general relaxation technique for children dealing with anxiety, and as a method for helping children fall asleep when they are having trouble doing so.

Using metaphorical stories requires planning and practice—it's not something that most counselors can do off the top of their heads. You need to have a clear idea of the purpose of the story, the message you want to communicate, the story outline, and the way you want to deliver the story. With practice, you will begin to feel more relaxed and confident about using storytelling, and become more spontaneous in generating metaphorical stories for specific uses, such as this transition technique.

References

Gunnison, H. (1990). Hypnocounseling: Ericksonian hypnosis for counselors. *Journal of Counseling and Development* 68:450–453.

Haley, J. (1976). *Problem-Solving Therapy*. New York: Harper-Colophon.

Whitaker, C., and Bumberry, W. (1988). *Dancing with the Family: A Symbolic-Experiential Approach*. New York: Brunner/Mazel.

9

Reading on the "Porch Swing"

Joan M. Doherty and Roger D. Phillips

INTRODUCTION

Ending play therapy—what we refer to as the "walk back"—is a significant time in the therapeutic journey, and a time that often receives less attention than the beginning and middle phases. At the end of play therapy, the child and therapist recognize the work that has been done; the journey has brought the child to a "clearing," a restoration of self-confidence about the pain or circumstances that led to the referral for play therapy. The child has a new sense of self, along with the learning and competence gained from the experience of sharing the journey with the play therapist. But there are fewer specific strategies and techniques offered for the termination of play therapy. We have found our book-writing and reading strategy, as if sitting together contentedly on a porch swing, to be a very productive and satisfying way to close play therapy.

RATIONALE

The beginning of play therapy is a time of realization, to become aware of the real world of the child who has come into our lives for a brief time.

Once the playroom is transformed by the child into a safe place, the child invites the therapist into the sacred and privileged environment of her/his own heart. During this middle phase of therapy, the child settles in and takes the therapist's hand, guiding the therapist on a path toward healing, with its own peaks and valleys, rough and smooth terrain. Ending play therapy, however, offers the child and the therapist something different: a chance to pause and savor the time traveled, and to anticipate the return home by sitting peacefully together on the "porch swing." This closing provides unique moments for consolidating a child's gains, launching her/him onto a new developmental path, closing productively a formative relationship, and most importantly, allowing the child to share her/his voice of wisdom.

DESCRIPTION

During this "walk back" in the last few sessions of play therapy, we ask, "What advice would you give another child who might be in the same situation as you, or had the same worry that you had?" Often we suggest that the child write a book that answers that question (with the therapist as scribe, if needed). The child identifies the story, we think about the reader, and collect supplies (paper, markers, crayons, etc.) to begin the writing and illustration process. We have rarely journeyed with a child who did not have a ready answer to this inquiry, as well as a generosity of spirit and willingness to share.

The last session is our "porch swing" session. We sit together and read the story slowly, sharing feelings and laughing about some of the fun times. Reading together provides a closeness and gentleness in which to accept that the journey is finished. The child's wisdom, in the form of a book, is her/his heartfelt legacy and memory of the journey taken.

One 8-year-old boy wrote the following book, including the lessons tagged at the end, as play therapy closed. He began treatment because of uncomfortable self-consciousness and teasing about his appearance, as well as confusion following his parents' intensely confrontational divorce and custody battles.

David and the Teasers

Once there was a boy who was always teased by other kids. David was 8 years old and lived in a town with his sister, brother, and his parents.

He hid the fact that he was being teased all the time. Nobody knew. He would hide his anger about being teased way inside himself.

He didn't want anyone to know how he felt. This worked for a long time. But the teasing continued.

Each day after school David rides the bus home. He is still being teased on the bus. Some boys tease him about being fat. They say, "You're as fat as a pig!" Then they laugh and laugh.

David feels awful and begins to cry. He hides his eyes with his hands so no one will notice his tears.

David ran inside his house and slammed the door as hard as he could. He wanted to make a really loud noise. He was VERY UPSET because he let all his anger out at once. He started to throw balls at the lamps on the tables in the living room. He still had more anger inside. Finally, his Dad picked David up and pinned him on the floor and said, "Calm down, you crazy boy!"

David didn't care that his Dad pinned him down because he already let out all of his anger that had been way down inside.

One night David was lying in his bed thinking about what he could do about being teased. Then David could hear his parents screaming at each other. Suddenly, he got really scared and started to cry. He finally fell asleep.

The next morning David saw his mom packing her clothes and he said, "Oh, it's all my fault?!" and ran out of the room. He grabbed his book bag and ran off to school.

David's mom shouted after him, "No, David, come back." David just kept running as he slammed the door shut behind him. He went on the school bus and the kids teased him even more.

At recess that day, one kid came up to him and said, "Look, the fat boy is coming." David got brave enough and he said, "I don't want you teasing me anymore." The boy looked surprised and said, "I never knew you felt that way." David said that to every boy that teased him. So, everyone stopped teasing David.

When David returned home after school he was in a good mood. He wanted to tell his mother what he had done at school, but she wasn't there. David asked his dad where Mom was. Dad said, "We have shared custody." David was glad because he gets to live with both parents.

David lived happily ever after.

Lessons

- *You should tell your parents and teachers if you are angry at getting teased instead of holding it in.*

- *Most parents know when something is bothering you, but they need you to tell them what it is so they can help you.*

- *Kids can learn how to stand up for themselves.*

- *Kids feel upset and scared when their parents split up.*

David's book and his last session contained a newfound confidence that he could handle teasing from peers, and that his advice to other children would be useful. David illustrated his book, as well as writing its story, and those pictures revealed poignantly differentiated feelings about both the choices that he could make for himself and the events over which he had little control. He left his final session with this comment: "Nothing can ever take away what happened here." David realized fully that our time together in play therapy was permanent and immutable, even in the face of many ongoing and future changes to negotiate.

APPLICATION

We have found our book-writing and reading strategy to have wide application, spanning children's age, difficulties, disorders, and even phases of treatment to some degree. For example, we have occasionally used book writing earlier in therapy, particularly if a child seemed stalled at a crossroad. In that context, book writing can become an exploration of alternative outcomes. If used earlier in therapy, then we might return to those productions during the "walk back," but focus solely on reading and looking back together, and affirming the new path toward well-being. We have found, however, our book-writing and reading strategy to be an especially respectful way to close the energies and commitments of play therapy.

10

Spontaneous Metaphor

William Walter Jenkins

INTRODUCTION

Conversation, if not communication, with adolescents is a challenge for even the most skilled adults. The adolescent is suspicious, out of control, withdrawn, insecure, often resistive, angry, uncommunicative, and in turmoil. Talking about what the teenager wants to talk about is disarming, cuts through the resistance, renders the adolescent amenable, and makes the job of healing so much more pleasant for everybody. Natural boundaries are reinforced and new ones built. When working with the displaced, disenfranchised, traumatized, attention-deficit youth, spontaneous metaphor makes the process seem natural. The technique is flexible, brings the adolescent to life in the therapy session, and provides a bridge for generalization and change. Therapist as metaphor is exercised as the instrument for change, as well.

RATIONALE

Consistency and creativity are key aspects of working successfully with adolescents. The adolescent wants to understand what is going to happen and have some control over the outcome. The experience can't be boring and must enhance the teenager's sense of power, and it must be exciting and pleasurable. To engage adolescents, you must meet them on their own turf. The spontaneity of the technique engages them at an emotional level and puts the message on a level of intensity that is irresistible. Setting limits and acceptance can be crafted in the same sentence.

Metaphor makes the teenager's images vivid and important and takes the abstract yearnings and makes them concrete. Metaphor is the handiest and most versatile tool we have for reconciling uncertainty. Metaphors can be used to build a careful foundation before we approach an idea.

DESCRIPTION

A strong belief in the healing power possessed by the adolescent is primary and necessary for the therapist to present at the first meeting. An air of confidence, as well as interest, humor, energy, and expectancy are important in sustaining a therapeutic conversation. The work begins with the physical and psychological presence of the therapist. You need to know where your boundaries are. Focus on need, wish, desire, and pain. Don't recoil from the truth or be soft, vague, or circumspect. Show respect, compassion, and acceptance by directly confronting both the demons and desires. A forthright acknowledgment will honor the situation and make the adolescent feel valued. With rapport intact and the adolescent feeling respected, you are on your way to creating a spontaneous metaphor. The therapist identifies feelings in a story and can point out special attributes of the adolescent. Metaphor is uniquely suited to bridging the known and unknown, the conscious and unconscious, the personal and universal.

Metaphors can be written down and reviewed. The past is now and persistent. Negative emotions can be modified. Therapists must accept limitations and set boundaries. When the dialogue with an adult is sustained, the adolescent feels supported and understood. Limits are set, and they are resolvable, metaphorically, with imagery that offers both natural consequences and success.

APPLICATION

Spontaneous metaphor can be used with children who have trauma and attachment problems. Learning disabilities and adopted adolescents get to express deep feelings while still maintaining the distance necessary for them to feel safe. The technique helps the therapist develop a third ear. It acknowledges the adolescent's fear in a nonthreatening way and suggests the possibility of alternatives. Attachment-deficient, traumatized adolescents can be helped with this technique. The metaphor bridges the thinking, emotions, and actions of this young person in the dialogue below. First, metaphoric rapport:

Adolescent: No sense being here. You can't change anything. All I care about is getting what I want. Do you see the truck across the street? It's hot, a 4-by-4, and red. You could buy it for me. You can afford to, you have lots of money, but you won't.

Therapist: Like I am the richest guy you know. You think that if I would give you that truck, it would prove that you're special, but you don't think you'll ever get it. If you get it, you would feel deserving, but it's like no one cares enough about you to help you.

Adolescent: All I want is a truck, a license, and money. My father won't sign for my license. He never helped me. He is nothing but trouble. He drinks and I hate his guts. I would beat him up if he were here.

Therapist: You want to get back at him for hurting you. You want nice things. You deserve to be treated better. You feel abandoned and angry.

Adolescent: I hope when he has nothing, is homeless, and asks me for some food, I'll give him garbage or tell him to go away.

Therapist: It is kind of gratifying to see him down and getting what he deserves. It was wrong for him to hurt you.

The adolescent tells more about his life, his vengeful feelings, and what he wants to do to people who have disappointed him. He wants revenge and he wants to be satisfied immediately. He is focused on the past. He finds no satisfaction in relationships nor does he recognize personal accomplishments. He has never thanked anyone for helping him because he feels oppressed and unworthy. Here is where spontaneous metaphor can be especially effective:

Adolescent: I keep thinking about the way my father abused me and got away with it.

Therapist: You keep thinking about the past and feel resentful and cheated; it's not fair. Your dad really hurt you. It is frustrating to want things to be better, but to feel helpless and undirected, like a rocket that is escaping gravity without guidance. There are strong forces pulling you off course, but you can't make corrections and can't use your power. You are powerless. You are being tossed and pulled by the past. You are vulnerable and that broken system is not getting fixed too soon. The thought of crashing and burning is terrifying and is making any positive change difficult. You want to feel powerful.

Adolescent: Well, sort of. I feel like a race-car driver who has gas, but has lost steering and is about to go off the road at 200 miles an hour. I can't get around the corner and am going to crash.

Therapist: At those speeds you are so frightened it's hard to think and you don't know how to ask for help. You have all of that power and excitement and no control. With the steering so damaged there seems to be little hope for the future. You are frightened and excited. You have a powerful car, but it's not working the way you want.

Therapist skill practice and acceptance of emotional turmoil is essential. With spontaneous metaphor the therapist and the adolescent begin to resolve helplessness, hopelessness, and the feelings of abandonment.

Bibliography

Jenkins, W. W., and Jenkins, T. (1993). *Recycling Paper and Things*. Scottsdale, AZ: Bill Jenkins.

Koop, R. R. (1995). *Metaphor Therapy: Using Client-Generated Metaphors in Psychotherapy*. New York: Brunner/Mazel.

11

Storytelling via Cartoons

Mary Ann Drake and David Drake

INTRODUCTION

Play therapy, by design, works for children and adolescents who are reluctant or unable to share their concerns and feelings verbally. Storytelling with the use of self-drawn cartoons is a venue that encourages children and adolescents to share what is going on in their lives and psyches without needing to rely just on verbal skills. The cartoons also provide insight for the therapist as to what is happening with the client and how the youngster structures and organizes her/his world. The cartoon strip allows the creator to move into a world of fantasy where characters and worlds are generated with a complete range of options, situations, and feelings in a way that is not personally threatening.

RATIONALE

Cartoons are an innocuous and familiar part of most young people's lives. To them, cartoons are fun and playful and do not carry heavy familial or psychological connotations. Cartoons are not considered to be fine art, and thus children and adolescents are not intimidated or resistant when asked to draw one. The sequential nature of cartoons reveals insights often not found in single-picture drawings. With a single static picture, the therapist can ask many questions about the story, about what is or has taken place in the picture. But in drawing a strip of pictures, the creator more concretely creates a process of thinking that involves looking at sequencing, consequences, and problem solving. As the child unconsciously utilizes these problem-solving skills, the skills become stronger in the individual. The process becomes an important adjunct to the story the child is telling. For some who have difficulty with these cognitive skills or are not conscious of such processing, the cartoon strips become an intermediate step in acquiring the skill of seeing an event or image as part of a whole.

Once the cartoon series is completed, young clients often feel free to share their work without inhibitions, often poignantly revealing feelings and experiences that otherwise might not be expressed in a milieu less familiar and comfortable than cartoons.

DESCRIPTION

Provide paper to be folded into division. Provide pencils or other drawing materials and ask the client to draw a cartoon strip like in the newspaper. The cartoon can be about anything the client chooses or the topic can be suggested. The drawings can be stick figures or they can be more sophisticated than that if the client so chooses.

After the drawing is completed, the artist talks about the drawing, telling the story, and perhaps sharing some feelings. The client can start with the first frame and move forward, or sometimes, the child begins at the end and works backward.

The therapist can help with questions: "What happens next?" "What happened before that?" "How does the character feel?" "What does the character wish had happened instead?"

As with any play technique, depending on the therapist, both the therapist and client can draw a cartoon strip and both can tell the story.

APPLICATION

This technique is applicable for use with children who are 4 or 5 years old (depending on their fine motor skills) and older. Again, the familiarity of cartoons makes this an especially applicable activity for most young-sters. The materials are few and the client can take the cartoon home, if desired. Cartoons generate wonderful and insightful stories, and some-times, depending on the emotional health of the client, terrifying and horrible stories.

One young client used the first folding technique shown above, which exposes a frame at a time. Each frame revealed a body part or part of a body part. When the entire cartoon was open, the body parts made a whole person. This young man had healed from having felt completely disconnected (because of abuse) from his physical body to the point of recognizing the wholeness of his body.

Another client, a severely depressed adolescent girl whose mother had not had the skills to care for her or protect her from abuse, also used the one-frame-at-a-time technique. As her frames were exposed, she revealed her fantasy wish to kill her mother and feel herself the victor. Her last two frames were of her mother being dead, with her holding the still smoking pistol, and then the gravestone of her mother, with her being free of her rage. In reality, this girl could not speak of her rage toward her mother; yet the fantasy cartoon freed her unconscious to allow these feelings to come to the surface.

The piece of paper can be folded and divided and used in several ways.

The paper is folded in half and in half again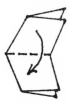

then in half a third time. 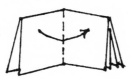 =

Folded this way, the cartoon strips can be presented in two ways:

1. As a four-frame or an eight-frame strip, opened flat.

 or

2. As a progressive unfolding strip with four or eight frames.

or

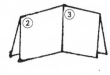 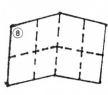 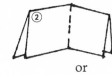

12

Expressing Grief through Storytelling

Hilda R. Glazer and Donna Marcum

INTRODUCTION

Storytelling can be a powerful intervention with children, and we have found that it can be a wonderful experience for both the teller and the child. Storytelling is applicable to individuals as well as groups. The narrative technique described below is one we have used and found to be effective in encouraging the processing of grief.

RATIONALE

The telling of one's own stories is part of mourning. In support groups the sharing of stories is a critical element of the group process (Harvey 1996). Telling one's own stories can be therapeutic for oneself in the telling and therapeutic in the knowledge that one is not alone in the feelings and experience of grief and mourning. An alternative to the telling of one's own story is the metaphor. Storytelling, or metaphor, is a literary technique in which one idea is expressed in terms of another (Pearce

1996). The listener draws unique and unpredictable meaning from metaphor (Pearce 1996). It can encourage the individual to consider the meanings for oneself.

DESCRIPTION

Muro and Kottman (1995) suggested that storytelling works best with children in the second grade or older. Their storyteller began the story, setting the stage, providing the beginning and the middle of the story, and then inviting the child to complete the story. Children were then asked to draw a picture of the story.

The story can be an existing story or a metaphor that is developed especially for the particular therapeutic goal. Numerous children's books address issues of loss and are valuable tools in working with grieving children. As the children's book market continues to grow, there will be books available for many of the issues facing children. Stories found in old books are beneficial because they are less likely to be familiar to a young audience. Children hearing a story for the first time can become involved in the content without a natural tendency to critique the story line. Stories created by the teller can be developed to meet the therapeutic needs of the children and can easily be edited for different age groups. Careful consideration must be given to the copyright laws, but we have found that many authors are willing to let us use their stories.

APPLICATION

In a study of the ability of children to express their grief through storytelling, a story was developed about a child who lost his father and then suffered the additional loss of his home and friends because of a move back to a family home. The child, upon reaching the new home, finds a tree perfectly built for climbing, which he calls his dreaming tree. The children were asked to finish the story from that point. Here is how two children finished the story:

Boy, 10 years old:

Hey, Mom, can we stay here for the rest of our lives? Well, maybe when you grow up, you might move, but we might stay here for a little, maybe for a lot longer. The next day, when Joey came home from his new school, he went up in his oak tree and did all the usual things, and his mom called him to tell him that people were coming to cut down the tree because it was dying, and he said, "Why do people have to take away things I (pause) like all the time?"

Girl, 9.5 years old:

Joey's friend came and they both played in the oak tree and they spent the summer there and they had fun. Joey wanted his friend to live there, but he couldn't. And Joey almost forgot about his friend because he loved the tree so much. The oak tree comes alive, and instead of being the oak tree it's Joey's friend. And he lived there forever being the oak tree and Joey's friend.

The children were also asked to draw the end of the oak tree story. While most children drew the tree, a few of the children drew the dream they had told.

Storytelling can be used as a group or individual activity. Storytelling can also be used in filial therapy as a joint parent–child activity. Complete stories can be told and the child could be asked to draw the story or a part of the story. Children are often able to express in their art what they are unable to express in words. For example, one first-grade child included her mother, as an angel, when she drew the garden in the story she had just been told. Stories can be told with children, with the therapist providing the setting and the beginning and middle, and the child finishing the story. Within the support group setting, we have worked with small groups of children to turn a story into a play and present it to the larger group. Other storytelling techniques are well documented. Narrative-based techniques can be easily integrated into group and individual sessions. There is no upper age limit for storytelling. We have found that adults, as well as children, enjoy and benefit from this technique.

Acknowledgment

The research on this technique was supported by a grant from the National Storytelling Association, 1998.

References

Harvey, J. H. (1996). *Embracing Their Memory: Loss and the Social Psychology of Storytelling*. Needham Heights, MA: Allyn & Bacon.

Muro, J., and Kottman, T. (1995). *Guidance and Counseling in the Elementary and Middle Schools*. Madison, WI: Brown and Benchmark.

Pearce, S. S. (1996). *Flash of Insight: Metaphor and Narrative in Therapy*. Boston, MA: Allyn & Bacon.

Resource

National Storytelling Membership Association, 116½ West Main Street, Jonesborough, TN 37659, (423) 913-8201, *nmsa@naxs.net* or *www.storynet. org*.

Section Two

Expressive Arts Techniques

13

Role Playing with Play Doh

Nancy M. Schultz

INTRODUCTION

In my roles as a counselor–play therapist in a school of 450 children, I often have just one or two sessions with a child who either personally asks to see me or is referred by a parent for brief counseling work. The self-referrals are often older students, in the third, fourth, or fifth grade, many of whom place a personal note in my "mailbag," which I hang in a central location in the school. Most of these self-referrals are about peer problems (having feelings hurt by a friend, having a conflict with others, failure to make friends, etc.). Occasionally, children ask to talk to me about a teacher problem, or even a worry that they have about a parent's health or welfare. Parent referrals are often about the child's difficulty with anger or concern about homework. Referrals that lead to longer-term counseling work are often related to a parental separation or divorce. A quick technique to use to establish rapport is role playing with Play Doh. I hand children a ball of Play Doh as soon as they sit down at my child-sized table.

RATIONALE

Role play is a technique largely attributed to the behavioral model of play therapy. It allows the child to express feelings about a particular situation and to practice new reactions and behaviors to this same situation. In addition, the child may easily play the role of others, allowing for empathy to develop, or at least for the viewpoint of others to be experienced. Using Play Doh is an easily applied technique that appeals to most children and taps into the unconscious mind as it is used as an art expression. Putting these two techniques together is a natural way to briefly address a child's problem.

DESCRIPTION

Usually I greet the child and gesture toward the can of Play Doh on the table. As the student begins to relate the problem or situation, he/she squeezes and manipulates the Play Doh. Most of the time, the telling of the story unfolds while the Play Doh acts as an energy outlet. Since most brief play therapy sessions involve a problem-solving component, I begin to use the Play Doh in myriad ways as part of the telling of the child's story and in the search for an idea to represent a solution. At times, the Play Doh (in my hands or the child's) becomes people in the child's story (sometimes just large or small balls). At other times, the Play Doh represents the child's day divided up into segments, as bigger and smaller balls representing the importance to the child of choices. A big ball represents a perfect choice or task, and smaller balls are less perfect yet more interesting tasks. The Play Doh becomes parts of the child's problem in a concrete yet loosely defined medium.

APPLICATION

This method is useful in briefly working with children with peer difficulties or conflicts, with sibling difficulties, and with school-related situational problems. Once I used it with a 9-year-old who was small for his age and needed to become more assertive on the school bus with children who teased him. He felt hampered by his size. Using Play Doh, he stretched himself to twice the size of the bullies and practiced speaking up to them. In another case, a girl with divorced parents who found herself needing to travel between two homes every four days used the Play Doh to represent the homes. One was a "flat" house, not much fun, and the other, represented by a Play Doh bowl, brimmed over with joy. She left the session seeming to realize for the first time the nature of the difference in her feelings in each parent's house. These representations can change over time, of course, as the child works through the emotional stages of her family's divorce.

The tactical touching and forming of the Play Doh often seems to trigger the workings of the unconscious mind as well. For example, a 10-year-old boy whose uncle had just been recently shot and killed in a drive-by shooting, constantly made bullet-like pellets from the Play Doh as he shared his feelings about the incident. His forming of the pellets seemed totally disconnected from his words, but it was obvious to me that the Play Doh was enabling him to express a metaphor for his grief and especially for his fears. In this case, I continued with his sessions for several weeks, always using Play Doh, with which he was obviously comfortable. The combination of the Play Doh sculpting of bullets and the verbalizing of both his imagined ideas of the actual shooting scene and the traumatic impact of this event on his life helped this child greatly with his emotions and well-being.

In still another case, a child living in a foster home for most of her seven years of life always made Play Doh "food" such as pizza, doughnuts, and cookies while talking about her foster families. Children in such home situations often have unconscious needs for nurturing, and are known to draw or play out food themes in play therapy. In the brief therapy sessions with this child, Play Doh proved to be the perfect medium for creating foodlike shapes and for acting out "eating" sessions. (Most children know not to put Play Doh in their mouths.) In still another case, the Play Doh was used to represent worms. The child told a story about the worms being mean to one worm who did not have any friends. With my reflecting, I guided the story to help the left-out worm speak up about his feelings. Since we know that children play out their conflicts in play therapy, presenting this Play Doh worm's friend problem was a metaphor for this child's peer problems. By providing the play medium of Play Doh, together with an accepting, nonjudgmental therapeutic relationship, the atmosphere for re-creating this child's conflict proved successful!

Play Doh role playing can be used with most school-aged children, and costs only the price of a can of Play Doh. (Properly closed tightly in a container, it remains moist and pliable.) It is especially useful to the play therapist who travels and needs to have portable toys.

14

The Parent–Child Clay Animal Activity

Carla Sharp

INTRODUCTION

One of today's most pressing issues in child and family psychotherapy is attachment and bonding. Repeatedly, therapists treat children with oppositional traits, running away behaviors, or severe aggression. These behaviors and many others may have at their root an inadequate attachment or a history of disrupted attachment. Beverly James (1994) believes that part of any child assessment must include an assessment of the bond between the child and the parents. In my experience, play therapy is the best modality with which to assess and treat this vital relationship. Certainly, the younger the child who presents with emotional/behavioral problems, the greater the need to determine the quality of this bond.

RATIONALE

Communication between parent and child occurs verbally and nonverbally. It has been well established that young children communicate naturally through the use of metaphor (Mills and Crowley 1986). Young children are less skilled at direct, verbal discussion of a parent–child problem. In addition, neither the child nor the parents can tell us what they do not consciously know.

Many parents seek counseling because they do not understand their children and are confused about their child's behavior. The goals of treatment for children and their parents often include increasing the parents' understanding of child behavior and enhancing the parent–child relationship. Therapists can foster increased insight and empathy among the child and parents. It is through play that the therapist can most readily see the underlying dynamics of this relationship. It is also through play that the family play therapist can effect the necessary changes to this dyad relationship. Eliana Gil (1994) states, "When adults are able to relate to children and enter their worlds, a dimension of contact is achieved which solidifies mutual relatedness or emotional connectedness" (p. 36). Simply put, when parent and child play together, a deeper emotional connection occurs.

DESCRIPTION

The Animal Creation Phase

The therapist invites the parent and child into the playroom together. The concept that the therapist can help parent and child understand each other better by having them play together should have already been explained by the therapist. The therapist then introduces balls of modeling clay and announces: "Today I'd like each of you to have some fun with clay. I'd like each of you to make an animal—any kind of animal you want. When you're done, I'll have you tell a story together."

While the parent and child are creating animals, the therapist can lead a discussion of how things are going at home, if this seems appropriate. The content of the discussion may appear later in the story. It is important to observe how parent and child relate to each other during the creation phase: Are they curious about each other's animals? How does the parent encourage or discourage the child? Does the child express surprise that the parent can play? When both state they are finished, suggest that each introduce his or her animal and say a little bit about it. Note to yourself the kind of clay animal made and the relationship these two animals would have in nature. For example, a cat and a mouse have a rather famous antagonistic relationship and very different from two kittens, who might easily play together. Also note if these two animals can occupy the same realm; for example, a fish and a lion would have difficulty finding common ground.

The Story Phase

The therapist instructs the parent and child to tell a story together. The therapist specifies that the story must have a beginning, a middle, and an end. This helps shape a more meaningful metaphor. Encourage the animals to have a dialogue. The therapist's role is to record the story. Note significant aspects of the content, the parent's and child's affect during the storytelling, and the central conflict in the story. Also, note if the conflict was resolved and how.

One mother–daughter dyad created a duck (mother) and a gorilla (11-year-old daughter). The duck and the gorilla immediately realized that they did not speak the same language. The duck quacked and the gorilla growled and they had to find a common language in order to understand each other.

Another dyad made a whale (mother) and a tiger (5-year-old boy). These two animals had to find a common meeting place, and finally decided to meet on a beach where the whale swam into shore and the tiger stayed on the sand. The whale offered to take the tiger for a ride on her back if he promised not to claw her. This parent–child dyad was able to play about the mother's fears of her son's aggression. The child was able to achieve the closeness he desired by curbing his aggressive impulses.

Yet another very conflicted dyad created a cat (mother) and a duck (10-year-old adopted daughter). They struggled to find a home they could share. The reluctant duck doubted they could ever live together. Eventually, the cat built a house (out of clay) and created a special pond for the duck. Thus they were able to live together. This metaphor directly addressed their tentative attachment, and the mother was able to demonstrate her commitment to this child.

Postplay Processing

The degree to which the therapist chooses to process the story depends on the age of the child, the stage of treatment, and the goals of treatment. The therapist usually talks about the story briefly while staying within the metaphor. The animal figures can be interviewed about their reactions to the events in the story and the feelings that emerged. By staying within the protection of the metaphor, the therapist can ask the duck how it felt to have her own swimming pond, made just for her. Parents and children are often more comfortable addressing an issue through metaphor than in direct discussion. Some parents acknowledge with a smile and a wink what is really being discussed, while the child is often less aware of the other level of meaning. This does not seem to impede the therapeutic effectiveness of the activity. During the postplay processing, parents may gain insight into their child's behavior. One father learned that his son was afraid of him during their storytelling. This knowledge helped him to alter his parenting style.

APPLICATION

This activity is appropriate for all ages of children and for parents who are capable of playing and who are capable of insight. It is not appropriate for abusive parents in the early phase of treatment, for the psychotic parent or child, or for any child who is not comfortable playing with the parent in the playroom.

This activity is quite useful during the assessment or the treatment phase. The therapist's role and amount of intervention will vary accordingly. When the conflict does emerge in the metaphor, the therapist can acknowledge to both parent and child that resolution of this conflict will be one of the goals of treatment. This can be done within the metaphor by talking to the animals. For some, it is appropriate to link the metaphor to the real-life situation. The therapist closes by thanking both parent and child for being willing to play together so that the therapist can better understand their unique relationship.

References

Gil, E. (1994). *Play in Family Therapy*. New York: Guilford.

James, B. (1994). *Handbook for Treatment of Attachment-Trauma Problems in Children*. New York: Lexington.

Mills, J.C., and Crowley, R. (1986). *Therapeutic Metaphors for Children*. New York: Brunner/Mazel.

15

Inside–Outside Masks

Theresa A. Kruczek

INTRODUCTION

Children are developing a variety of cognitive and affective capabilities. Children participating in counseling are commonly struggling with two specific areas of development: self-concept and regulating emotions. Children in counseling often present with a narrow self-concept consisting of the negative labels that have been applied to their problem behaviors. Additionally, they have difficulty identifying and regulating their emotional experiences. Children can use mask-making activities to expand their self-concept and capacity to identify their feelings. Older children can use the activity to begin to understand the complexity of their emotional experiences.

RATIONALE

Making masks is a creative art activity to engage children in a nonthreatening and enjoyable way. Children are comfortable with creative art activities, as they often use them in other settings such as school and community activities. Counselors can use art activities to help the children expand their communication repertoire. Children are typically less defensive when engaged in the art activity, and they are able to clearly and comfortably communicate using expressive arts. Additionally, use of creative arts helps the child concretize and organize (cognitively) their experiences with a naturally playful medium.

DESCRIPTION

The mask-making activity can be simple or sophisticated, depending on the counselor's budget, capacity to plan ahead, and the developmental level of the child. Simple masks can be made with construction paper and tongue depressors or string. More sophisticated masks can be made from the ceramic or paper masks that can be purchased at craft stores. Craft stores have paints to decorate these more sophisticated masks. Most often in individual counseling I make the simple, construction paper masks. I have made ceramic masks in a group setting with older elementary school children and adolescents.

To make simple masks, draw an oval on a piece of construction paper. Next, draw two eye holes at the midpoint of the oval. Then draw a mouth about halfway between the eye holes and the bottom of the mask. Depending on the motor skills of the children you may need to help them cut the eye and mouth holes. You can either glue a tongue depressor on the bottom of the mask or make two small holes at the edge of the mask, about even with the eye holes. You can use yarn or string to make ties for the mask. I often let the child choose two different colors of construction paper and glue the two sheets of paper together before cutting. In that way there is a different color representing the inside and the outside of the mask.

You then direct children to decorate the outside of the mask by making a collage. Use child-appropriate magazines to cut out pictures and words for the collage. If you are trying to elaborate self-concept, the children are to choose pictures or words that represent how the outside world sees them. When they have completed decorating the outside of the mask, they decorate the inside of the mask. The inside of the mask represents who they are on the inside. You may need to direct them to expand the inside of the mask beyond negative labels. You can prompt them by asking them to include things they like, things that make them feel good, things they are good at, things they enjoy doing, and aspirations for the future.

The counselor and the child can then use the pictures and words chosen as the basis for further discussion. The counselor can help children recognize their strengths and expand their self-concept beyond negative labels or behaviors that brought them to counseling. The counselor can also help them understand the importance of having others recognize more fully who they are. The counselor and children can explore ways the children can show others the "inside" of who they are. Color choices for the inside and outside can also serve as a metaphoric basis for discussion.

If you are trying to elaborate feelings, have the children put pictures and words representing the feelings the outside world sees on the outside of the mask and the feelings they experience internally on the inside. You may need to use lists of feeling words to help them identify different feelings. Depending on their developmental level, they may need a higher level of direction from the counselor. For example, with young children the counselor might need to go through the feelings list and first ask if they can define the feeling. With young children, the therapist may want to limit the feelings to the basics: happy, sad, mad, scared. When children understand the feeling, the counselor can then ask if they often have that feeling. If they do, then they decide if it is more often a feeling that stays inside or is shown outside. They then search for pictures or words to represent the feelings to paste on the mask. Older children may need only the latter prompt (inside or outside), if any prompt is necessary.

The counselor and children can again use the mask as a basis for discussion. The counselor can help the children recognize that certain internal feelings may be manifest externally as other feelings. The counselor can help the children understand that many people who come for counseling develop rigid and stereotyped ways of expressing emotion. The counselor can then help the children identify and recognize all the different types of emotions they experience by referring to the feelings identified on the inside and outside of the mask. The counselor can also teach the children how to use "I" statements to clearly identify and communicate their feelings to others. The counselor asks the children to use each feeling identified on their mask in the following sentence: "I feel _____ when _____ ."

APPLICATION

This technique is applicable to all children. It can help children articulate and expand their self-concept. It can also help children identify and understand their emotional experiences. The self-concept mask is particularly useful with children who have been labeled "difficult." The feelings mask is helpful with children who demonstrate tendencies toward either internalizing or externalizing behavior problems.

Case Examples

An 8-year-old girl had been identified as "painfully shy" by her teacher and was referred to the school guidance counselor. Initially, the girl was reluctant to talk and interact with the counselor. The counselor used the inside–outside mask to help the girl elaborate her self-concept. There were very few pictures and words on the outside of the mask. With minimal prompting the girl was able to extensively decorate the inside of the mask. Using the mask as the basis for discussion enabled the girl to begin to share verbally with the counselor. Initially, the counselor was able to help the girl identify one peer to begin to share the "inside" mask with. The counselor supported the child to continue to talk about herself with peers.

An 11-year-old boy was referred for counseling to help him manage frequent angry outbursts at home and school. His environment was described as fairly chaotic. The boy used the inside–outside feeling mask to identify his feelings. With the aid of his counselor, he created a mask that contained primarily angry words and pictures on the outside. However, his inside pictures represented feelings of confusion, fear, guilt, and being out of control. The counselor encouraged him to use his angry feelings as a sign he might be feeling one of the other "inside" feelings. His counselor shared with him that the "flip side" of anger is often feeling out of control (Gil 1983). He was instructed to use "I" statements to understand the inside feelings. He was to complete the "I" statement sentences with the inside feelings when he began to feel angry on the outside. For example, when beginning to feel angry, he was to say to himself, "I feel out of control when _____ ." He was coached to use his response to attempt to gain some understanding and control over the situation.

Reference

Gil, E. (1883). *Outgrowing the Pain*. New York: Dell.

16

School Backpack Kit

Mary Anne Peabody

INTRODUCTION

Play therapy texts, regardless of theoretical orientation, often include a preferred list of toys to use with children in therapy. The toys are generally selected for their ability to help children express their feelings, needs, or experiences. Selected toys should allow for exploration and encourage interaction between the child and therapist.

Children use pretend-fantasy toys to explore different roles and relationships, express feelings, experiment with alternative behavior, and act out situations they observe in real life. Much like a doctor kit helps children explore and express medical concerns, a school backpack kit helps the child play out the real-life experience of school. By providing this opportunity, the therapist is better able to enter the school world of play with the child.

Schaefer (1993) describes fourteen "therapeutic powers" of play that have one or more curative functions. These therapeutic factors often overlap or co-occur, depending on the approach the therapist uses. Each child in therapy is unique, with unique difficulties or disorders. Depending on the treatment plan of each child, various therapeutic powers of play may be used at some point in treatment. Because the school backpack kit can be used in both nondirective and directive play therapy, it inherently brings out several of the powers of play, depending on the approach the therapist uses. The therapeutic powers I have seen most often with children using this technique include fantasy, communication, creative thinking, role play, relationship enhancement, the mastering of developmental fears in the case of school-related anxiety issues, and overcoming resistance. Catharsis, abreaction, and positive emotions may be evident in the play of some children needing to release negative emotions, work through trauma, or express positive emotions about their school situation.

RATIONALE

In treating children, the therapist must be aware of the child's "ecosystem." The impact of all systems, including school and peers, must be taken into consideration. For the school-age children, school is where they spend a large portion of their time. School can be a place of joy and learning, or a place of frustration and peer conflict. Understanding the experience of school is vital to understanding the world of the child. This is especially important if the presenting problem relates to school situations or is affecting how the child is functioning at school.

As a prescriptive approach, a school backpack kit can be used in a nondirective approach or in a more directive approach, as described below. This technique allows the skilled play therapist to adapt the technique to best meet the presenting needs of the child and goals of a comprehensive and cohesive treatment plan.

Kuhli (1997) recommends having two houses as standard equipment in a playroom. Changes in family structure, relocation, loss, and trauma were just some of the situations that children could play out with the availability of two separate houses. In my playroom I have one traditional dollhouse and one empty dollhouse. The empty structure allows children to create any type of space they want.

When using the school backpack kit technique, I ask the child to create the scenes in the empty dollhouse structure. If there is only one house available, the child could arrange the contents of the kit in the sandbox, build a school structure from available blocks, or simply set up the school on the floor. The technique allows for versatility.

DESCRIPTION

Inside a regular-sized plain backpack, I have a variety of school-related doll-size furniture, desks, chairs, people figures, and animal figures. I have also included some school-related accessories: miniature books of notebook paper, small toys (yarn jump rope, rubber balls, cars), maps, chalk and chalkboards, cursive writing or printing sentence strips, a flag, a globe, and charts. Small blocks of wood serve as desks, tables, or places to lean the maps against.

Much of this school backpack kit can be inexpensively made from craft supplies or computer clip art programs. Homemade or commercially purchased playground apparatus, long tables for the cafeteria, and a school bus can be used in the technique. Although the kit could be arranged in any container, the children associate the backpack kit with their own personal backpack that they bring to school each day.

If the school backpack kit is simply one of several choices in a child-centered approach, children would use the kit just as any other toy choice in the playroom. The kit is available on a playroom shelf and children may or may not choose it as a modality in which to do their work.

If the children's needs and the treatment plan call for a more directive approach, then I have used the school backpack kit in the following ways:

- I ask children to show me and describe a typical school day, including leaving the house, waiting for the bus, the bus ride, the classroom experience, lunch in the cafeteria, recess, and the trip back home.

- I ask children to role play a typical scene in the classroom, cafeteria, or playground. Then I ask them to role play the ideal way or how they wish things were in the classroom or playground.

- If a child is involved in a conflictual situation, we re-create the situation with the figures, and the child attempts to come up with alternate ways to solve the problem. I can also provide different endings to the story as a way of teaching coping skills.

- I ask the child to select a figure to be the adult in the scene (bus driver, teacher, playground monitor) and to create a pretend skit with the figures.

- I have adapted questions from the school kinetic drawing technique (Kottman 1995) by asking children to create their classroom and include themselves, their teacher, and two friends doing something. I then ask, "What is this person doing? How does this person feel? How do you feel about this person? How does this person get along with other people?" An additional question might be: "If you could change anything about this class, what would you change?" Kottman (1995) lists other questions in the school kinetic drawing technique discussion.

APPLICATION

I have successfully used this technique with a wide range of school-age children to gain insight into their thoughts, feelings, and wishes about school. It is especially useful with children who are dealing with school-related issues, such as school anxiety, separation anxiety, learning difficulties, attention-deficit disorder (ADD), attention-deficit/-hyperactivity disorder (ADHD), or low self-esteem.

References

Kottman, T. (1995). *Partners in Play: An Adlerian Approach to Play Therapy.* Alexandria, VA: American Counseling Association.

Kuhli, L. (1997). The use of two houses in play therapy. In *Play Therapy Techniques*, ed. C. Schaefer and D. Cangelosi, pp. 63–68. Northvale, NJ: Jason Aronson.

Schaefer, C. E. (1993). *The Therapeutic Powers of Play.* Northvale, NJ: Jason Aronson.

17

Reverse Report Card

Mary Anne Peabody

INTRODUCTION

School-age children receive a report card several times a year with grades from their teacher. It is a concept with which most children are fairly familiar. In an effort to have children report to me their thoughts and feelings regarding significant people or experiences in their world, I created a reverse report card, on which the child is the one giving out the grades. I have found that children enjoy the role of being the "teacher" and like to have the opportunity to grade others. This technique allows for expression of feelings and is a vehicle for children to communicate about their world.

RATIONALE

Some children have difficulty verbally expressing feelings, thoughts, and concerns. Using a structured technique gives the therapist a direction in helping children communicate about the people and situations in their world. However, direct questioning is often too threatening for most children. Finding playful and creative ways to help children verbalize in a nonthreatening presentation provides the therapist with a structured way to gather information from the child.

I want children to feel that their life inside and outside the playroom is important to me. When I ask them to grade and talk about the different aspects of their day-to-day life, it lets them know that I am interested in their world. Combining open-ended questions with the grading techniques deepens my understanding of their perception about themselves, others, and their environment.

DESCRIPTION

I have designed a report card template out of oak tag cardboard. I leave the categories blank, so that I can tailor the card to suit each child. I ask if the child is familiar with grades and report cards in general. As we go through the report card together, I write down the categories to fit the situations the child is experiencing. The grades are set up like a five-point Likert scale, with 1 being positive, 3 in the middle, and 5 being negative (Figure 17–1). I ask the child to grade the situation or person in the last few weeks. The therapist could vary the time question to include grading today, over the last week, and so on, depending on the concept of time that the child would comprehend. The child then marks the square with a check or uses a stamp and stamp pad to place the stamp under the grade. If you have a few different stamp choices and stamp pad colors, it adds to the technique. After every grade I ask more clarifying questions to better understand why the child chose to give that particular grade.

Because so many adult–child interactions are filled with questions, the therapist should be careful to monitor the child's nonverbal reaction to the clarifying questions. The pacing of the questions is an important variable. The therapist should avoid overwhelming the child with question after question. With some children I only ask them to grade a few sections per session, allowing them to see changes over time.

Graded by _____

Date: _____

	(+) 1	2	3	4	5 (−)
Your younger brother					
Your older sister					
Mom					
Dad					
Grandma					
Grandpa					
Day-care kids					
Day-care provider					
Teacher					
Bus stop					
Bus ride					
Recess					

Figure 17–1. Reverse report card.

Categories

Home based: Mother, father, siblings, grandparents, pets.

School based: Teacher, cafeteria, waiting at the bus stop, bus ride, school peers, recess, gym, art class, principal.

Other: Day care, after-school activities, neighborhood peers.

APPLICATION

This technique is applicable to a wide variety of school-age children dealing with various issues. It is best used with children who have at least beginning reading skills.

It can be used at various times during treatment to see how thoughts, feelings, or situations change over time. Depending on the child's age, developmental level, and attention span, the technique can be varied and broken down into smaller time frames. For example, the therapist may choose to have the child grade only a few areas per session, carrying the technique over several sessions. Or the therapist may use the technique at the start of each weekly session, as a review of the week. Children then are provided with a structured way to share with the therapist their thoughts, feelings, and perceptions of the past week. The technique can be used at various times during treatment to see how the children's thoughts, feelings, or situations change over time.

18

Drawing for the Child

Deborah B. Vilas

INTRODUCTION

This art therapy technique uses therapist-made art as a way of helping children connect to, express, and process feelings that have not yet been accessible to them. I have used this technique successfully in my work as a child life specialist with hospitalized children, and as a teacher and therapist in a therapeutic nursery to communicate with emotionally disturbed 2- to 5-year-olds.

This technique is also described by Lesley Koplow (1996), who calls the technique "The Purple Crayon," based on a children's story (Johnson 1955), in which a boy's fantasies are given life through his drawings.

RATIONALE

Although play is a child's best and most natural form of communication, there may be times when a child is unable to use play or words to access his emotions without intervention from a therapist. Whether a child is withdrawn, in an agitated or unreachable state, or speaks a different language, this technique creates almost instantaneous feelings of validation and connection for the child. It provides the child with access to issues that may not yet have reached symbolic expression.

DESCRIPTION

The therapist uses plain white drawing paper and markers or crayons to draw the child. The child can be drawn in his present state, or the therapist can choose to draw something that has happened previously in therapy or in the child's life. Artistic talent is not important. However, details such as eye and hair color, skin color, facial expression, and color and style of dress should be accurately represented. The child should never be depicted as a stick figure.

If the child shows interest and is able to interact, the therapist should ask for the child's input during the drawing. The therapist can do this by narrating her drawing process and interjecting questions. If the child is unable to contribute, the therapist can make appropriate guesses about what the child may be feeling or thinking. Often, the child will enter willingly into dialogue, if just to correct a therapist's interpretation. The following is an example of a drawing dialogue:

Therapist:	Okay, I'll make you standing by the door and me next to you. You are wearing a blue shirt and jeans. What color shoes do you have on?
Child:	(No answer.)
Therapist:	Let me see. Black shoes. Now, I'm drawing your face. What kind of mouth should I draw? A sad mouth? An angry . . . ?
Child (interrupting):	SAD!

The therapist continues to draw the child and then adds other characters or background to depict a particular scene. When the drawing is done, a thought or word bubble is added, and the child is encouraged to fill in the words, thoughts, and feelings to the scene. Sometimes a child becomes involved in the drawing itself. For example:

Therapist: So, here you are crying. I wonder what you're feeling in this picture?

Child: Angry and sad. Draw the door and the wall and the door to the outside and you coming in and the plants are there. I'm here, crying near the wall. You're smiling a little, right?

Therapist: You remember that I was smiling, but you were feeling sad and angry. What are you thinking in this picture that is making you so sad and angry?

Child: I'm sad and angry because you are telling me I have to stop playing.

This technique can also give the therapist a glimpse into the impenetrable world of psychotic children. One such child, a 4-year-old girl, was jumping up and down and loudly singing in jargon. She was unresponsive to several verbal and nonverbal attempts made by the therapist to establish contact. The therapist then drew a picture of the child in mid-action (Figure 18–1). The child stopped jumping and yelling and came over to see what the therapist was doing. She then dictated the following monologue to accompany the picture:

Child: Habadibada! Come with me, come on pumpkins. My mama gets so prickly. Takes my money out my hand, and take a break of my mommy crack me. And my mommy hit me with a ball-headed pot. She bunked me in the head and I flat on the window. And she smacked me in the butt, with my shoes falling down in the window. And my mama cracked my arm. I don't know why.

At times, this drawing technique is validating in and of itself and opens communication sufficiently between patient and therapist. It can also be paired with other dramatic techniques such as puppet and doll play to further explore the issues presented.

Figure 18–1. The therapist's drawing of a child in mid-action.

APPLICATION

This technique has been used successfully with preschoolers; psychotic, autistic, and traumatized children; as well as children with pervasive developmental disorder and overall developmental delays. It may also be used with older children.

In addition, the technique has been helpful in bridging communication gaps between hospitalized children and hospital staff. For example, a 5-year-old hospitalized deaf child was inconsolable after seeing her mother wheeled away, sick in a wheelchair. A child life specialist knew no sign language, and the child could not lip read. The specialist drew a picture depicting the child crying and the mother being taken away in the wheelchair. The child expressed immediate relief when she saw that the specialist knew what was upsetting her.

Some therapists may worry about inhibiting the child's own artistic work by presenting them with an adult model that they can't match. Therapists should clearly explain to the child when and where it is appropriate for the adult to draw for the child and when it is not. As with all techniques, therapists should use their knowledge of the child and their intuition to judge when the time is right to draw for a child. There will be times when children are receptive and the intervention will resonate for them. At other times and with particular children, the technique may be too intrusive or threatening in its directness.

References

Johnson, C. (1955). *Harold and the Purple Crayon*. New York: Harper.

Koplow, L. (1996). *Unsmiling Faces: How Preschools Can Heal*. New York: Teachers' College Press.

19

Feeling Stickers

Liana Lowenstein

INTRODUCTION

Many children have difficulty identifying and expressing their feelings, because they have limited verbal abilities, they are reluctant to self-disclose, or they feel anxious about the therapeutic process. Activities that are concrete and play-based help children express their thoughts and feelings with lowered levels of anxiety. As most children enjoy using stickers, this activity is an engaging and valuable therapeutic technique.

RATIONALE

When children are limited in their ability to verbalize their feelings, it can help to combine discussion with engaging play-based activities. Feeling stickers is a technique that has several therapeutic purposes: (1) The activity helps children identify and express feelings. (2) The exercise provides valuable assessment information for the therapist. (3) The practitioner can use the activity as an opportunity to normalize and validate children's feelings. (4) The activity enables children to understand that people experience various feeling states in different parts of their body.

DESCRIPTION

The therapist and child sit on the floor. The therapist has a large piece of butcher paper available (large enough to trace the child's body outline), markers, and a variety of stickers (preferably happy faces, bees, lizards, and stars). The therapist introduces the activity by stating, "Today we are going to do an activity that is going to help us talk about feelings. Everyone has feelings. Sometimes we experience comfortable feelings, like happy or proud. Sometimes we experience uncomfortable feelings, like sad or mad. It is normal and okay to have both comfortable and uncomfortable feelings." Next, the therapist spreads the butcher paper on the floor, has the child lie down on it, and traces the child's body outline onto the paper. The child can personalize the body outline by coloring in the face. The therapist then guides the child through the activity as follows:

Therapist:	We are going to use stickers to help us talk about different feelings. First, we are going to talk about happy feelings. What makes you feel happy?
Child:	When my mom buys me a treat.
Therapist:	Where in your body do you feel happy?
Child:	All over.
Therapist:	You can use the happy-face stickers to show where you feel happy in your body. (The child then sticks the happy-face stickers on the body outline.)
Therapist:	What about sad feelings. What makes you feel sad?
Child:	When other kids won't play with me.
Therapist:	Where in your body do you feel sad?
Child:	In my heart.

Therapist:	You can use the upside-down happy faces to show where you feel sad in your body. (The child then sticks the upside-down happy faces on the body outline on the heart.)
Therapist:	We all get mad sometimes. What makes you feel mad?
Child:	When my brother changes the channel when I'm watching TV.
Therapist:	Where in your body do you feel mad?
Child:	In my throat because I yell at him! (The child puts the stickers on the body outline.)
Therapist:	The lizard stickers are for scared feelings. When do you feel scared?
Child:	When Mom and Dad are fighting.
Therapist:	Can you tell me more about that?
Child:	They fight a lot, and Dad makes Mom cry.
Therapist:	Why do you think Mom cries?
Child:	Because Dad is mean to her.
Therapist:	What does Dad do that is mean?
Child:	He punches her, and yells a lot.
Therapist:	Where in your body do you feel scared?
Child:	My eyes, because I get scared when I see it. (The child sticks the lizards on the body outline on the eyes.)
Therapist:	Lots of kids would feel scared when they see their parents fighting. What advice would you give to another child who also felt scared when his mom and dad were fighting?
Child:	I would tell him to call the police.
Therapist:	That's good advice. The last stickers, the stars, are for proud. When do you feel proud?
Child:	When I get a good report card.

Therapist: That is something to feel proud about! Where in your body
               do you feel proud?

Child: Everywhere. (The child then places the star stickers on the
               body outline.)

Therapist: You did a good job talking about your feelings today!

The child is then provided with paper and a variety of stickers to make
a sticker book to take home at the end of the session.

APPLICATION

This activity can be modified for use with various age groups, and can
be used with a wide range of client populations, including children
dealing with abuse, domestic violence, divorce, grief and loss, chronic or
terminal illness, substance abuse, and placement in out-of-home care. The
technique serves as both an assessment tool as well as a treatment
intervention. As an evaluation and diagnostic tool, the activity elicits
valuable information that can be integrated into the child's overall
assessment. During treatment, the activity facilitates affective expression
and cathartic release. This activity also gives children a sense of mastery
and control as they decide which feelings and experiences to discuss.

This is a concrete intervention that helps bring the child's issues and
concerns to the surface. The practitioner can use the exercise as a point of
departure to further explore and discuss the child's feelings. Through the
use of open-ended questions and supportive comments, the child's
openness is encouraged.

20

The Gingerbread Person Feelings Map

Athena A. Drewes

INTRODUCTION

This technique can be utilized by children who have difficulty identifying and integrating their feelings. It has been successfully utilized with traumatized children in a residential treatment setting; however, it can be used in any setting and with any age group.

RATIONALE

Children who have been traumatized often have difficulty expressing and identifying feelings within them, especially when dealing with emotionally charged situations or memories. They often revert to saying "sad" or "mad" to express many feelings that may be going on inside of them. Children particularly have difficulty conceptualizing that many feelings could be occurring simultaneously within them or that they may feel ambivalent. Often they are not well integrated with their body and do not understand how their various feelings may be felt in various parts of their body. I have found using this simple expressive arts technique helpful both as a diagnostic tool and as a visual aid for helping children better understand and integrate their feelings.

DESCRIPTION

I use the shape of a gingerbread person with eyes, nose, and a smile. Next to the outline are the words, happy, sad, afraid, angry, love, and worried (Figure 20–1). I usually have several reproduced blank forms

Figure 20–1. Gingerbread person—blank form.

available to use, but you could also just quickly draw the gingerbread shape spontaneously during a session, as the need or opportunity arises. I also ask children to try and add one or two other feelings to the list. By asking them to include another word or two, I help them expand their "emotional vocabulary." It also gives them some control over the task, and they feel they are an active participant in the process. I have also found this task very helpful in quickly gathering informal information on the child's cognitive skills and underlying concerns. Over the years, I have been amazed at the choice of feeling words children have added to the list, such as petrified, anxious, stupid, tense, and confused.

The child then chooses a color for each feeling listed and makes a small line with the marker, crayon, or colored pencil next to the feeling word. It is interesting to see the choices made, rather than having preselected colors filled in on the drawing. Many children I have worked with have come up with nontraditional colors for happy and angry, such as using blue for happy and yellow for angry.

I then use an emotionally upsetting situation the child was talking about as a reference or I have the child think back to a particularly emotionally upsetting event in school or at home. Then I ask the child to color inside the gingerbread person where he may experience each feeling listed (both in the situation we've talked about and in general). Once completed, we process the drawing. I pay particular attention to where in the body anger is expressed and how that might play out in the child's world in responding to situations and point this out to the child. I look for discrepancies, such as where the child may have colored in happy feelings on the face, but anger in the hands, feet, or body. We then talk about how the child may present to others as calm, but inwardly he is seething, or perhaps manifesting his anger through hitting or restlessness in his legs. We look at where he put love (usually drawn as a heart) and how it may be "walled" off by layers of scared, hurt, and angry feelings.

Children enjoy the visual aid in being able to see where they feel and express their anger, as well as their love and happy feelings. This aid then becomes a good starting point for helping children work on better ways to express their feelings and handle situations as well as help integrate the children's affect.

APPLICATION

I like to use this technique in the initial stages of individual play therapy, early in the relationship, to help assess how emotionally constricted children might be, how aware they are of their inner life of feelings, and how connected or disconnected they may be from their body. It also is a fun activity and helps early on to lessen anxiety about the ways in which we can talk and deal with feelings and emotionally charged situations. As a way of measuring therapeutic progress, I will repeat this exercise again six months later as a way to see how therapy may be helping and if there is progress in the child's awareness and integration of feelings. After we've looked over and talked about the new gingerbread person coloring, I will bring out the first one the child completed and compare it, with the child assisting. Children enjoy being able to see the differences, and discuss progress that has been made in feeling better integrated with their affect and in handling their feelings.

Case Example

Nick was a 10-year-old boy who often would walk around with a smile on his face, appearing happy, but at the slightest frustration or teasing by a peer he seethed with anger, ready to fight. In therapy, he often angrily spoke of his longing for his mother to get off drugs and become the nurturing and protective mother of his dreams. When asked to explore his feelings, Nick had difficulty expressing his ambivalence. We utilized the gingerbread person drawing and Nick quickly could see how many different feelings he had and where he experienced them. He also was surprised that the drawing had a smiling face when in fact it had so many angry feelings inside, and commented that it should really be frowning. He quickly changed the mouth to a frown (Figure 20–2). Then he spontaneously made the connection that he always walked around with a smile, when in fact he really did not feel that way inside and others must think he was happy when he wasn't. It was the beginning of helping him realize the incongruity of his happy face masking his emotions of fear, loneliness, anger, and love (Figure 20–3). Over the next six months, Nick was able to integrate his affect and feel more in control of his anger.

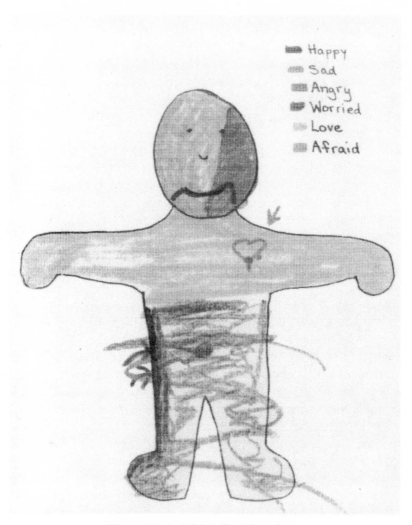

Figure 20–2. Nick's first drawing.

Figure 20–3. Nick's second drawing.

21

The "Feeling" and "Doing" Thermometer: A Technique for Self-Monitoring

James M. Briesmeister

INTRODUCTION

Depending on their cognitive levels and individual abilities, young children typically do not have an adequate capacity for appraising themselves and their behaviors. This is particularly true of children prior to the full acquisition of Piaget's third level of cognitive development, concrete operations (Flavell et al. 1993, Ginsburg & Oppler 1988). Children, at best, have undeveloped and inadequate abilities of self-perception and self-monitoring. They do not yet recognize the complex range of their own behaviors and emotional expressions. The use of the "feeling" and "doing" thermometer within a play therapy format offers a concrete behavioral technique for developing self-evaluation and, thereby, improving self-perception, self-control, and self-competence.

RATIONALE

Young children are limited in their ability to appraise the range and intensity of their behavioral and feeling states. By the very nature of their early developmental levels, they tend to think in black and white extremes. They do not yet appreciate the subtleties and gradations of a full range of emotions. Children do not fully grasp the notion that emotions exist on a continuum, ranging from mild to severe. For instance, when asked to describe their feelings, children frequently speak in generic, but age-appropriate and all-encompassing single-word responses, such as "good," "yukky," or "bad." In a similar manner, when asked, "How sad (happy, angry, upset, etc.) do you feel today?" the youngsters usually respond in absolutes by saying, "I'm *real* sad." By integrating the feeling thermometer within a play therapy modality, children can learn to identify and monitor a much wider range of affective experiences.

Schaefer's (1993) systematic taxonomy and analysis of the therapeutic factors in play include the development of a sense of competence that results in improved self-esteem. Play techniques that facilitate self-perception and self-monitoring foster the child's sense of competence. The ability to evaluate one's actions and emotions is essential to self-management and the resultant sense of self-efficacy (Bandura 1977). Through the use of the feeling (or doing) thermometer we can strengthen the child's self-competency by facilitating the self-evaluative process. Improved cognitive monitoring of feelings and actions can lead to better understanding, behavioral control, and a heightened sense of self-efficacy.

DESCRIPTION

Most children have had experiences with a thermometer. For instance, they will say, "Mommie uses it to see if I'm sick." They may also state, "You put the thermometer in your mouth to see how hot your head is." Therapists who work with children can capitalize on the youngsters' familiarity with this measuring instrument. A large thermometer can be drawn on an artboard or piece of cardboard. Gradations from 1 to 5 are drawn on the outside of the thermometer. The bottom section is cut out and a smaller strip of red construction paper (or red artboard) is placed behind the cut-out section. The red strip is mobile and can slide up or down a gauge from the lowest point, number 1, up through 2, 3, and 4, to the highest point, number 5. Children can be instructed to measure the perceived level of their own feeling states or to evaluate their behavioral performance on any given task by sliding the red mark on the thermometer to the corresponding point. A small range of gradations is suggested. If too large a range is used, it may become confusing and overwhelming to young minds.

In the initial stages, children often will encounter difficulties in appraising the levels and intensity of their own emotional status. Therefore, the therapist could offer an external and, perhaps, less threatening source of affective display by using puppets to stage various degrees of happiness, sadness, anger, and the like. The child can be taught to evaluate the level of the puppets' feeling states. For example, the youngster could be instructed to move the red mark to 1 if the puppet is only a little bit angry, or 2 if more angry, or all the way to 5 if the puppet is the most angry it can possibly be. The therapist, of course, could model this perceived appraisal of the puppets' emotional levels. After a few demonstrations, children can then begin to appraise and monitor the range of their own feelings.

The artboard drawing can also be dubbed the "doing" thermometer. If using the same thermometer confuses a very young child, a second drawing can be constructed using a strip of blue movable construction paper, thereby offering two separate measuring instruments. In a similar manner, the child can be taught to monitor levels of behaviors, performance, social-interpersonal interactions, and the like. The parents can enter into the therapy session and with the aid of this measuring instrument they can also gauge the intensity of their child's most recent temper outburst or expression of sadness. This adult feedback affords children an invaluable opportunity to compare their interpretation and appraisal with that of their parents (therapist, teachers, peers, etc.). Congruence or marked disparities between the child's perceived evaluation and that of another person can offer crucial therapeutic information and serve as the content for future sessions.

By engaging in this comparative process and being given feedback, children become cognizant of the consequences and social impact of personal moods, feelings, behaviors, and interactional styles. It places the individual's self-evaluation within a social context. Youngsters can learn to identify and monitor the degree of reciprocity and fair play that is present within a game with their peers. They can be asked to rate themselves as they imagine a favorite playmate might evaluate them.

This not only encourages a more accurate self-perception, it also enhances perspective-taking and helps children to appraise the impact that their actions and moods might have on others.

APPLICATION

Cognitive-behavioral play therapy incorporates a wide and diverse array of techniques, such as storytelling, puppet play, role playing, verbal games, mirroring, and modeling, to name but a few. The feeling and doing thermometer is a concrete and visual adaptation of a ranking or rating scale. The gamut can be incorporated into a wide expanse of cognitive-social-behavioral play approaches. It has been used to help children with conduct disorder, impulse control problems, temper outbursts, attention-deficit/hyperactivity disorder (ADHD), and related dysfunctional behaviors identify and monitor the intensity of their disruptive actions. They also gain a better understanding of the impact their behaviors have on others, such as their parents and peers. Youngsters can be taught to rate (assess) their performance in a game as well as evaluate the extent to which they lost control and acted out (e.g., shouting, pushing, fighting). They can also become more aware of their individual and therapeutic progress by auditing their attentional levels: their gains in anger management, sharing, and fair play; and the degree to which disruptions have decreased.

This self-monitoring technique has also been very useful with depressed children who have difficulties in identifying and determining the intensity of their personally experienced negative affect (Briesmeister 1997). Once children learn to evaluate the level or degree of sadness, they can gain some sense of mastery over the mood state. Children are encouraged and enabled to recognize progress when, for example, they are able to say, "Last week my sad feeling was a 5, today it's only a 2; that's a lot better."

In addition to reducing the symptoms of depression as well as acting-out disorders, the self-evaluative technique can also be used in treating shyness and social inhibition, selective mutism, and obsessive-compulsive/perfectionist tendencies. Similarly, it can be an effective aid in reducing the incidents and intensity of childhood fears. The ability to rank a hierarchical sequence of fears is an essential component of progressive desensitization. The thermometer technique affords even young children a method for assigning a specific ranking to their fears and phobias. A growing appreciation and gradual attainment of self-awareness, self-control, and self-competence are inherent goals of all play therapy approaches. Therefore, the feeling and doing thermometer can be incorporated into various play therapy situations and can be prove an invaluable adjunct in treating diverse childhood diagnostic categories and disorders.

References

Bandura, A. (1977). Self-efficacy: toward a unifying theory of behavioral change. *Psychological Review* 84: 191–215.

Briesmeister, J. M. (1997). Play therapy with depressed children. In *The Playing Cure*, ed. H. G. Kaduson, D. Cangelosi, and C. E. Schaefer, pp. 3–28. Northvale, NJ: Jason Aronson.

Flavell, J. H., Miller, P. H., and Miller, S. A. (1993). *Cognitive Development*, 3rd ed. Englewood Cliffs, NJ: Prentice Hall.

Ginsburg, H. P., and Oppler, S. (1988). *Piaget's Theory of Intellectual Development*, 3rd ed. Englewood Cliffs, NJ: Prentice Hall.

Schaefer, C. E. (1993). *The Therapeutic Power of Play*. Northvale, NJ: Jason Aronson.

22

Medicine Bags

Theresa A. Kruczek

INTRODUCTION

Children often need assistance in generalizing from one learning situation to others. Two natural ways to facilitate this process are use of transitional objects and positive associational cues. Transitional objects are tangible representations of someone or something that children carry with them to remind them of the object represented. Similarly, positive associational cues are tangible representations for children, but they serve a slightly different purpose. Children who have had traumatic life experiences often have frequent and strong anxiety reactions. Those anxiety reactions are precipitated by negative associational cues or environmental triggers associated with the traumatic event. Positive associational cues are calming and soothing triggers developed to counteract the negative associational cues. Counselors can use medicine bags as containers for transitional objects and positive associational cues.

RATIONALE

Medicine bags can serve as a bridge between the therapeutic environment and children's outside world. Children and counselors can create symbols and reminders to place in the children's medicine bag. The children can take these symbols/reminders with them in their daily functioning environment. The symbols and reminders can concretize and reinforce images and strategies developed in the counseling process. Further, the symbolism inherent in the medicine bag can be healing for children.

DESCRIPTION

Counselors either can have medicine bags on hand to distribute to children, or can have the children make the medicine bag in the therapy session. To make the medicine bag, children need sufficient fine motor skills and the ability to follow directions. The medicine bags are simple drawstring pouches about 3 by 5 inches (see Appendix A for a pattern). There are advantages and disadvantages to counselor-made or child-made bags. The advantage of the counselor providing the bag is it can become a transitional object for children between the therapeutic environment and their daily functioning environment. The advantage of having the children make the medicine bag is that successful construction can be an esteem-enhancing task.

Whichever mechanism is utilized, counselors explain to the child that Native-American "medicine men" used medicine bags for healing. Healing symbols or tokens were placed in the bag and worn close to the person to aid the healing process. Then counselor and child can create healing symbols within the context of therapy. You are only limited by your own creativity in developing healing symbols. Symbols can be powerful animals, superheroes, or mythic creatures. They can be helpful people like police officers, firefighters, doctors, or nurses. You can use guided imagery to have the child envision safe or calming places and make drawings of those places. You can even include reminders of cognitive and behavioral strategies. Children can also be encouraged to add symbols to their bags with the aid of parents and other important adults. These latter symbols can be reminders of positive, happy events and activities.

APPLICATION

This technique is particularly useful with children who have been traumatized or who have significant anxiety. It is also beneficial for children whose environment is chaotic. With all these children, the symbols included in the medicine bag can serve as a bridge between the safety and security of the therapeutic environment and their daily functioning environments. The bag can be a container the children can carry with them. It can contain the positive and adaptive coping strategies developed within the context of counseling.

Case Example

A 9-year-old girl was brought to counseling by her mother. Her mother had been recently diagnosed with breast cancer. Approximately two weeks after the parents disclosed this diagnosis to their children, the girl attended summer day camp. She was stung by a bee in the outdoor toilet at camp, on two successive days. At the time of referral, she was refusing to go outside and evidenced fear of going to the bathroom at home. The child presented as a bright, creative, and engaging child. On inquiry she identified her fear of the outdoors as an exaggerated response to the bee stings. She indicated the bee stings had triggered a fear of death. That is, she was afraid she was going to die. She also described a dream where she and her mother were encircled by dinosaurs and there were giant prehistoric insects trying to attack them. In counseling, we connected her recent "traumatic" life events (the bee stings and mother's diagnosis) and her current fears. We sewed a medicine bag and put in drawings of the dinosaurs. She additionally included pictures of birds (as predators of bees) and insecticide. She wore the medicine bag on a string around her neck. She shared her fears with her parents. Within a few weeks she was able to go outside and was no longer afraid to go to the bathroom at home.

APPENDIX A

Medicine bag sewing instructions:

1. Fold short ends under ¼ inch (wrong side of fabric).

2. Fold long top down ½ inch (wrong side of fabric).

3. Stitch at bottom edge of long top draw string sleeve.

4. Fold right sides of fabric together at center line.

5. Stitch ½-inch final seam along outside perimeter starting at bottom edge of drawstring sleeve.

6. Turn pouch right side out.

7. Feed drawstring through sleeve. Tie off end of drawstring.

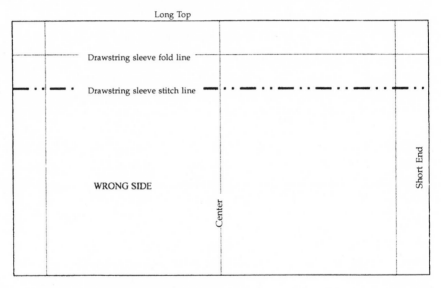

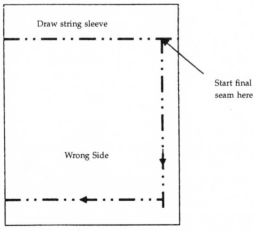

23

Feeling Flowers/Healing Garden

Tamra Greenberg

INTRODUCTION

This technique can be used to enable children to correctly identify and appropriately express their feelings. When working with sexually abused children, this technique enables them to process and work through traumatic experiences. Expanding on the "Color Your Life" technique introduced by O'Connor (1983), it includes a creative and tactile component so often beneficial in working with survivors of sexual and/or physical abuse. Further, there is opportunity for transformational work with this technique as the flowers/garden can be an ongoing creation reflecting progress over the course of treatment.

RATIONALE

The betrayal so commonly experienced by sexually abused children often leads to difficulty in interpersonal relationships. This difficulty may manifest itself as impairment in the ability to form attachments and/or an inability to trust. Relating to such patients through the use of play therapy can be a more natural and less threatening form of interaction. Consequently, the therapeutic alliance is strengthened and the child has the opportunity for a corrective relational experience. The powerlessness often present in sexually abused children can surface as anxiety, and the children need assistance in facing their fearful feelings and memories. Using play as a method to aid children in exploring and sharing their abuse experience, this technique helps to reduce anxiety, thereby making children more available to working through their trauma. Creating the "feeling flowers" helps them to identify and express their thoughts and feelings within a safe environment. Further, the development of a "garden" provides the opportunity for transformation and mastery.

DESCRIPTION

The therapist provides clay in an assortment of colors. Sitting with the child, the therapist presents a feelings list. It is helpful to have ready-made lists available that are either age appropriate or specific to the clinical issue at hand. Alternatively, the child can be invited to assist the therapist in creating his or her own feelings list. Using the chosen feelings list, colors are then paired with feelings. For example, blue is paired with the feeling sad, red with angry, yellow with happy, and so on, until each feeling is paired with all the colors of clay available. The play then proceeds as follows:

Therapist: We are going to use this clay to make some flowers. And each flower will represent a feeling for you. So we'll use our feelings list to match the feelings with the different colors of flowers. For example, if you feel sad today, we'll make some blue flowers. And if you also feel angry, we'll make some red flowers. We'll make however many red flowers to show us just how much anger you feel today. Okay?

Child: Okay, can orange be worried?

Therapist: Sure! You feel worried?

Child: Yeah! There are some new Pokemon cards out today, and I might not get there in time!

The therapist will continue to explore the child's thoughts and feelings by going through each of the feeling/color pairs and helping the child to make the flowers that show her feelings. Initially, the therapist may use this technique to explore feelings in general. In later sessions, it may be used to explore feelings and thoughts specifically about the abuse, as follows:

Therapist: Remember how we used the flowers to talk about feelings?

Child: Yes. I had a lot of orange flowers that day!

Therapist: Well, we're going to make flowers again today. But today I want you to think about what your uncle did to you, and we'll make flowers that show your feelings only about what happened then.

Child: Okay, but I'll need a lot of red flowers!

Therapist: You feel very angry. I wonder what's making you so angry.

Child: What my uncle did to me makes me VERY angry!

At the end of the session, the child will have created a bouquet of flowers that represent her many feelings and have aided her in identifying and appropriately expressing her feelings and thoughts about her abuse.

With older children, this technique may be expanded to include the creation of an entire garden. In this case, we would incorporate the use of items such as weeds and rocks in addition to the flowers to demonstrate how the child feels about herself or her life before, during, or after the abuse. The garden would remain intact in the therapist's office and be made available to the client during each session. Over time, with the child tending to his "garden," rocks and weeds give way to blossoms and flowers, with the flowers continuing to represent a range of feelings about the abuse and the self. As the child works through the pain of the abuse and begins to refocus on the positive aspects of the self, a garden once dominated by red and blue flowers (anger and sadness) may change over time to a garden of yellow and pinks (happiness and love).

APPLICATION

The feeling flowers/healing garden technique is particularly useful with victims of childhood sexual abuse. Identification and appropriate expression of the feelings involved in such abuse can be extremely difficult for these children for a number of reasons. Although the technique could certainly be used with any child, victims of sexual abuse—often having undergone numerous investigations—will experience this as far less threatening than direct questioning. Consequently, the child will be able to connect with her feelings, develop a trusting relationship with the therapist, and at that point be more available to develop necessary coping skills and to work through the abuse.

Reference

O'Connor, K. J. (1983). Color your life technique. In *Handbook of Play Therapy*, ed. C. E. Schaefer and K. J. O'Connor. New York: Wiley.

24

Sharing Feelings through Clay

Debra Atchison

INTRODUCTION

Sharing feelings is a basic component of therapy. Yet sharing uncomfortable feelings is a difficult task for most of us, adults and children alike. When asked to describe or discuss difficult feelings, children benefit from the concreteness and the sense of focus that clay can provide. That is, the clay can be a metaphor for feelings, yet at the same time it serves as a tangible item that is visible, changeable, and under the child's control. A child can look at the clay, focus on it, and avoid direct and sometimes intimidating eye contact with the therapist. The clay can be manipulated, squeezed, and pounded, which will help to reduce anxiety as a child broaches what is many times a difficult subject. If he chooses to not verbalize, the clay can serve as an object onto which the feelings are projected.

RATIONALE

Sharing feelings through clay is a directive approach useful as an assessment or treatment tool. In assessment, simple statements, such as

"Tell me about the happy feeling or sad feeling that you have right now," can be used. Other directives that might follow include "Tell me when you've had that feeling before? How long did you have it? Who made you have that feeling? Show me how big (small, strong, weak, etc.) it was." In treatment, reflections might include statements such as "Let's decide some ways you can make this bad feeling smaller, or this good feeling larger; if you talked to this feeling, what are some of the things you can say (do) to it?"

In both assessment and treatment, the feeling focus is on the clay. As the client moves further along in treatment, he can begin to take more ownership of feelings and begin to personalize them. For instance, reflections might include "Remember when we worked with the clay and you described your feelings using the clay? Without using the clay, tell me how you feel right now." "Remember when you told me you wanted to tell the piece of clay that you hated it for hurting you? Without using the clay, tell me how you felt when that person hurt you. Tell me how you feel right now."

Clearly, this process can be used with children who have experienced abuse. However, sharing feelings through clay can serve as an assessment and treatment tool for adults. The playfulness of the activity helps to reduce defense mechanism including those such as intellectualizing and rationalizing. For instance, victims of domestic violence could focus on the clay and project their feelings onto it. Victims of natural disasters, divorce, or grief could benefit from sharing feelings through clay. The tangible nature of the clay and the hands-on and the here-and-now experience facilitate the affective side of a client. As treatment progresses, the client should be able to take ownership of feelings, express them in session, and bring resolution to them, which is what we want all clients to do.

DESCRIPTION

Even during a first session, the topic of feelings is introduced. For instance, I say to the child, "This is a time and a place for you to feel safe, to talk about whatever you want to talk about." If a child seems to get stuck and can't move on to a higher level of dealing with an incident, I might suggest that he tell me how he's feeling right at that moment. If he can't verbalize his feeling, he can draw, paint, or act it out. However, if the child still isn't able to express himself I use the sharing feelings through clay technique.

Holding a fistful size of clay in my hand, I ask the child to hold out his hand and take the clay. I tell him that all his feelings (sad, angry, scared, and happy) are like the lump of clay. I pull off a portion of the clay and tell the child that it's like sharing a feeling, that when he shares he doesn't have to carry around the big lump alone. I then ask the child if there are any feelings that he wants or needs to share. The first time he may be hesitant. If so, I do not force the issue but introduce it again in following sessions. At some point, I have found that many children will respond.

By giving me a portion of the clay, the child has chosen to trust me by sharing a feeling. I encourage verbalization and attempt to track what the child says. However, if he only hands me a piece of clay and doesn't give verbal information, after a few seconds of silence I reflect to him that "in my playroom you can choose to talk or you can choose not to talk." All the time I'm hoping that he will verbalize his feelings, if not then, then perhaps in the future.

APPLICATION

The technique works best with children who are reluctant for various reasons to talk about their feelings. Even happy feelings are sometimes difficult for children to talk about. I also use this technique to talk about bad dreams or anything that is difficult for children to verbalize. The idea is to have the child share part of the "burden" with you as the therapist, to contain and hold it for him.

Some children have become accustomed to sharing their feeling through clay. On entering the playroom, they immediately pick up clay and begin to hand me portions of it, telling me about their feelings. Some will use the clay (labeled with a feeling) in cooking, making various types of foods with good feelings or bad feelings. Children sometimes mix various feelings together, which is a metaphor itself for having many mixed-up and confused feelings or having many conflicting feelings at the same time. I've found this metaphor especially useful in working with children who have anger issues with a parent whom they love and dislike all at the same time. Or in the case of adults, the mixing of feelings may describe an abusive spouse who is still loved but simultaneously disliked.

25

Weights and Balloons

Celia Linden

INTRODUCTION

A common challenge when working with children is how to make the information they need to learn in treatment accessible and meaningful. Many therapeutic constructs are abstract and difficult for the young child to comprehend. The theoretical information may be valid and necessary for the child to master in order to attain her/his therapeutic goals, but frequently the clinician struggles with how to make this information readily available for the youngster.

Practical activities children can playfully experience are often a good way to teach important therapeutic concepts. Experiential learning and hands-on techniques are cornerstones of current educational philosophy, which can be applied to learning that occurs in the playroom as well. When a child can participate in the process of acquiring a new skill, it will be a more meaningful experience and will assist that child in retaining the information. Props and play are an ideal combination of techniques to make important therapeutic material accessible to the young child.

RATIONALE

Cognitive-behavioral treatment techniques are extremely useful in treating children with depression; however, some of the ideas involved are complicated. When working with young children, the more concrete and easy the information is to apply, the more likely the child will be able to utilize that technique in a real-life situation, making the therapy more effective.

DESCRIPTION

To use this technique you will need the following things:

About a dozen helium balloons

Paper and pen

Weights of some kind (rocks, paperweights, blocks, etc.)

The therapist and the child first work to generate a list of the negative and positive thoughts the child has about a particular situation or in general about their lives. The lists are to be kept separate either in columns or on different pieces of paper. When the lists are completed, the therapist will explain how negative cognitions feed the feelings of depression and weigh us down. Then a list of positive thoughts is created, and the therapist explains that these thoughts help to lift our spirits and help us feel good. The therapist at this point can explain the theoretical notion that our thoughts directly affect our feelings and that we can change the way we feel by changing our thoughts.

Once the lists are completed, the therapist will assign each negative thought a weight and each positive thought a balloon. The therapist will demonstrate at first how it feels to hold each of the objects, letting the child get a sense of the physical sensation of each object. If the child is able, the therapist can elicit how it feels to hold each object at this time, to assist in the processing of this activity when it is finished. After the child experiences each of the objects, the therapist will talk about each negative thought and assign its weight. For a more sophisticated child, the weights can be incremented to represent more serious negative cognitions. After the negative thoughts are completed, the therapist and child can process what it feels like to carry the weight. The child can try to move about the office carrying the weights or go for a short walk to further illustrate the sensation of being burdened down.

An additional part of this activity can involve the child carrying around these negative thoughts (the weights) for a while to experience how it feels to hold onto negative thoughts. When the child is asked to put the weights down (or told to let go of the negative cognitions), the child can feel what it is like not to carry around these feelings any more. The therapist and child will process this after the task is accomplished.

Next, the positive thoughts are each assigned a balloon. These can be given to the child to hold or tied onto an arm. The therapist can discuss the "weightlessness" of these thoughts and assist the child in understanding how these positive cognitions are helpful. The following is an example of how this technique can be used in a play therapy session. It was taken from a session with a depressed adolescent patient.

Therapist: Today I brought some things to help us continue our work on changing those negative thoughts that are making things gloomy and difficult. Here's what we are going to do. First we'll pick something that is bothering you.

Child: OK. Start with school.

Therapist: Sure. What about it?

Child: I always pay attention to the bad grades I get. When I get a bad grade, I think it's the worst thing in the world. I really don't think it's anything good when I get a good grade.

Therapist: Tell me what you hear yourself say to yourself when you get a bad grade.

Child: I'm dumb. Everyone else is smarter than me. The teachers think I am stupid and I don't study. I'll never go to college. Who cares about the good grades anyway?

Therapist: Wow! Those are pretty heavy thoughts. Here. For each of those statements I am going to give you a rock (therapist

	gives the child five weights to hold). Take these for a walk around the room (the child does). Now put them in your pockets. How do they feel?
Child:	Heavy.
Therapist:	What do you think it would feel like to carry these all day every day at school? What if you had to hold them in your hands all day?
Child:	How could I write? They would be in my way.
Therapist:	Exactly. These heavy thoughts get in your way. They weigh you down and make things difficult for you. Now let's change those thoughts into positive messages you can give yourself.
Child:	Ummm . . .
Therapist:	It's easier for you to think of the negative ones. You are used to listening to these.
Child:	Yeah.
Therapist:	Let's see. What can you say to yourself about your grades that would lift you up instead of bring you down?
Child:	Well, I guess I could say "Good job" if I got a decent grade.
Therapist:	All right! Here, let's put this on your wrist (therapist ties a balloon onto the child, providing the child has no issues with this type of touch). What else could you say?
Child:	Well, I am not perfect and I won't always get everything right.
Therapist:	Good! Here are two more. How about another?
Child:	I am still learning.
Therapist:	Right!
Child:	That's all I can think of.
Therapist:	Now take a walk around with these. How does it feel?

Child: Different. Kind of funny.

Therapist: Imagine having these on all day.

Child: That would be weird.

Therapist: These thoughts are the kind that lift you up. When we give ourselves these kind of messages we can actually help keep ourselves positive. You can feel the difference, right? Now pick up the rocks while you have the balloons. Which do you feel more?

Child: The rocks.

Therapist: These negative thoughts really want you to notice them. Now put them down again.

The therapist and child could continue to play with the objects to further illustrate the difference in the cognitions and how they affect the child's functioning. In this session, homework was given to the child and the parents to notice any negative statements the child makes at home. The child was to be given a rock to hold at the moment any negative statement was made. Similarly, the parents and child were told to notice positive statements made at home. When one was noticed, the child was to be given a balloon. The child was asked to keep a log of these for a couple of days and bring it to the next session. At this point work on these thoughts would continue.

APPLICATION

This activity is particularly useful for children who struggle with depression but can also be used with all children to illustrate the effect of cognition on affect.

26

The Child's Own Touching Rules Book

Frances L. Strick

INTRODUCTION

An increasing number of prepubescent children, some as young as 3 or 4 years old, are referred to play therapists because of precocious or sexually acting-out behaviors. Most, although not all, of these children have histories of victimization (Araji 1997). A traumatized child needs to heal from his traumatic experiences (Gil 1991), but he must also terminate his inappropriate behaviors. We cannot allow the traumatized child to continue to act out his own experiences against other children who may in turn act out against others. Sexually acting-out children may progress in their behaviors until they become adolescent, and then adult, sexual offenders (Groth 1994). Treatment for sexually acting-out children should include the same critical elements as treatment for adolescent and adult sexual offenders: overcoming denial, increasing victim empathy, and developing a treatment plan (Salter 1991).

RATIONALE

A child-centered approach is frequently very effective in assisting a child in working toward resolution of traumatic experiences, and may be effective in phasing out sexually inappropriate behaviors. However, a directive approach that focuses on immediate termination of the sexual acting-out behavior can be effective in preventing many other children from being victimized (Salter 1991). Directive techniques can be implemented by the same therapist prior to the child-centered session, thereby addressing both survivor and victimizing treatment needs. The therapist emphasizes that during the first part of the session they will be working together, and for the remainder of the session the child will get to do pretty much whatever he would like to do. I have adapted Anna Salter's technique of assisting the child as he creates his own book of behavior rules so that it can be used with very young children.

DESCRIPTION

Following intake, at the beginning of the first regular session, the therapist asks the child to sit next to her. The location, an office separate from the playroom or an area in the playroom, will be the same for the focused part of each session. The therapist explains to the child that she has heard that he has been getting into trouble for touching other children in a way that is "not OK." It is important that the child understand that they are working as a team on his "touching problem" so that he will not upset any other children or grown-ups through his behavior. The technique proceeds like this:

Therapist: You know many rules about touching. (I have never seen a child who had not been taught something about this subject.) We are going to make a book about your rules so that you will remember them very well. Here is the paper. You can choose to staple it or use tape. (The child does the stapling or taping, with assistance, if necessary.) What would you like to title your book?

Child: "No More Ugly Stuff!" (The child is allowed to title the book something that is meaningful to him, even if, at first glance, it is something that the therapist would like to correct.) The child writes the title of the book and his name on the cover, with assistance if necessary. He may add a picture or a design.

Therapist: What is a rule about touching that you have learned?

Child: Do not put your hands in other people's underwear.

Therapist: You remembered an important rule! What could you draw so that you will remember this rule?

Child: (Draws a pair of underwear and traces his own hand. Together the child and the therapist read the title page and first rule.)

Therapist: It is important that you remember the rule. You will be asked to "read it" at the next session.

During the remainder of the session the therapist uses a child-centered approach. At the following session the child reads the book title and his first rule, and then adds another rule in his own words with his own picture. The child or the therapist prints the rule. Another example of a specific rule created by a child is, "Do not touch tongues with other people," accompanied by a picture of a person's face with a large mouth and a protruding, red tongue. Rules are added until the child cannot think of any more. At this point the therapist may add a rule about maintaining his own safety, such as the well-known "Say 'No'! Run! And tell, if someone approaches you in a sexual way." Prior to termination, the child shares his book with a parent or caregiver just as an adolescent or adult sexual offender shares his prevention plan with family members.

APPLICATION

This approach may be used with children as young as 4 or 5, as it relies on the child's own input and drawings and does not impose information that is beyond the child's cognitive level. It serves to overcome denial and assist the child in remembering his rules because he is the person who suggests the rule, and he feels supported by the therapist and his family in his efforts. The child in foster care can carry the book with him through any relocations and share it with his new families. His own "Touching Rules Book," although just a part of treatment, is an important part of his prevention plan.

References

Araji, S. K. (1997). Closing the cracks, systemic wide response needed. In *Sexually Aggressive Children*, ed. S. K. Araji, pp. 193–218. Thousand Oaks, CA: Sage.

Gil, E. (1991). *The Healing Power of Play*. New York: Guilford.

Groth, N. (1994). Intervention in child sexual abuse: victims, offenders, and survivors. Workshop conducted in Mobile, AL.

Salter, A. (1991). Treatment of child sexual abuse. Workshop conducted at the University of Alabama, Birmingham, AL.

27

Party Hats on Monsters: Drawing Strategies to Enable Children to Master Their Fears

David A. Crenshaw

INTRODUCTION

Children often resort to the defense of magical thinking: "If we don't talk or think about the problem, it doesn't exist." This is especially true of anxious children who are extremely reluctant to confront their fears and worries. The party-hats-on-monsters technique is a drawing strategy intended for preschool and school-age children. This intervention enables children to face their fears in a gradual and less threatening manner. It has been helpful with a wide range of anxiety disorders in children, including the catastrophic fears often associated with separation anxiety. It has also been useful with generalized anxiety disorder and posttraumatic and acute stress disorder. Titrated exposure has been shown to be the most effective way to reduce anxious and phobic symptomatology (Barlow 1988, Silverman and Kurtines 1996). Exposures to the feared objects or images can involve both in vivo ("live") and imaginal forms (Silverman and Kurtines 1996). The empirically supported treatment of anxiety disorders in children includes learning to handle their fears or anxiety through gradual exposure. Children typically find it reassuring that they are not expected to face their worst fear or anxiety immediately. The step-by-step success experience with the anxious event or feared object increases their confidence and sense of mastery.

RATIONALE

Children need gentle but firm encouragement to confront the scary external events, or thoughts, fantasies, and dreams that occupy the internal space of their minds. Most young children enjoy drawing and coloring pictures, and this technique engages them in a playful activity that typically is less threatening than direct verbalization of their fears and worries. Mills and Crowley (1986) delineated helpful drawing strategies that they called inner resource drawings to enable children to cope with pain associated with injury, burns, or medical procedures. These strategies not only aided in desensitization but also increased hope in these children by having the child drawing their pain looking "all better." As Mills and Crowley explain, by asking children to draw how their pain or worry would look "all better," the therapist is suggesting that "all better" does exist, which helps to build hope in the child. Mills and Crowley place emphasis not only on the drawings releasing pent-up feelings but on the simultaneous activation of inner resources and strengths. Their work draws on the writings and teaching of Milton Erickson (1980) with his emphasis on the positive forces for healing in the unconscious and the potentials rather than the pathology of the person being the focus.

DESCRIPTION

The therapist sits at the same level as the child, either at a table or on the floor. The therapist has drawing paper or a sketch pad available along with pencil, markers, and crayons. The therapist could expand the choices if desired to watercolors, finger paints, or clay. Choices are very important to anxious children since it reinforces their sense of personal control. The drawing strategy proceeds as follows:

Therapist: First I would like you to draw something that you choose (again giving the child choices and control; if the child seems unsure what to draw, the therapist can suggest): Perhaps it could be a picture of your favorite toy or a picture of you doing something you really like. Or it could be a picture of something that makes you feel really good or very safe.

Child: I'll draw a picture of me shooting hoops.

Therapist: That's fine!

After the child finishes the drawing and the therapist has engaged the child in relaxed conversation about his drawing of a favorite activity, the therapist proceeds: "Now I want you to think about the scary things that have happened to you or the scary thoughts or dreams. I don't want you to draw the one that scares you the most; rather, I would like you to draw one that scares you *only a little.*"

If the child hesitates, the therapist states, "I've used these drawings with lots of children. These children have discovered that when they draw their scary thoughts or the thing that happened to them, it's not so scary anymore. When they put it out here on the paper, they can step back from it and to their surprise it's not as scary to them as it was when it was just in their mind. Also, when they put it down on paper and share it with me they don't feel so alone."

Child: I'll draw a green monster who scares me in my dreams.

Therapist: Good! Let's see that green monster in the light of day! (Therapist expresses confidence that the frightening image can be faced. Also, scary images and thoughts are typically more frightening at night.)

After the child has drawn the scary green monster, the therapist continues: "Good job! Now I want you to change the green monster in some way. You can shrink him and make him smaller. You could put a party hat on him so he doesn't look scary anymore! You can draw one of your favorite superheroes who arrives on the scene and tames the monster, or you can change it in some way that *you choose* that makes him less scary to you!"

While the child is doing the modification of the drawing, or afterward if it is distracting to the child, the therapist can add, "The amazing thing that so many children have discovered is that when they realize that they can change the picture out here on the paper, they can also change it in their head so they don't have to be afraid anymore!"

In the event that the child is trying to come to terms with his fears about an actual event in his life, he may be instructed to draw the event itself and then to draw it looking "all better" (Mills and Crowley 1986). Alternatively, the child could be asked to draw a picture of himself or his family looking "all better."

Making a hierarchy of the child's fears will allow the therapist to proceed at a pace that the child can tolerate. Also the child will gain confidence as he achieves mastery over the less intense, frightening thoughts, fantasies, or events.

APPLICATION

This strategy is useful with all children in facing their common fears, but especially useful with children experiencing anxiety disorders. It allows children a considerable degree of choice and control, pacing in keeping with the child's needs and gradual exposure and desensitization in the context of a playful activity that most children enjoy. The children gain mastery and confidence in facing even their most scary imaginary and external events.

References

Barlow, D. H. (1988). *Anxiety and Its Disorders. The Nature and Treatment of Anxiety and Panic.* New York: Guilford.

Erickson, M. (1980). *The Collected Papers of Milton Erickson on Hypnosis,* ed. E. L. Rossi. New York: Irvington.

Mills, J. C., and Crowley, R. J. (1986). *Therapeutic Metaphors for Children and the Child Within.* New York: Brunner/Mazel.

Silverman, W. K., and Kurtines, W. M. (1996). *Anxiety and Phobic Disorders: A Pragmatic Approach.* New York: Plenum.

28

The Feelings-Thoughts-Needs Inventory

Barbara A. Turner

INTRODUCTION

In my work with adults over the years I have frequently given them what I call an inventory assignment. Several times each day they are instructed to take a brief personal inventory of (1) their feelings, (2) their thoughts about their current situation, and (3) what they might need to preserve their sense of wholeness in relation to this situation.

RATIONALE

Many clients have suffered developmental deprivations that prohibit taking their subjective experience into account. Frequently their skill building was concerned more with surviving dysfunctional environments than it was with building healthy self-awareness tools. I assure the clients that with awareness of these three elements of personal experience, they will be able to set appropriate boundaries for themselves in any circumstances. It has been deeply gratifying to witness many examples of adult clients' increasing subjective awareness, while simultaneously enhancing their capacities to feel safe and to remove themselves from abusive relationships. An easy translation of this valuable tool was made for children through an interactive drawing.

DESCRIPTION

When the child presents with a perplexing or unresolved dilemma, the therapist can write the problem situation on a piece of paper and draw a hasty, full-bodied figure of the same gender and approximate age of the client. Drawing a large heart in the middle of the body, the therapist asks, "What is he [or she, depending on the gender of the child] feeling about this?" The child can write in words, color it in, and so on. Younger children may limit themselves to colors. The shared experience of the activity allows the therapist to talk with the child about his or her feelings and to model, or play-act the affect connected to the event with the child. The third-person reference to the child in the drawing—"What is he/she feeling or thinking?"—provides a more comfortable distance for the child to more easily access his or her subjective experience than would asking directly. The simplicity of the drawing also works to make the activity relaxed and nonthreatening.

Drawing a thought balloon emerging from the figure's head, the therapist then asks, "Now we know what he/she is feeling, what do you think he/she is thinking about this situation?" Again, the child is free to write thoughts that emerge from their discussion, or the therapist may write them for the child. The therapist's interaction and the concrete movement to another region of the drawing associated with the bodily experience begin the important work of distinguishing between feelings and thoughts.

The therapist then draws a large sign board in the hand of the figure and writes upon it, "What I need here is . . ." Talking to the child the therapist says, "Well, now we know what he/she feels about this and what he/she thinks about it. So, now we're ready to find out what he/she needs." The child or the therapist then writes down what the needs of the child are in the particular situation. Awareness of the feelings, thoughts, and needs associated with the child's problem facilitates discussion about problem solving, behavior change, boundary setting, and so on.

APPLICATION

The feelings-thoughts-needs inventory is a fun interactive psychoeducative tool that can provide children with the essential self-awareness skills they need to form healthy, reciprocal relationships. The shared experience of the drawing allows the therapist to comfortably meet the client at his or her level of awareness and to facilitate their emerging self-awareness. Since developing the inventory drawing for children, I have found it to be a great resource for adult clients as well. Although I prefer the spontaneity of doing the drawing with the client present, it is certainly possible to make and photocopy some outline templates in advance (see Figure 28–1 for some suggestions).

CASE EXAMPLES

In the middle of a session, a 5-year-old boy looked me directly in the eyes and said that his kitten had run away. Using the feelings-thoughts-needs inventory drawing, he said he felt sad, and proceeded to color in tears flowing from the eyes of the figure (Figure 28–2). He spontaneously colored in a green heart at the bottom of the drawing, saying, "I miss my kitty." As the child spoke and colored, I wrote in his feelings. He drew a "card" at the top left of the drawing, saying, "I love my kitty," then drew his loving rendition of his beloved, "Max."

I next sketched a thought balloon, asking, "What does he think about his kitty running away?" He quickly said that he wanted a new kitty. When asked what he might need about this problem, he said, "I need a kitty for Christmas!" With the full solemnity of his 5-year-old wisdom, he spontaneously added, "I wish he didn't run away. I hope he found a good home."

Another client, a 10-year-old boy facing multiple losses, required more coaxing from the therapist. Using the feelings-thoughts-needs inventory drawing to explore his experience of his father's recent relocation across country, all he could do was color a small dark blur of overlapping orange, purple, and green in the heart area (Figure 28–3). I quietly re-

Figure 28–1. Feelings-thoughts-needs inventory templates.

sponded, "That looks pretty sad to me." Picking up the cue, the client then said, "I'm very sad." "Also, I'm scared for Dad, because it's dangerous in Chicago." He proceeded to tell me about gangster movies he had seen set in Chicago. This gave rise to a reality check and a discussion about Chicago. Asked if he felt anything more, he said, "I'm

Figure 28–2. Feelings-thoughts-needs inventory: 5-year-old boy.

confused, too. He said he will come back in two years, but I don't think he will."

When asked what this boy thinks about his father moving so far away, he wrote in the words, "He misses me, too." By this point in the exercise

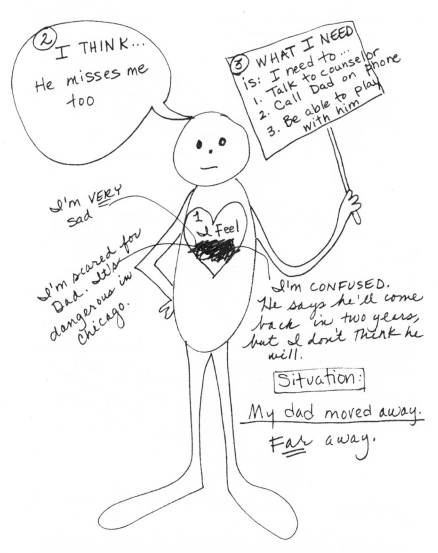

Figure 28–3. Feelings-thoughts-needs inventory: 10-year-old boy.

this boy was more forthcoming. He wrote in three things he needs regarding this situation of his father moving so far away. "I need to (1) talk to counselor, (2) call Dad on phone, (3) be able to play with him."

In both of these examples, the feelings-thoughts-needs inventory drawing permitted entry to an in-depth exploration of the children's subjective experiences of loss. At the same time the use of the inventory modeled self-examination skills that are applicable to other life circumstances. Whether used as a psychoeducational tool, or as a means of affective exploration and expression, the feelings-thoughts-needs inventory drawing is a valuable and engaging therapeutic tool with multiple applications in the play therapy setting.

29

Variation of the Family Attribute Game

Erika L. Surkin

INTRODUCTION

Initial assessment of the child and the family is necessary for all clients. Understanding the child's point of view regarding each family member and typical interaction often includes clear reference to presenting problems stated by parents. This technique often provides a rich source of information as therapy proceeds.

RATIONALE

Children who have not examined the role of each family member in creating a home environment may be unaware of their own contribution to difficult situations as well as their parents' efforts to cope. New patterns of interaction may begin to emerge through verbalization of the child's perception of temperament, behavior, and social style. Cognitive-behavioral therapy may then be used in an effective manner through play techniques, as outlined by Susan M. Knell (1993). This technique may be used during the assessment phase to understand the child's perspective on family dynamics. Later, reference can be made to these attributes, as provided initially, to elucidate the thought-feeling-behavior connection and create new self-talk.

DESCRIPTION

As part of the assessment process, a family drawing can be used to begin the process of the child's exploration of her own perceptions. The child is provided with a blank sheet of paper and drawing materials to depict the family "doing something." Children experiencing separation or divorce struggle with inclusion or exclusion of parents. The child who draws an intact family despite the reality of life communicates the often-unvoiced desire to undo the split between parents. Choice of activities, location of each family member in the drawing, and the size, shape, and choice of color provide information, as do body language and facial expression. Artistic talent is irrelevant.

Once the drawing has been completed, the therapist produces attribute cards, which are colorful 3" by 5" index cards. Each card has a general attribute written on it, such as "the most fun to be with," "the saddest," "the strongest," and "the one who cries a lot." The child creates a pile for each member of the family. Each pile can be placed below a name or drawing on a white board. These premade cards should contain generic statements applicable to most families and should include both positive and negative attributes. Once the child has assigned the premade stack of cards (enough to assign two or three cards per person), the child is invited to create her own cards. The therapist may explain that the cards were made for any family and may not give a good picture of the child's family. It is important for the therapist to write down whatever description the child offers in her own words and without comment. Most children run out of words. Use of a feelings chart may help to elicit responses.

Use of a different color for the cards created by the child will facilitate later assessment of the child's responses. Generally, the first one or two cards created and the order in which attributes are assigned provide vital clues about family dynamics. Once the cards have been sorted, a rubber band wrapped around each pile will allow later assessment of the order of sorting as well as keeping each pile intact.

APPLICATION

Assessment of children's perception of each family member is important in setting therapy goals for many different populations of children. I have used this technique effectively with children experiencing separation and divorce in order to explore current relationships as well as to determine "red flag" issues surrounding family dynamics. It is particularly effective with latency, preadolescent, and adolescent clients who may not be able to articulate family dynamics directly. Frequently, families with erratic practices of reward and discipline create a triangulation dynamic in which the child is the apex. This environment may be intolerable to the child, who carries an enormous burden in the life of the family. Understanding the role of each family member through the eyes of the child is key to understanding and helping to create a healthier environment for all.

Reference

Knell, S. (1993). *Cognitive-Behavioral Play Therapy*. Northvale, NJ: Jason Aronson.

30

How Am I Doing?
A Self-Evaluation Technique

Ellen M. Stickney

INTRODUCTION

An important part of the therapy process is ongoing review of progress. This is emphasized especially in brief therapy approaches and is often necessitated by managed care procedures. Play therapy is no exception. This review is generally done with a child's parents. The child can also greatly benefit from inclusion in this evaluation as she receives feedback on change and learns to identify her own growth. Her input can also provide the therapist with valuable information regarding future treatment objectives and/or readiness for termination. "How Am I Doing?" is a technique that provides a way for children to communicate these ideas concretely.

RATIONALE

Children tend to be cognitively concrete. It may be difficult for them to conceptualize growth and change and find words to describe it, especially in any measurable way. Using pictures and drawings provides children with a developmentally appropriate and meaningful way to become involved in the process of self-evaluation.

DESCRIPTION

This technique is first introduced in the assessment phase of treatment with the child. In a first or second session the therapist draws the following picture on a piece of paper:

She then explains: "You [or your parents] have said that you feel [angry, sad, worried, scared, wiggly] a lot of the time. In the first bucket, draw a line that shows me how much of that feeling you think you carry with you most of the time. Now, in the second bucket, draw a line that shows how much of that feeling you wish you had in your bucket." The therapist thanks the child and explains that playing and talking can help children feel better and that they will be meeting every week to have a special time together.

When the therapist wishes to evaluate progress, the above drawing is repeated with the addition of a third bucket. The first bucket recalls the level of feeling when therapy began, the second where the child feels it is now, and the third the end goal. The therapist can then ask the child these questions: "How did you get rid of that much of the feeling? Where did it go? What things are you doing differently?" These questions empower children to see the change as something they have accomplished rather than something someone else has done to them. Then the therapist asks, "What do you think would bring the level down to here [indicating a line halfway between the current level and the end goal]?" When the child has indicated he has reached his end goal, the questions become: "What do you think will help you keep your bucket of [anger, sadness, worry, fear, wiggles] at this level? What do you need from other people? Whom can you ask for help when you need it?"

APPLICATION

This technique can be used with children ages 4 to 10 throughout their therapy process to evaluate progress and further treatment needs. It can be especially helpful for children dealing with grief and loss issues, anger management, anxiety, and attention-deficit/hyperactivity disorder (ADHD). It can help them to communicate their feelings in a tangible manner and empower them to see their own role in the healing process.

31

The Nightmare Box: Empowering Children through Dreamwork

Deborah Armstrong Hickey

INTRODUCTION

Nightmares accompany many of the problems that influence children, especially those who have suffered from trauma, abuse, and other forms of victimization. Even children who are simply reacting to less severe stressors in life, such as moving or the death of a pet, are often plagued by an increase in nightmares, which may become a lifelong pattern of sleep disruption.

Still, it is rare that a child therapist will work directly with the symptom of nightmares, likely due to inexperience and lack of training in working with children's dreams. This technique originated as a simple expressive arts technique that facilitates children's (and adults') expressing their fears, creating a container for holding those fears, and then changing the environment that holds the fears so that children can tame what is frightening to them. Of course, taming the fear opens up space for processing and healing from what has influenced the onset of the fears (nightmares) in the first place.

The technique involves having children choose a box in which they create a representation of their nightmare. Collage materials and objects are placed inside and out, expressing their personal experience of the nightmare. The process involves choosing materials and preparing to make the nightmare box, making the box, and then playing with and/or changing the box in some way that makes the box and what it contains less frightening to the child.

I experimented with this technique in my work with adults and then used it with children. What I found was that children and adults both reported a decrease in nightmares along with changes in behavior during waking (increase in positive social interactions, less influenced by fears during the day, and less influenced by feelings of victimization).

This technique can help children feel less frightened of sleep and become generally less fearful, and may facilitate their healing from whatever trauma they have sustained in a way that allows some distance from the event itself.

RATIONALE

Developmentally children seem to be at risk for nightmares. Their cognitive understanding is that dreams are real, and they usually feel quite powerless in influencing their dreams. Much like in their waking lives, children often feel at the mercy of events and influences that appear to control, or possibly hurt them.

Dreams are one of the first places where children's daily concerns and more significant traumas or hurts express themselves through image. While dreaming, children's defenses are down, thus permitting even the most disturbing of thoughts and memories to emerge; hence, the increase in nightmares during times of change, trauma, or other daily events that seem out of their control.

Children do not have the cognitive grasp on where these images are coming from, or how to reduce or cope with them. The nightmare box can be a physical container into which the child can place the terrifying images for either storage or exploration and eventual processing. Expressing fears in a concrete form can provide immense relief for children whose internal images have become so frightening as to interfere with their daily lives in school and at home.

Making the nightmare box also provides an opportunity to master materials, to create a rich and often powerful mirror of one's internal experience in a safe place, and finally to discharge some of the pain with which these images/experiences have become imbued.

After making the nightmare box, children often like to create a symbol or figure that can provide strength and guidance as needed. Creating this figure or symbol can lead to an internalization of some control and ego strength.

For the child therapist, the child's dream expressed in such a medium is a rich and evocative representation of the child's inner life, strengths, vulnerabilities, and capacities to connect with resources. It is a wonderful assessment tool!

DESCRIPTION

Materials required for this technique include the following:

boxes of many different sizes, with and without lids

glue/glue sticks

paint and brushes

pictures (cut out/without words)

collage materials, including yarn, materials of different textures, nature items, and so on

plastic objects including people and animals

jewels and stones

objects brought from home

clay

This technique may take several sessions to complete, depending on the child's approach to making the box. This technique should only be used after excellent rapport has been formed with the child. The therapist and the child most often have already engaged in some play or conversation about the nightmares the child has been experiencing. The therapist may have even read the child a story about dreams, dream catching, or nightmares.

The therapist can begin by letting the child know that in some countries, such as Malaysia, children (and adults) are encouraged to talk about and make a home for their scary dreams during the daytime. Furthermore, the therapist can inform the child that some cultures even insist that children (or adults) who are having the scary dream demand (emphatically) a gift from the scary "monster" in the dream because it is really not okay for someone or something to scare a person the way that the nightmare is scaring them.

The therapist can ask the children if they are interested in doing this with the therapist there to protect them and help them. If they agree, the therapist invites them to create a place for the nightmare and monster in a box that they choose. It should be emphasized that this is the child's choice and that given the nature of the inner material that the child might be influenced by, the child should not be forced or even pressured to agree to make the box.

The child can then make the box. Sometimes children first like to tell the dream to the therapist while the therapist writes the dream down in bold print on a big sheet of paper. Then, the children can begin to prepare to make the box. Often children will take an entire session to choose the materials. These may be placed carefully into the box they have chosen and kept until the following session.

Children often create the scary figure out of clay. The therapist should be very aware and responsive to the child, which is what the child may need in order to feel safe during the process. Sometimes a child may want to take a break from making the box for a session or two. The box should be kept in the therapy room, protected, but easily available for when the child wants to work with it.

Once the box is made, the child can be invited to create a protector figure who can help him/her during the nightmare, a gift from the scary figure to the child, or a power object to heal the scary figure from what ails him or her. Of course, the child can speak to the figures from the nightmare and sometimes may want to destroy them. The child should be encouraged not to destroy the scary figure itself, but perhaps to create another image in a drawing to destroy, or to save the remains of the scary creature, so as to be able to re-create it in another, less frightening form later on.

APPLICATION

The technique can be helpful with any child who is under the influence of nightmares, both severe and chronic, as well as those that are moderate and reactive. It can be particularly of value with children who are generally fearful and who have strong, supportive families. It gives children the opportunity to creatively express their nightmares in a container that allows them to feel protected and safe. It allows them to play, change, or simply view the nightmare from a more powerful position.

For those children who have sustained some trauma or victimization, it is imperative that the therapist have excellent rapport with the child and that continuity of the therapy is ensured. A contraindication to this technique might be those children who may be experiencing symptoms of a thought disorder.

The nightmare box technique is best used with children ages 6 to 12 or older, but modified versions (simpler, fewer materials) can be used with younger children.

Bibliography

Foreman, M. (1982). *Land of Dreams*. New York: Holt, Rinehart & Winston.

Garfield, P. (1984). *Your Child's Dreams*. New York: Ballantine.

Ginsberg, M. (1979). *Ookie-Spooky*. New York: Crown.

Kincher, J. (1988). *Dreams Can Help*. Minneapolis, MN: Free Spirit.

Siegal, A., and Bulkeley, K. (1998). *Dreamcatching*. New York: Three Rivers Press.

Spurr, P. (1999). *Understanding Your Child's Dreams*. New York: Sterling.

West, K. (1978). *Crystallizing Children's Dreams*. Lake Oswego, OR: Amata Graphics.

Wiseman, A. S. (1989). *Nightmare Help: For Children from Children*. Berkeley, CA: Ten Speed Press.

32

The Title of Therapy

Dee Ray

INTRODUCTION

Play therapists observe and note themes that run throughout the child's therapy. Directive therapists develop treatment plans and specific activities from the observed play/expressive art themes. Nondirective therapists simply note themes or comment on them to the child. However, it is often difficult for the child to develop an awareness of these themes. In addition, the child has difficulty recognizing progression in these themes. The "title of therapy" technique allows the child to review the course of therapy and comment from a current perspective.

RATIONALE

In the concrete world of children, I have found that it is helpful to offer them a concrete example of the continuity in their treatment. Artwork is a visual and concrete way to track a child's course through treatment. Especially effective for third-grade children and older, the title of therapy technique is designed to demonstrate weeks of therapy to the children, who can then look over where they have been and compare it to where they are now. Titling each piece of artwork at the termination of therapy allows children to look at their progress from a fresh, healthier perspective. This technique also offers children the opportunity to comment on their time in therapy, including commenting on the relationship with the therapist, which is often formidable for children to address directly.

DESCRIPTION

During the course of treatment, the therapist consistently offers art time for the child during counseling sessions. The therapist may occasionally request a specific drawing, such as a picture of self or family. The therapist asks to keep the drawings. It is important that the therapist assure the child that the drawings will be kept in a safe place and that the child can look at these drawings at any time. The therapist should also pencil in the date on the back of the drawing.

In the final two counseling sessions, the therapist presents all of the drawings to the child and asks the child to review them. This often encourages children to discuss how they were feeling and what events were taking place at the time of the drawing. They also have the opportunity to express how they feel currently about the time of the drawing. The therapist then asks the child to title each of the drawings. After the child titles the drawings, the therapist and child lay out the drawings in chronological order on the floor. This action usually produces much discussion as the child recognizes and verbalizes certain themes. If not, the therapist could prompt the child by asking, "Do you notice anything that is the same or different in your drawings?" The therapist responds by reflecting and clarifying the observations of the child. The children may decide whether they want to take home the drawings. Often, children are completed with their work in therapy and have no need to keep their artwork.

APPLICATION

This technique is based in expressive arts but introduces the cognitive component that encourages the child to recognize and verbalize issues and the impact of therapy. I have used this technique in school counseling and private practice. Children in concrete operations, and even more so in formal operations (Piaget 1954), enjoy pointing out the themes and reviewing their past artwork.

One of my clients is the founder of this technique. She was a sixth-grade student whose mother had abandoned her and left her with a stepfather who she had just recently discovered was not her natural father. Her drawings were filled with self-hatred and chaos. I kept her drawings because she never took them with her, and yet they were very interesting. In our last session, she asked if I had kept her drawings. When I responded, she was quite excited and asked to see them. I laid them out on a table for her. She proceeded to focus intently on each one, discussing how she felt at the time of the drawing, then titling each one. When she finished, I asked if we could lay them out on the floor. She agreed.

A few of her titles were "Family," "Colliding Cultures," "Myself," "Our World," "The Real One," and finally "Leaves Falling to Water." As we both looked at the drawings, she noticed the dark, heavy painting and lack of distinct figures on the first few. For example, "Colliding Cultures" and "Our World" were a mix of dark colors with no lines of distinction. She then noted how much she hated her mother when she drew these pictures. The later drawings were lighter in color and included formed figures yet still depicted chaos. "The Real One" was a drawing of herself, who, she explained, was behind a mask. The mask was covered with gashes of paint across the face. At this point, she noted that in recent weeks, she was feeling better about herself, doing better in school, and getting along better with her stepfather. Although looking at the artwork did not define the success of therapy, her explanation and awareness of her issues was clearly a sign of progress. Her last activity of therapy was to spontaneously draw a picture for me, which included distinct, lightly colored tulips. She explained it was for me because I "helped kids grow."

Since my introduction to this technique, I use it regularly with older elementary-school children, especially in the school environment. Older children are often embarrassed to take their artwork with them during school hours. This technique provides an outlet to reflect upon their art and gather greater meaning for themselves.

Reference

Piaget, J. (1954). *The Construction of Reality in the Child*. New York: Basic Books.

33

Be True to Thyself

Richard Bromfield

INTRODUCTION

We often encounter children who are on the fence between a decent and an immoral life. As we try to grasp that piece of humanity and build upon it, we must rely on the child's own sense of honesty and responsibility, for, as our grandparents could have told us, people don't change unless they want to, and they usually don't want to until they clearly see something in themselves that they no longer like or are willing to live with. The be-true-to-thyself technique helps children begin to realistically see what is true. This technique is titled solely for the purpose of this book. The technique should be seamlessly introduced into therapy without any reference to its title.

RATIONALE

Without honesty most therapies are doomed to failure. This technique provides an opportunity for stealing, lying, and otherwise externalizing children to face themselves in our presence in a manageable and

self-controlled way. By experiencing our tolerance for their own assessment of their behavior, they come to trust us and to see our belief that the
road to rehabilitation lies within themselves.

DESCRIPTION

The therapist gives the child pen and paper and invites him to take a
seat in as private a spot of the office as there is (i.e., where the therapist
cannot see what the child writes). The therapist says, "I know some
people have said you have a problem with stealing [for example]. I don't
want you to tell me what you steal right now. But I want you to take this
paper and write down everything you've stolen in the past week. Take
your time, and remember, I'm never going to read this. When you are
done, you can rip the paper into a million pieces and take them with you,
if you like."

The therapist patiently waits, keeping in mind what a remarkable
thing this is (i.e., the child, merely by virtue of doing this, is admitting a
lot to the therapist and himself). When the child is done, the therapist
asks: "Is that everything? How honest do you think you've been to
yourself?" If the child says perfectly honest, the therapist acknowledges
this, and asks about the child's own reaction to seeing the list. This may
lead to the child's stating a wish to be better, to not steal. If the child says
it is not honest, the therapist gently wonders aloud what could make a
child lie even to himself. If the child offers to show the therapist the list,
the therapist might well consider declining, stressing that the child will
have plenty of time to share what he's done in future sessions.

This is a powerful technique that propels the delinquent-prone child
toward more open self-examination and to owning and assuming responsibility for the work and goals of therapy.

APPLICATION

This technique can be used with children who steal, lie, use drugs, or
behave in any kind of immoral and irresponsible way, and who tend to
take little blame for what they do.

34

Dreaming Pots: A Natural Healing Approach for Helping Children with Fears and Trauma

Joyce C. Mills

INTRODUCTION

Often in the face of trauma, pain, and fear, the visions of our dreams and our sense of identity can get shrouded in an all-encompassing feeling of hopelessness. It is at these challenging times that the symbols in our dreams must be reawakened and brought forth to help us manage and heal from the struggles that temporarily blind us to the possibilities, solutions, and simple joys of life. The imaginative creation and playful activity of "dreaming pots" is a stepping-stone for helping children and families escape their fears and traumas and embrace a sense of empowerment and well-being (Mills 1999).

RATIONALE

On September 11, 1992, Hurricane Iniki struck the small Hawaiian island of Kaua'i with ferocious force—wind gusts measuring up to 227 miles per hour. Kaua'i was left without electricity and telephone, along with limited food and water supplies for close to three months. This event was particularly meaningful for me, because my husband and I had just moved there ten days earlier.

In response to the community's need for specialized, culturally sensitive services, I was asked to be the director of a project for the remote Westside area of Kaua'i. The program I ultimately developed was called the Kaua'i Westside Ohana (Family) Activities Project, sponsored by Child and Family Services of Kaua'i and funded by the Office of Youth Services. This program provided counseling services and community activities, which were both healing and preventative, to the youths and families living in Westside. Along with myself, there were three outreach workers who were from the local community.

The program provided opportunities for the youths and their families to move past the focus of posttraumatic stress disorder (PTSD) and into a model more focused on healing and prevention, which I called posttraumatic stress healing (PTSH). Under the PTSH model, three programs were employed: (1) natural healing activities, (2) parent talk-story groups, and (3) the talk-story (counseling) center.

While these services focused on a safe and respectful atmosphere in which natural healing from the trauma of Hurricane Iniki could occur, they also included education, activities, counseling, and support for those youths and their families who may have had preexisting traumas or problems. The project's goals were empowerment, cultural appreciation, and community involvement for the youths and families of Westside. One of the natural healing activities used with the children and community was "dreaming pots."

Natural Healing Activities

Natural healing activities can be defined as experiential and learning projects for youths and their families that promote an activation and reintegration of inner strengths and emotional resources. Natural healing activities are based on the principles of Ericksonian hypnotherapy and the therapeutic and culturally respectful use of storytelling, artistic, and living ritual metaphors (Mills 1989, 1992, Mills and Crowley 1986, 1988).

DESCRIPTION

Dreaming Pots: From Seed to Fruition

Before bringing any activity into my work, I first experience it on a personal level. A main principle of my philosophy is to enter the world of the child. Dreaming pots (Mills 1989, 1994, 1999) derives from an idea I had after seeing a pottery exhibit of the Mimbres Tribe at the Heard Museum in Arizona. The pottery bowls were distinctively painted with symbolic designs that told the story of everyday life and ceremonies. What sparked my attention were the holes in the bottom of each bowl. Although little is known about the bowls, it is known that they were placed in the burial site when a person died. One hypothesis is that the bowls were placed there to bring good spirits to those who had died, and the holes allowed the departed spirit to travel freely and unconstrained. The holes also allowed negativity to be released as the person made his or her journey to the spirit world.

The experience of hearing the story and seeing the pottery stayed with me long after I left the museum. I began to wonder how can we use the idea of pots such as these in life. I wanted to be able to use them personally, as well as with the children, families, and individuals with whom I worked whose dreams were dimmed by the traumas of life.

I reviewed the story in my mind. I began to think of death as a form of sleep, and when we sleep we dream. Hence, "dreaming pots."

Ready-made clay pots with the holes in the bottom can be purchased cheaply at a flower nursery. They can be decorated with beads, feathers, and paint. Decorating the pots with dream symbols fosters a sense of relaxation and enjoyment.

Steps for Making a Dreaming Pot

This stepping-stone exercise is designed to help children reconnect to dreams that bring joy, empowerment, and self-appreciation. Dreaming pots can be created in one of two ways: (1) by a hands-on approach, using a clay pot, paint, and other supplies; or (2) by using the dreaming pot drawing provided here.

The Hands-On Version

Use a small clay pot with a hole in the bottom. Decorate it with paint, pebbles, shells, flowers, sand, earth, and so on. In the therapy session ask the child to hold the pot in her hands, close her eyes, take a few slow deep breaths, inhaling through her nose, and exhaling through her mouth. Thus the child makes a connection with the pot. The child can say, "Hello, I am Joyce and I have come here to share my dreams." Ask the child to think of images and symbols from her good dreams or things she likes to do. When the images are clear, the child opens her eyes and begins creating her own dreaming pot using the art supplies you provide (Figure 34–1).

Figure 34–1. Hands-on dreaming pots.

You can ask the child to draw a picture of what she wants in her life now. Place the finished drawing in the pot, and tell the child to place the pot near her bed at night and "enjoy your dreams while you sleep. In the morning you can take the picture out of the pot and put it in an album, thereby creating a dreaming pot journal."

The Drawn Version

Apply these same steps to having the child draw a dreaming pot similar to the one shown in Figure 34–2. The only change is to ask the child to imagine holding the pot in her hands before she begins to draw it. All else remains the same (Figure 34–2).

Figure 34–2. Drawn version of a dreaming pot.

APPLICATION

At a local neighborhood center, I told the story of the dreaming pot to a children's group. Then the children were supplied with small clay pots and asked to hold their pot in their hands, close their eyes, take a few "magic happy breaths" (Mills 1992), and let the symbols of their good dreams come into their minds. When their images were clear, the participants were asked to open their eyes and begin to decorate their pots.

This activity was significant to the children and their parents because many of their homes were destroyed in the hurricane and they were sleeping on the floor or in tents. They experienced nightmares and fears of going to sleep. By making their own dreaming pots, the children could put them by their sleeping places and be reminded of their good dreams. They were told that the holes in the bottom were there to let all the bad dreams pass through and that the pot would hold all their good dreams. To date, over five hundred families on the Westside of Kaua'i have dreaming pots in their homes.

Using dreaming pots in individual play therapy is also particularly useful with troubled adolescents who may have limited visions or goals. They can create their own dreaming pots as part of the therapeutic process. Adolescents struggle with low self-esteem, anger, truancy, or substance abuse, at times resorting to noncompliant, socially deviant, and violent behavior. While it is critical for teens to develop appropriate social skills, I believe that without hope and vision this goal cannot be accomplished. Dreaming pots offer these children a tangible yet symbolic means of representing the hope that is within each of them.

In family therapy, a larger pot is supplied and all family members are encouraged to add the symbols of their dreams, hopes, hobbies, and so on. My focus is always to bring out the inner resources of a family so that they can be fortified to face struggles, conflicts, or traumas.

There is no interpretation of symbols by the therapist in this process. Children or families can interpret the meanings of their own symbols if they so wish. By joining the child in the process, there is no resistance. The meanings of the symbols ascribed by the child also provide seeds for future storytelling metaphors that can be developed in play therapy. Sometimes a child creates a dreaming pot in silence, without any interpretations expressed. This, too, needs to be fully accepted by the therapist and not interpreted in any way as resistance or denial. The atmosphere is always one of play and acceptance.

I have used both the hands-on and drawn versions of dreaming pots with children ranging in age from preschool to adolescents, and within a variety of settings—classrooms, hospitals, group homes, residential treatment facilities, and individual play therapy sessions.

Acknowledgment

Natural healing activities were developed within the scope of a three-part program, The Kaua'i Westside Ohana (Family) Activities

Project, sponsored by Child and Family Services of Kaua'i and funded by Office of Youth Services (1992–95).

References

Mills, J. C. (1989). No more monsters and meanies: multisensory metaphors for helping children with fears and depression. In *Brief Therapy: Approaches to Treating Anxiety and Depression*, pp. 150–169, ed. M. Yapko. New York: Brunner/Mazel.

———. (1992). *Little Tree: A book for children with serious medical problems.* Washington, DC: Magination Press.

———. (1994). *Ericksonian play therapy.* Paper presented at the 6th International Congress on Ericksonian Approaches to Hypnosis and Psychotherapy, Los Angeles, December.

———. (1999). *Reconnecting to the Magic of Life.* Kaua'i, HI: Imaginal Press.

Mills, J. C., and Crowley, R. J. (1986). *Therapeutic Metaphors for Children and the Child Within.* New York: Brunner/Mazel.

———. (1988). A multidimensional approach to the utilization of therapeutic metaphors for children and adolescents. In *Developing Ericksonian Therapy: State of the Art*, pp. 302–323, ed. J. Zeig and S. Lankton. New York: Brunner/Mazel.

35

The Draw-Your-Bad-Dream Technique

Nancy Boyd Webb

INTRODUCTION

Nightmares and bad dreams are typical problems for children. Whereas the reasons for them vary, the experience of waking up in fear can be very upsetting to both the child and the parents. Although all children have occasional bad dreams, especially during the preschool years, when they may occur on a nightly basis and require repeated parental involvement, professional help may be necessary.

In my practice I have found bad dreams to be part of the reason for referral in children who have been traumatized, in bereaved children, and in children who have separation problems. Anxiety that the child manages to control during the day erupts at night when the child is sleeping and emerges in the form of vivid, scary pictures. Often the child runs screaming into the parents' bedroom, and disrupts everyone's sleep.

RATIONALE

When the child can take the "picture" in his head and transfer it onto a piece of paper, it becomes an object for action. The very process of drawing the dream gives the child control and mastery over it. Art therapists (Di Leo 1973, Malchiodi 1998) refer to this as "externalization," meaning that what was previously an internal representation, through drawing becomes external, and less fearful.

The draw-your-bad-dream technique is a directive play therapy method intended to relieve a distressing symptom. The therapist initially asks the child to draw his/her dream. Then, depending on developmental factors such as the child's age and level of cognitive development, the therapist decides upon an appropriate action and instructs the child accordingly. For example, for a child under 7 years of age and who still believes in magical thinking, the therapist tells the child that he can choose a method to "destroy the dream" (picture), and get rid of it, so it will never bother him again. If the child is older, more advanced cognitive methods can accomplish the same goals, for example, asking the child to draw the happy dream he would *like* to have, and/or a picture of himself waking up in the morning after a peaceful night's sleep. These latter techniques rely on the cognitive process of thought substitution and positive restructuring.

Regardless of the method, it is important for the therapist to convey a matter-of-fact, positive, upbeat attitude that this drawing method really works to help children with their nightmares.

DESCRIPTION

Step 1: Engagement and Contracting

After greeting the child and clarifying that the therapist is someone who helps children with their troubles and worries, the therapist tells the child that she knows from the child's mother that he is having some difficulty sleeping at night. The child typically nods in agreement, giving the therapist the opportunity to universalize the problem: "A lot of kids who come to see me also have bad dreams at night." Usually this raises the child's interest, and the therapist then says that she knows some ways to help kids get rid of their bad dreams. The therapist then asks if the child would like to have some "help to make the bad dreams go away." When the child agrees, the implementation phase begins.

Step 2: Draw the Dream

The therapist takes out colored markers and drawing paper and asks the child to draw the scary part of the dream. If the child says, "I can't draw well," the therapist says, "That's OK. You don't have to be an artist to do this. Just do your best, and show me the very scary part." During the drawing the therapist can ask for clarification: "Tell me about this part." "What is this here?" Depending on the child's age and the situation, the therapist might make a validating statement: "No wonder you were scared. That looks pretty frightening!" This should be followed immediately by a statement directed at the dream: "We're not going to let you, Mr. Werewolf, continue to wake Danny up any more!"

Step 3: Destroy the Dream

Looking at the child, the therapist asks, "What could you do to destroy this horrible wolf?" The child usually doesn't know at first what the therapist means. So the therapist continues, "Well, you made this drawing, it's yours, and you can do anything you want with it. Some kids like to rip their scary drawings into a million-zillion pieces and throw it in the trash. Some want to scribble all over it with black, so nobody can see it anymore, or some just ask me to keep it in my office, locked in the file, so it can never get out. It's up to you to decide how to get rid of this."

Step 4: Resolution

The child decides, and the therapist encourages him to "really get rid of that horrible dream." Whatever the child decides, the therapist says, "This horrible werewolf will never, ever bother Danny again. He is going to have a wonderful sleep tonight and from now on, with no more bad dreams."

Step 5 (Optional): Dream Replacement

Depending on the circumstances, and the judgment of the therapist, it may be helpful to ask the child to draw a happy, peaceful dream to replace the nightmare. If the child does this, he should be encouraged to take the picture of the happy dream home and hang it up near his bed and to look at it just before getting into bed.

APPLICATION

This technique can be used with all children. However, it is especially useful for children with anxiety problems and with traumatically bereaved children. I presented a detailed case example of its use with a 10-year-old girl (Webb 1996). I recently used it by explaining the method to the parents of a 6-year-old boy who was dying of cancer. He was having horrible nightmares, but after they helped him draw his bad dream, the nightmares stopped, and he died peacefully. I have also used it with my 5-year-old granddaughter. I believe strongly in this technique and my belief has convinced the numerous children with whom it has been effective.

References

Di Leo, J. H. (1973). *Children's Drawings as Diagnostic Aids*. New York: Brunner/Mazel.

Malchiodi, C. (1998). *Understanding Children's Drawings*. New York: Guilford.

Webb, N. B. (1996). *Social Work Practice with Children*. New York: Guilford.

36

Color Your Feelings!

Hilda R. Glazer

INTRODUCTION

The development of a feeling vocabulary and understanding the way in which the individual expresses feelings is an important developmental process. Helping children to visualize the seat of emotions in the body often helps them to understand the emotions and the way that emotions are expressed. I have used a technique that has come to be called "Color Your Feelings" with both school-age children and teenagers. The discussions that follow completion of the drawings are often quite revealing to the child.

RATIONALE

While frequently we do not have a wide feeling vocabulary, we are often able to easily identify where emotions sit in our bodies, how we feel the emotions internally, and how we express the feelings. That is, what we cannot name or describe, we can show visually through our drawings. Particularly for children who have lost a loved one, the emotions surrounding grief are new and hard to understand let alone to verbalize. I have found that encouraging the expression of emotion through drawing can facilitate the process of understanding and growth.

The exercise calls for the selection of colors for the feelings selected. While there is some convention about colors, and as Allan (1988) noted, there is reliability in the interpretation of color, my experience has been that there is no pattern in the matching of emotion words and colors. The freedom of choice of color matches is an important element of this experience for the child.

DESCRIPTION

Clients are told that they are going to do an art exercise in which they work with feelings and where they "feel" the feelings in their bodies. If questions are asked, further explanation might be given on how we locate different feelings or respond internally to different feelings in different parts of our bodies. Depending on the client and whether this is a group or individual session, a body outline of the client might be drawn on a large sheet of paper, or a computer-generated body outline on an 8½" by 11" sheet of paper is given to the client. The decision to make a full-body outline should be based on the relationship with the client, the issues that have arisen in therapy, and the child's comfort level with the process. I always ask permission to draw the body outline and fully respect the wishes of the child. In some cases, the adult who brings the child to the session may be asked to help out if the child prefers.

Clients are first asked to select five feelings that are connected to an issue in therapy. If the client, as is often true of school-age children, is unable to select five feelings from memory, then a feelings chart or feelings cards may be used to facilitate the process. Next the client is asked to match each of the feelings with a color selected from the variety of colors provided in crayons or markers. A color mark is placed by each feeling name to identify the choices. Thus, there is a feeling key on the paper for the client to follow. Next, the client is asked to work through the list of feelings, coloring in the parts of the body where the feeling is located. In my experience there has never been a situation where a school-aged or older child has not been able to do this exercise.

Debriefing of the exercise follows, and will differ depending on the theoretical orientation of the therapist. In debriefing, I ask the child to tell me about the colors and then reflect on the expression of feelings. With parent–child dyads, I also encourage discussion about similarities and differences. Depending on the depth of the discussion and particularly with teens, I might ask if the client has learned anything through this process.

This was an insightful experience for a 13-year-old girl whose presenting issue was the chronic illness of her mother and her reaction to the disease process and the impact it was having on the life of the family. The girl had recently begun to hurt her mother by hugging her too tightly or squeezing her arm when she helped change the IV bag. These incidents were becoming more frequent and were upsetting to both mother and daughter. We did a body outline on large brown paper, and she had no problem picking feelings or colors to go with the feelings. The first feelings was anger and the color was purple. She colored her mouth purple and then colored her hands purple. She then said in animated tones: "My anger is coming out in my hands, that's why I hurt her!" The coloring and subsequent discussion focused on what she was learning about herself by doing this. The next session she reported that she had shared the drawing with her mother, and that she had not hurt her mother since the last session. The behavior did not reappear during the remaining time she was in therapy.

APPLICATION

I have used this exercise in a variety of ways with a wide range of age groups. It has been an effective way for grieving school-age children to process the feelings associated with their loss and to understand more about these often new and unpleasant feelings. In elementary school grief groups this has been an effective way for children to understand that they are not the only ones with these feelings or that they are not the only ones who feel grief in the various ways in their bodies. This has been a normalizing experience for grieving children in groups. And as with the girl in the above example, it is possible to gain insight about one's behavior by visualizing and externalizing an internal process.

Another use has been as a family exercise. Here the impact has been an increase in understanding of the feelings of the others and/or how each of us may internalize feelings and express feelings differently. Given that we do not often have either breadth or depth in our feeling vocabulary, the use of art to express and externalize feelings can be a powerful experience for the individual and the family.

Reference

Allan, J. (1988). *Inscapes of the Child's World*. Dallas, TX: Spring.

37

Postcards in Motion

Paris Goodyear-Brown

INTRODUCTION

This technique was developed in the treatment of a group of adolescent girls who were interested in the arts. To fully engage these teenagers, an exercise that combined guided imagery, movement, writing, art, and performance was created. The idea of generating material in this way came from Liz Lerman, a modern dancer who uses combinations of movement and text to develop new dance themes.

RATIONALE

While each of the modalities combined here (writing, art, and movement) has intrinsic therapeutic value, the unique integration of expressive modalities increases the likelihood that the client will experience a sense of competency/accomplishment in at least one area, thereby enhancing self-esteem. Moreover, the structured nature of the exercise creates a level of safety in teenagers that allows them to relax into their experience/ memory. Teenagers often feel overwhelmed by traditional talk therapies, particularly those in which the teen leads the way. They feel like they have to come up with something. This technique provides a framework and some projective stimulus on which the teenager can build. The client uses "the place" as the reference point throughout, removing the young person one step from the actual event or trauma that occurred in the place. Teenagers are given an opportunity to make mind–body connections through this exercise. The body movements can help teenagers get past their defenses and connect more intimately with their feelings.

Teenagers get to practice their newfound ability to think abstractly while also manipulating symbols (a vital component of play therapy with younger children). They create an active symbolism as one layer of abstraction, text, is transformed into another level, image, and finally into a third level, movement. The teenager is given at least three different opportunities to create and re-create meaning. In my own practice this exercise has proved to be cathartic and therefore healing in itself.

DESCRIPTION

The following directions are for working with a group, although the same exercise can be used with individual clients.

Step 1

Lead the client through a guided imagery with the following directions. "Remember a place where you felt safe." (You can substitute different feeling words each week, but it is best to help clients learn the steps of the exercise with "safe" as the stimulus.) Some teens will have no memories of safe places and they should be encouraged to "*imagine* a place where they *could* feel safe."

Step 2

Invite clients to explore the place in their minds. Ask questions that will help clients focus on the colors, shapes, sights, sounds, and smells of their safe place.

Step 3

Ease the clients out of the visualization and ask them to "write a postcard from your safe place." It is important to have form postcards available, as they provide a clean, projective, yet concise space in which to write.

Step 4

After clients have completed the text, have them turn the postcard over and draw an image of their place on the front of the postcard. There are no rules, although they may ask for some.

Step 5

Direct clients to put their postcards aside. Have them visualize their place again. Give them a piece of paper and ask them to write numbers 1 to 4. Then ask them to pull out four words or phrases of the following types from their safe place:

1. an architectural element,

2. a small detail,

3. a main element (the thing that sticks out most to them),

4. the mood or feeling of the place.

Step 6

After clients have generated their lists, ask them to come up with four body gestures, one to represent each of the four things that have been listed (you can liken it to charades).

Step 7

The next step is to have them decide in what order they want to string their gestures together. Have them practice doing the gestures in that order. In the group setting, clients can partner up and practice with each other.

Step 8

Finally, have the clients do the movement sequence while the postcard is being read out loud. You may want to videotape the clients doing their "postcard in motion."

APPLICATION

This technique can be used in group settings for specific populations. All group members would create a series of postcard that reflected, for example, various aspects of a trauma that they had experienced. It can be used as an initial assessment tool, and new postcards in motion can be generated throughout the course of therapy to assess the client's therapeutic gains. The technique can be empowering to victims of trauma, in that they are completely in control of how deep they want to go with the work.

This technique can also be used for time-limited groups. An entire 6- to 8-week anger management group could be constructed using the postcards in motion as the main intervention. Each session could involve the creation of a postcard based on a place where the client felt angry. After the postcards/gesture sequences were shared, discussions could include how their bodies respond to anger, what perceptions led to anger (in their place), what they would do differently next time, and so on.

The postcards in motion are also helpful in building a feelings vocabulary for clients. Each week, postcards that focused on different feelings are created. "Remember a place where you felt happy, mad, sad." Have clients discuss commonalities in the physical expression of these feelings each week. By the end of the group, clients will feel a stronger kinesthetic connection to their feelings and will have expanded their feelings repertoire. This technique can also be used with individual clients dealing with trauma, grief, and loss. It can even be used as a form of desensitization training with sexual abuse survivors.

Section Three

Game Play Techniques

38

Emotional Bingo

Heidi Gerard Kaduson

INTRODUCTION

Emotional recognition and differentiation in self and others develops through a sequence of levels, as it moves from concrete and egocentric to complex, abstract, and other-oriented. This is characterized by Harter (1983) as the young child's growing ability to understand feelings. As children get older, there is increasingly more differentiation between self and parent and an understanding of the attributes of others. However, children find it difficult to talk about feelings to others. But there is a less threatening atmosphere in a game format, and children can express themselves with more ease.

RATIONALE

Being able to express emotions in a safe environment is therapeutically beneficial for children as well as adults. In a group, several other benefits occur. Children can hear that others have the same feelings that they do. Therefore, children do not feel alone in their suffering or joy. A sense of

173

cohesion develops in the group, which allows for the group process to flow. Children can easily report when they felt a certain way as long as it is "only in fun" or "the rules of the game." Children are more likely to be able to express feelings with the help of peers and the therapist. Once feelings are expressed, there is a release of affect so that children may feel less burdened by their problems after releasing the information. Many children feel very comfortable and less threatened about answering questions in a game format due to the distancing they feel from reality.

DESCRIPTION

Materials needed:

Bingo game

Poster board to represent the emotions in written and picture form

Cards to draw and write emotions on

Velcro attachments

Bingo chips

The therapist makes a Feeling Chart on poster board. This chart has the numbers to be used in the bingo game associated with a specific feeling, both in words and in pictures; for example, B1 = happy, B2 = sad, B3 = lonely, B4 = excited, B5 = angry, I16 = frustrated, I17 = bored, I18 = proud, I19 = overwhelmed, I20 = scared, and so on. There are fifteen numbers under each letter in bingo, for a total of seventy-five feelings. The therapist can create all seventy-five, or minimize the number by using only five or ten under each letter. This Feeling Chart would represent the numbers in emotions to be used when the number is called, and acts as a master for the children to look at so that reading is not needed.

The therapist also makes "calling" cards with the same words and pictures on them. These can be made from cardboard or labels with hard backs so that they can stick to the Feeling Chart. Therefore, the therapist would say the number, attach it verbally to an emotion, and stick the calling card onto the Feeling Chart with tacks or Velcro attachments. The Emotional Bingo game is then ready to use. The therapist hands out bingo cards to the group members. They are also given bingo chips to place on the square of the number called after they state when they had that feeling in their own life.

The therapist says:

> I am going to play Emotional Bingo with you. I will call out the number, and say the feeling along with it. If you have that number, raise your hand. When I call on you, you must tell me a time you felt that way, and then you get to put the bingo chip down on that number. Remember, the first one to get a line filled down, across, or diagonally will be the winner. Everyone pick up a bingo chip and put it on your free space, which is the center square.
>
> B2 = sad. Does anyone have B2? If you do, raise your hand and tell me a time when you felt sad, and then put your chip down.

Children are allowed to pass or choose not to put a chip down, but most of the time they have no trouble thinking of a time when they felt a certain way.

In group, this game can take the entire session. It doesn't matter if no one wins, because the process of the game is what is therapeutic.

APPLICATION

This game is therapeutically useful for group work, whether the children are internalizers (who hold in their feelings) or externalizers (who act out their feelings). Because of the fun quality of the game, the children find it easier to express emotions and are more likely to be empathic to others who experience the same types of feelings that they have.

Reference

Harter, S. (1983). Cognitive-developmental considerations in the conduct of play therapy. In *Handbook of Play Therapy*, ed. C. Schaefer and K. J. O'Connor, pp. 95–127. New York: Wiley.

39

The Photograph Game of Emotions

Harvey Payne

INTRODUCTION

A common problem with young children, and especially children with developmental disabilities and older children with aggressive reactions, is the accurate identification and response to social-emotional cues by others. Social-emotional cues of the face are often missed or misinterpreted. The use of photographs of the significant individuals in the child's life with a range of emotional expressions can help heighten awareness, specificity, and more adaptive responses to social-emotional cues.

RATIONALE

Play is a therapeutic medium that allows social-emotional processing and learning to take place with less resistance and anxiousness, and more fun and repetition. The photograph game allows children to interact with and respond to emotions in a safe environment in which the emotions feel less powerful and more manageable, and new ways of responding can be tried. Emotional distinctions, such as mad versus serious, can help children lower their arousal state or startle reactions to adult interactions, such as with compliance requests. The use of the photographs of significant people in a child's life helps with generalizing to the real world what is learned in the therapy session. The use of the photographs also helps evoke specific emotional responses to these people in a way that allows the child to play and verbalize more adaptive responses.

DESCRIPTION

Request permission to take, or have taken, pictures of key family members and school staff expressing a variety of emotions. Have individuals give both exaggerated and normal facial expressions for the emotions of happy, sad, mad, fearful, concerned, serious, silly, and others based on the needs of the child in therapy.

The first step is the identification of emotions, and this can be done in a number of game-like ways. Shuffle the pictures and place them between the therapist and the child. Each one picks one picture and tells who the person is and the feeling expressed. Tokens or stickers can be used for correct answers or attempted tries. A brief statement about the feature of the face that helps us know the emotion should be given: "Your mom does look sad. See how her mouth points down?" Other games such as using the cards as flash cards and having the child quickly name the emotion expressed with each photograph can be played to help with quickly scanning and processing social-emotional cues.

The next step is to use the cards to come up with situations or stories about the person and the feelings. "This is my teacher. She is happy because I did all my work today." As the child develops in her skill, additional photographs can be added for stories that include different feelings or people interacting with each other. "Mom is mad. Sis is being silly. Mom is mad because Jill won't clean her room and she's running around looking silly." The therapist can model appropriate emotional responses, or highlight specific areas of concern in his stories of the photographs, similar to Richard Gardner's (1971) mutual storytelling technique.

At times, this process can evoke important emotional responses in the child, including refusal to look at the photograph. Working with the child to play out and verbalize these emotional responses can lead to better understanding and healing:

Therapist: You don't like that picture.

Child: I can't stand him. He always does that.

Therapist: It's hard when your father is mad.

Child: It's hard when he is never around.

Finally, the cards can be used to help the child learn more adaptive responses to the emotional reactions expressed in the photographs:

Therapist: When Dad looks serious, are you in trouble?

Child: All the time!

Therapist: Dad looks to me like he can't figure something out. Like he's thinking really hard.

Child: What do you mean?

Therapist: Like he had a problem at work, and he's still thinking about it. Maybe you are not in trouble.

Child: I don't know.

Therapist: Do you ever think about something that happened at school? How do you look?

APPLICATION

This technique grew out of teaching children and adults with pervasive developmental disorders about emotions and appropriate social skills. Many children enter therapy without these skills of accurately identifying and adaptively responding to emotions. This technique can be helpful in these cases.

Reference

Gardner, R. A. (1971). Mutual storytelling: a technique in child psychotherapy. *Acta Paedopsychiatrica 38*: 253–262.

40

The Feeling Checkers Game

Michael Kantrowitz

INTRODUCTION

Children often have significant difficulty in verbalizing their emotions. They are often anxious and at times even suspicious of treatment and therapists. Questioning children regarding their family or behavior may further alienate them, as adults most likely have already questioned them in relation to situations and how they feel about what is transpiring in their lives. Feeling Checkers are used mostly with children of age 7 and older, although younger children often benefit as they learn about feelings and how to verbalize them. Feeling Checkers was first created to help a teenager express her angry feelings she had manifested for her father who was an alcoholic. Her father and mother had been divorced for a number of years, but the father's infrequent and inconsistent contact with her generated many conflicting feelings that were difficult for her to verbalize. Feeling Checkers created and opened the doorway that allowed her to express these buried emotions.

RATIONALE

Play is the most natural and efficacious theoretical approach to help children grow. It allows them to focus on an activity that is fun while decreasing anxiety and paving the way for expression of their emotions, which facilitates healing. One of the most interesting aspects of playing with children is their ability to recognize an intrinsic need for self-worth. Since many children who enter into therapy have such a need, they often tend to gravitate toward play experiences that provide opportunities to gain self-esteem, such as games. Hence, interactive board games that provide the necessary elements for a therapeutic growth experience can be essential for children and adolescents.

For years psychologists and therapists have been using the game of checkers to create rapport with their patients. Feeling Checkers adds dimensions of feelings and communication. One of the goals of therapeutic games is to remove all aspects of competition. As a natural consequence, one of the simplest ways for children to gain self-esteem— winning a game—is precluded. Since the goal of checkers is to win, the same goal has been kept intact in Feeling Checkers. This low-level competition keeps the child interested in playing as self-esteem is gained with every checker captured and every victory the child experiences. This is important, because if children stop playing the game for any reason, such as it's boring or they are unable to gain self-esteem, the healing process may come to a halt.

DESCRIPTION

Feeling Checkers is played just like checkers. To prepare the game, the therapist chooses from the eighty different feelings included in each version of the game (for ages 6 to 8, 8 to 10, and 10 to adult). Each feeling tab (word) slips underneath a checker. Every checker has a different feeling. The game is played on a regular checkerboard and is played just like checkers with one difference: when players capture the other player's checker, in order to keep the checker they must turn the checker over, read the feeling out loud, and report a time when they felt that feeling.

Since both players must verbalize feelings, communication and understanding occurs in a nonthreatening manner. As in the game of checkers, whoever has the most checkers (feelings) at the end of the game is the victor—of increased self-esteem. (Of course, this is always the child.)

Therapists may also model appropriate feelings in appropriate situations when it is their turn. The therapist should not ask the child questions regarding the feelings or situation that was just reported, as this will remove the safety zone that the world of play provides.

To allow for more flexibility, blank tabs are included so the therapist may address specific areas of concern. For more than two players, teams can be formed and players on each team may alternate sharing feelings and moving checkers.

APPLICATION

Feeling Checkers may be used with clients with almost any type of problem: phobias, conduct disorders, attention deficit disorders, divorce or relationship issues, impulse control disorders, and so on. No matter what the child's issues are, sharing feelings and learning how to appropriately deal with feelings helps children understand their internal emotional world and grow. Feeling Checkers is currently used all over the world in a multitude of settings and with a broad spectrum of cases. The client must be verbal to an extent and be able to comprehend the emotions being reported. If the child has difficulty reading or understanding the feelings, the therapist may facilitate in these areas. Feeling Checkers provides the medium that allows a true emotional connection to develop between the therapist and the child. To date, I have never won a single game of Feeling Checkers, unless you define "winning" as watching a child heal.

Feeling Checkers may also be used in marital/couples therapy to improve communication between two adults. Adults will find the age 10 to adult version interesting and challenging. One might be surprised to see that many adults often have difficulty reporting their feelings while playing Feeling Checkers. Using this game in couples therapy often produces fertile material for exploration in therapy.

Resource

The Feeling Checkers game is available from The Feelings Company. An on-line catalog is available at www.feelingscompany.com. Mail order: 30101 Town Center Dr., Suite 110, Laguna Niguel, CA 92677, phone (949) 363-0202, fax (949) 363-0206.

41

Monster

Steve Harvey

INTRODUCTION

"Monster" is a series of basic expressive play activities in which children and their parents both create and chase a monster away. These activities are constructed in such a way that the monster can become a metaphor for feelings of anxiety within the child. As the child and parent (or in combination with other relevant family members) develop dramatic activity to chase the monster away, the metaphor is extended to master anxiety. Furthermore, as parents and children become more mutual in their play together, their relationship can be enhanced as well.

This game entails dynamic play (Harvey 1994, 1997). Dynamic play is a family-centered intervention style in which family members are coached to develop expressive improvised play together, which has relevance to emotional problems of children as well as to the relational conflicts among parents and children. In this therapy style, parents and children are helped to use creative dramatic, artistic, movement, video, and storytelling activity in an integrative fashion. One of the basic principles of dynamic play is that families are asked to begin play using a basic activity structure. It is expected that children and their families will then develop deviations in this basic structure that are related to their underlying emotional experience. The play therapist then helps the families incorporate their deviations into a more unique and personal version of the structure. These developed play episodes are used to help families address their problems. Such coaching is seen as essential to help families, especially those with significant conflict, begin to learn how to play together improvisationally to express and organize their emotional experience. The play which results from the beginning structures is guided to have personal relevance, catharsis, and help families engage in creative problems solving. (Also see Volcano, Chapter 42.) Monster is such an initial structure.

RATIONALE

When children experience anxiety, they often use the play image of a monster to express such feelings. Stories of overcoming and defeating monsters of all sorts abound in fairy tales and children's literature. Usually in such stories, the protagonist is threatened and then must use several abilities such as cunning, courage, and resourcefulness to overcome the challenge of the monster. By employing the universal image of the monster and the theme of defeating the threatening object, children can be helped to master their internal fears. This is accomplished using the generalized scenario of chasing a monster away and helping children then make this story and image have personal relevance.

When parents are included in the story, whether as active partners in helping their children meet the challenge of the monster or in the role of a witness, the relationship between parent and child can be positively enhanced as well. As parents are included in developing improvised play around the theme of chasing the monster away, goals of reducing anxiety as well as improving parent–child interaction can be addressed.

DESCRIPTION

To begin, the play therapist asks the child and the parent to first choose something from the playroom to be the monster. Several large stuffed animals, puppets, scarves, or other movement-oriented play props are offered. If the parent and child have difficulty choosing, the therapist suggests a stuffed animal. Once the action has begun, another monster can be chosen by the family members that better suits their needs. The parent and child are then told to prepare a gesture and short phrase, such as "Go away, monster" or simply "Stop," that will cause the monster to move away and leave them alone. The therapist then begins to move the monster toward the parent and child and carefully watches how they react.

In this game, the monster never does get to the parent or child, and the therapist uses the family's reaction to the approach of the monster as a cue as to how to develop the next part of the monster story. Usually the parent and child do not complete the physical and verbal actions together, if at all, as the monster approaches, and the therapist stops the game with the monster a short distance from the child and parent. The therapist then uses their reaction to develop an approach to how the parent and child can chase the monster away. The game is changed to accommodate the new cues. The therapist keeps stopping the approach and changing how the monster will be chased away until the parent and/or child becomes actively engaged in the chase on their own. This can take several attempts before the parent and child improvise their own response to the monster story in a more spontaneous way.

The therapist can look in several places to help the family develop this next step toward improvisation. If the parent and child are stronger in their verbal response, they are encouraged to use their voice and/or verbal means to tell the monster to go. However, if the parent or child appears more able to use physical means, then the parent and child are coached to exaggerate and enlarge their gestures. Sometimes the child shows physical movements that are unintended with the approach of the monster. The therapist looks for such movements, particularly in the extremities, such as in the fingers or feet. If this occurs, the child is then helped to enlarge such movement into activities such as kicking (if the feet were moving as the monster approached) or pushing (if the hands or fingers were so used) the monster away.

Two extremes can occur, especially with children who experience high levels of intrusive anxiety, such as in the case of those who have posttraumatic stress disorder. These extremes include those children and parents who totally freeze when the monster approaches and show little or no movement, and those children who attack the monster very aggressively and show little or no awareness of what their parents are doing. For those children who freeze, the therapist becomes very observant of any unconscious movement including breathing to use as cues to expand a next step. Along this line, some parent–child dyads have been coached to "blow the monster away." As one child became more confident with his blowing, he spontaneously began to sing commands to the monster approaching him. A general strategy for the children who attack the monster has been for the therapist to become an announcer along with the parent and cheer on the children as they attempt to meet the challenge.

As children and parents become more independent in their play, the action can be extended using art and storytelling. Children are encouraged to draw or otherwise construct their monsters and then develop an ending such as put the monster in a jail, rip it up, or throw it out the door. Parents can also be instructed in helping their children make up their personal fairy tales about defeating their monster.

APPLICATION

Monster activities are particularly useful in helping children who have experienced traumatic events. Often the development of the metaphor of mastering the challenge of the monster with creative play can be directly linked to mastering the fear associated with the experience of the overwhelming event. In these cases, the changes within the monster story become the center of the progress of the therapy.

Monster activities were used in the therapy of a 7-year-old boy who was sexually assaulted by his father throughout his preschool years. The father had developed elaborate threats of animals watching the boy to keep him from telling of the abuse. The boy had developed a very constricted emotional style and had several anxiety-related symptoms including severe nightmares, difficulty eating, and many somatic concerns. He initially chose scarves as the monster. Both he and his mother were unable to generate much spontaneous activity to chase away the monster at first. As sessions progressed, however, he developed a story in which he would run away and under the scarf to keep it from touching him. He made several safe lands with pillows where the monster could not hurt him once he was there. He then taught this to his mother, and they both began to run and jump into the pillow piles of the safe lands together. Gradually he would begin to venture in more of the room as the monster scarves would be thrown into the air. His anxiety-related symptoms decreased with this expansion of play.

References

Harvey, S. A. (1994). Dynamic play therapy: expressive play intervention with families. In *Handbook of Play Therapy*, Vol. 2, ed. K. O'Connor and C. Schaefer. New York: Wiley.

————. (1997). A dynamic play therapy response to divorce. In *Play Therapy Theory and Practice: A Comparative Presentation*, ed. K. O'Connor and L. Braverman. New York: Wiley.

42

Volcano

Steve Harvey

INTRODUCTION

Volcano is a game often used with the dynamic play approach to intervention (described in Chapter 41). It is one of the initial games that can be used to help children and their families address the difficulties associated with basic emotional experiences of rage, withdrawal, and other more undifferentiated negative experiences. Typically children who are experiencing such strong emotional states have had histories that include abuse and significant losses, and they have significant feelings of insecurity that leave them with little ability to trust. Such children can present with high levels of anger and aggressive acting out. Parents and other adults typically report difficulty talking with their children in meaningful ways about personal experiences. Interestingly, the volcano game has also proven effective with children who present as very withdrawn as well.

RATIONALE

Often when children, especially at younger ages, experience traumatic events of separations from or loss of primary attachment figures, they become overwhelmed by their emotional reactions. In the face of the death of a family member or victimization from physical or sexual abuse, children may become unable to verbalize or even understand the strong emotions they experience. Such children may become distractible, aggressive, and distant from the remaining adults in their lives, even if provided sensitive and positive caregiving. It is not unusual for some children to become withdrawn on some occasions only to become very aggressive to other family members at other times for no seeming reason. In such cases aggression or withdrawal seems to become the only avenue of interaction a child may have while experiencing overwhelming emotions. Acting-out behavior can continue despite a family's use of consistent behavior consequences or attempts at verbalization. In this situation a family's interactions can easily become characterized by negative feeling and a lack of support. A child's play, especially in interactions with family members, can likewise become negative and lack the resources usually associated with play.

The activities of the volcano game are designed to help children and their family members make their expressions with each other more authentic, positive, and meaningful. The activities are built around the basic metaphor of personal emotional experience as being inside and the eruption as being the expression of such feeling. As the volcano metaphor is extended through physicalization, art, competition, video, and storytelling, the complexities and unique emotional experience of an individual child and family can be explored in ways that have personal relevance. Finally, when a child and parent(s) can begin to play with more improvisation and enjoyment, their relationship can improve.

DESCRIPTION

The activities of the volcano game can be played out with children individually (at least initially) along with the play therapist or with one or both of the parents, depending on the therapist's judgment of the child's needs. When the child is seen individually, the play therapist usually prepares the child to play the volcano game with his parents at a later time with the thought that he can teach his parent how to play. The first part of volcano, whether played by the child with therapist or in a family setting, is a physical activity beginning with the child being told that he can become a volcano by lying down on a large pillow while the play therapist and possibly a parent piles other pillows on the "mountain." Care is taken at this point to make sure that the child has the ability to ask for how many pillows to place on the mountain or to decide if his face is covered or not. Some children prefer to leave their face uncovered, while others want to be totally inside the pillow pile. Likewise some children desire only a few pillows to be over them, while others ask for several. Finally the child is also asked if the parent should join him under the pillows or not.

This part of the game can be used with children aged 5 and under if care is taken not to overwhelm them with too many pillows or by separating them from their parent prematurely. This problem can be solved easily by ensuring the child enjoys the activity by using only one or two pillows in the initial pile and by having the parent lie down next to him and assist in the "erupting" part of the game.

Once all these arrangements are completed, the volcano is told to begin erupting by kicking all the pillows off. The therapist (and parent, if the child is a solo volcano) then throws the pillow back over the child while the volcano keeps erupting by kicking pillows off. Various extensions can be added to this part of the game to provide a competitive element. Such competition usually helps increase the child's intrinsic engagement. The child (or child and parent) is asked to try and get all the pillows off in 30 seconds or a certain number of minutes (usually 1 or 2) while the therapist attempts to throw the pillows back on. The child may also be asked to make as large an eruption as possible by kicking the pillows to the wall of the room or away from the therapist. While the child (or child and parent) usually wins this part of the game easily, care is taken to ensure that adults do not hold the pillows down while covering the child. In this activity, adults are required to throw pillows back onto the child for him to kick/push off. A few adults want to hold the pillows on the child despite this rule. If this happens, the adult is told to stay several feet away from the volcano to ensure that the child can continue an eruption of kicking or pushing the pillows.

Some children change to kicking during the eruption phase through their very unique game performance. Such deviations are noted and the play therapist then incorporates such action into the story of the eruption. For example, some children want to stand up rather than continue lying down to better push the pillows off, while others stop kicking and want to hide under their mountains of pillows. Such developments are then reframed as part of the story of the volcano (see Harvey 2000, for an extended case study description).

As the action of the volcano comes to a close, the child is then asked to draw a volcano with the lava inside and then draw the eruption to create a visual metaphor of the physical action. The child and parent are then asked to create a story of the eruption. A video of the physical action can also be made and used as a source for a story as well. Such extensions of the volcano activity have proved very helpful in encouraging both expressive metaphor making as well as creativity. Following such extensions, the child and other family members are asked to use their videos and artwork to help describe and label the feelings they have inside them. The family's play behavior during the eruption part of the games or the various art and story metaphors can then be used to help children verbalize their more private and/or overwhelming experiences. The child and family are then asked to note when their volcanoes happen at home, in an effort to connect the play action with home behavior. Often the volcano game is then played again using the real-life circumstances related from daily life.

APPLICATION

The clearest uses of volcano are for those children who find it impossible to verbalize or express their emotional experience and in families that have difficulty with emotional expression. Such children have typically experienced psychological trauma and/or loss of significant attachment figures. In such interventions, volcano has been very helpful in helping children and their parents gain some understanding as they develop an organized expression together. The volcano game can be used with children aged 5 through 12. Specific adaptations can be made for use with younger children.

Volcano was successfully used with a 5-year-old girl who had recently been sexually assaulted by a middle-school boy. During the sexual episodes the girl had been physically restrained while the older boy lay on top of her. The girl had been increasingly aggressive with her older sister, had difficulty sleeping, became very moody, was becoming increasingly withdrawn and angry with her mother, and was having extended tantrum behavior in the home. During the first several sessions, she requested to be by herself with only one or two pillows placed over her when she was the volcano. She also asked that her face not be covered. During her several performances of the eruptions, she began to enjoy kicking the pillows as far away as she could and keeping them off her. As her mood changed, she asked her mother to jump on her as the volcano kicking began and then she stood to push the pillows off. The girl was able to begin to draw many pictures of the eruption and later more direct representations of the sexual episode at home following her acting out. She then began to verbalize her anger with the older boy more directly. Concurrently, she also began to express far more positive feeling toward her mother as well.

Reference

Harvey, S. A. (2000). Dynamic play with families. In *Current Approaches in Drama Therapy*, ed. P. Lewis and D. Johnson. New York: Charles Smith.

43

The Bat-a-Feeling Game

Joyce Meagher

INTRODUCTION

I have found that children in psychotherapy are often hesitant to directly express their feelings, especially in a sit-down, direct-eye-contact format. Early in play therapy, when children are "checking out" the therapist for trustworthiness, it is helpful to have available several casual, spontaneous, and fun activities. Children who are anxious or angry or have attention-deficit disorder usually are guarded or easily distracted unless the discussion of feelings is eased into in a relaxed fashion. Also, most young children participate in one or several forms of team sports, so they are eager to latch onto a familiar activity to achieve feelings of mastery to counteract their anxiety about being in a new situation. The Bat-a-Feeling game is a natural way to ease children into a more comfortable expression of their feelings.

RATIONALE

Children naturally express their feelings through play, by communicating orally, through body language, and symbolically through their representative play activities. When children are playing a game, they are less defensive about discussing their feelings because they see their answers as just one part of the game. In the Bat-a-Feeling game, children can control how often they express a feeling because they have the choice to hit the feeling ball and use it or not, and only are obligated to express a feeling when they miss the pitched ball. As children get into the game, they will often more freely choose to express feelings that are pertinent to their issues, whether or not the ball is missed.

Also, the physical activity helps promote the release of feelings, because the child feels empowered to control the activity, plus gain self-esteem as mastery of more pitches occurs.

It can help the therapist to assess the strength of feelings by observing a child's body language while batting. The child may show great determination to swat one certain color of ball repeatedly, leading one to comment on that pattern: "I notice whenever the red ball is pitched to you, you really try hard to hit it!" Often, children have said, "I don't want to miss it, because I'm not ready to talk about what makes me angry," or "I feel good when I really whack the angry ball, 'cause it makes me feel less angry!" Thus, just whacking the feeling itself can be a helpful release!

DESCRIPTION

Nerf bats and balls are kept in an open basket in the room, available at any time for children to play catch or to bat, with the therapist pitching. Often, children will swap positions, asking the therapist to take a turn at bat. After playing awhile in this manner, it is very natural to lead into the Bat-a-Feeling game.

Three different-colored balls are available, and the colors are matched to basic feelings by the therapist: the red ball is "red-hot," or angry feelings; the yellow bat is "sunny," or happy feelings; and the blue ball is "feeling blue," or sad feelings.

When a ball is pitched, if the batter hits it, he or she can choose to go on to the next pitch, or express a time that feeling was felt, according to the color of the ball hit. When a pitched ball is missed, the rule is that the feeling is to be expressed regardless.

If the therapist is asked to bat, it can be very helpful if feelings are expressed that align with the child's issues: "I feel sad when none of my friends can spend time with me." The child will often follow with a similar acknowledgment that opens up discussion pertaining to a current problem he or she has.

APPLICATION

This is an easy technique to introduce passively (if the child picks up the ball or bat and asks to play), or actively (as a directed activity). It can be adapted to group play by taking turns at bat, or can be altered by having a circle and taking turns throwing the different-colored balls to one another and responding with the feeling that is "caught."

Children with attention problems, conduct problems, or anxiety do very well with this game, because it is very active, and less threatening than direct conversation. It is also useful in family therapy sessions, to help promote exchange of feelings between parents and child, and between siblings.

44

The Topple-a-Feeling Game

Joyce Meagher

INTRODUCTION

Children in psychotherapy often respond best when they are put in a casual, non-threatening, and fun situation, especially when expression of feelings is the goal. If a game is played in its regular format, it is often already known and enthusiastically approached. Children who are anxious about trusting a new therapist, or about being in a new situation, will relax when playing a game that easily encourages mastery, with minimal skill variation. It is then quite natural to ease into another way of playing it that can pique a child's interest and that can seem relaxed to the child. The use of primary colors of the playing disks to describe feelings is easily understood and assimilated by children as young as age 3 (if fairly verbal); older children and even parents find this language a common one for mutual understanding, also.

RATIONALE

Children naturally express their feelings through play, by communicating orally, through body language, and symbolically through their choice of play activities. When children are playing a game, they are less defensive about discussing their feelings because they see their answers as just one part of the game. In the Topple-a-Feeling game, children can control which feeling they express because they have the choice to pick the feeling disk color, and can use the same one repeatedly. As children get into the game, they will often more freely choose to express feelings that are pertinent to their issues, especially when a variety of feeling disks are used by other players or the therapist.

Also, the excitement of trying not to topple the playing board helps promote the release of feelings, because the child feels empowered to control the activity, plus gain self-esteem as mastery occurs in placing the disks strategically to keep the board balanced.

It can help the therapist to assess the strength of feelings by observing a child's choice of disks used; the child may show great determination to use one certain color of disk repeatedly, or avoid one particular color, leading one to comment on that pattern: "I notice you really have used a lot of blue disks this game!" Often, the child comments, "That's because I have lots of sad feelings!" Thus, an opening can be made to naturally learn more about what the child's issues are.

DESCRIPTION

The purchased game of Topple is used and initially played the normal way. The object is to earn points competitively by placing disks evenly around a spinning board on a pinnacle base, without toppling the board. Then, the therapist suggests playing it a special way called "Topple-a-Feeling."

About twenty each of four different-colored disks are available, and the colors are matched to basic feelings by the therapist: The red disk is "red-hot," or angry feelings; the yellow disk is "sunny," or happy feelings; the blue disk is "feeling blue," or sad feelings; and the green disk is "green with envy," or jealous feelings (I explain this feeling to young children: "You wish you had something someone else has, or could do something someone else gets to do").

When a disk is placed on the Topple board, the player reports a time he or she has had that feeling. The player can choose any color disk from the pile, with no limit on repeating or ignoring certain colors.

When the therapist takes a turn, it can be very helpful if feelings are expressed that align with the child's issues: "I feel sad when none of my friends can spend time with me." The child will often follow with a similar acknowledgment that opens up discussion pertaining to a current problem he or she has.

Points can be earned similarly to the original game rules, or the board can just be filled until it topples.

APPLICATION

This is an easy technique to introduce passively (if the child picks up the game and asks to play), or actively (as a directed activity). It can be adapted to group play or a family therapy session. (I have used this game with adolescents and adults, also.)

Children with attention problems, conduct problems, or anxiety do very well with this game, because it is very active, and less threatening than direct conversation. There is usually giggling and a sense of lightness because the board threatens to topple unless it is kept balanced. Thus, one can also learn about a child's spatial awareness, patience, and ability to concentrate and be calm in placing the pieces on the board. Encouraging patience can lead to increased self-esteem as mastery occurs.

Children who play this game often will invite a parent or family member to play it in a future session, and are excited to explain the rules to the newcomer! It is a very popular tool in the playroom for comfortable expression of feelings.

45

The Slow-Motion Game

Heidi Gerard Kaduson

INTRODUCTION

Many children with social skill deficiencies seem to also have trouble with self-control and management of their activity level. In group settings this can be a problem for the child both in and out of school situations. To make children aware of their activity level, The Slow-Motion Game was created to help them focus on this particular skill. It can be seen by many therapists who work with active or impulsive children that they learn best by doing. Therefore, this game was created to have them do slow motion rather than just talk about it.

RATIONALE

Learning by doing is a very active process. Children with disabilities find it difficult to learn something unless they are actively involved in the learning. Many cognitive-behavioral approaches teach children what to do, but even though the children know the right answer, they have difficulty actually doing the right thing. This technique has children do the exercise over and over again until they become aware of the slow motion that they have self-control over. The term *behavioral self-control* refers to the implementation of self-monitoring, self-evaluation, and self-reinforcement procedures. "Self-monitoring" refers to maintaining an active awareness of the occurrence of certain targeted behaviors or thoughts; "self-evaluation" involves judging the rate or quality of the behavior being modified against some existing standard or criterion; and "self-reinforcement" refers to the individual administering his or her reinforcement if a certain standard of behavior has been achieved. This technique can help the child make strides in the right direction by illustrating to the child how to do the exercise within a playful format.

DESCRIPTION

Materials Needed

Stopwatches (for each child)

Laminated cards (see below)

Die

Poker chips

Paper

Coloring materials

Achievement awards (Figure 45–1)

Process

The children in the group are introduced to the game with the instructions about what self-control is. Many of the children are asked to contribute what they think self-control might be defined as. The therapist then turns the discussion to activity level, and how difficult it is to have self-control when we are moving too fast. The children are asked to illustrate on a piece of paper what fast moving might look like. Any art is acceptable, and the children are praised for whatever their illustration demonstrates. Once the group has an understanding of the premise, each child is handed a stopwatch. In the center of the table are cards created by the therapist with different scenes that the child will act out in slow motion. These cards are made from Avery labels, which have the lamination attached and can be computer printed so that they last longer. Children will play the game if they believe it is a game that "everyone" has played. The cards might have situations such as the following: throwing a basketball, running a race, raising your hand, playing baseball, having a shoot-out, playing soccer, doing a math test, doing jumping jacks.

The therapist then has the children roll the die to see who goes first. The highest number goes first, and that child picks a card and goes to the head of the room with the therapist. The therapist tells the group what that child is going to do in "very slow motion." The children have to start their stopwatches all together when the therapist says, "1, 2, 3, start." After each ten seconds, the children report the time passed to the child who is performing the task. He or she must keep doing the task for an entire minute in slow motion (with the help of the therapist's guidance when the motion is too fast). When the child has reached the full minute, the other children yell "Stop." Having successfully completed the task, the child earns a poker chip. Then the next child goes (working in a clockwise direction). He or she picks up a card, comes to the front of the room, and the play starts again.

When each child in the group has done the first task, the time is increased to two minutes for the second round. At the end of the second round, the players would all have two chips each, and a treat or snack is given as the reward along with a certificate for "Achievement in Slow Motion" (Figure 45–1). The therapist may go on to a three-minute interval if the children are still excited about playing.

APPLICATION

This technique can be used in small group settings or in classrooms where self-control is a problem to be worked on. It has been done successfully with children with attention-deficit/hyperactivity disorder, Asperger's syndrome, and conduct disorder.

Figure 45–1. Model of award to give children.

46

Make Me Laugh

Risë VanFleet

INTRODUCTION

Make Me Laugh involves the therapeutic uses of an age-old childhood game. It is useful for serious or withdrawn children; that is, children who are very reserved or who have difficulty smiling. The therapist and the child take turns trying to make each other smile or laugh.

RATIONALE

We sometimes encounter children who rarely smile or who may resist smiling. They have difficulty experiencing, expressing, or acknowledging happy or joyful emotions. The reasons for this behavior can be quite varied. These children might be experiencing depression, anxiety disorders, oppositional disorder, posttrauma reactions, or perfectionistic or obsessive-compulsive disorder. The Make Me Laugh technique is useful for all of these, but should be used as part of an overall treatment plan to assist the child's particular problem.

The purpose of the technique is to provide the child with an opportunity to experience and express joyful or silly emotions. The immediate focus of the game is on the person who is trying to keep a straight face, but the primary therapeutic benefit comes for the person who does silly things to make the other laugh. The simple act of doing something silly can be very therapeutic for these children. It can assist them in feeling less self-conscious and in learning that having a good time and playing without any serious purpose is not only acceptable, but desirable.

DESCRIPTION

The therapist explains that the players (the therapist and the child) will take turns trying to make the other smile or laugh. The straight-face player starts the game by gruffly saying, "Make me laugh." He must keep a serious face and under no circumstances smile or laugh. He must look at the other player's face and maintain eye contact for the duration of his turn.

The other player must then do whatever she can to try to get the straight face to smile or laugh. She is not permitted to physically touch him, but she may make faces, tell jokes, make strange noises, or engage in any silly antics that might make him laugh. She may move close to him, but no touching is allowed.

The therapist starts the game by allowing the child to choose which role he would like to play first. The therapist ensures that the child is successful or has a positive experience with whichever role he selects. For example, if the child decides to be the straight face first, the therapist goes through various antics but within the bounds the child is likely to be able to tolerate. It's important for the therapist to model some silly behavior without overwhelming the child. If the child smiles, the therapist laughs and then says, "OK, now it's time for you to make me laugh." Some children need encouragement in making faces and noises. The therapist needs to maintain a lighthearted atmosphere and at no time should the child be cajoled or subtly shamed into being silly. The therapist can provide some little cartoons or jokes for the very timid child to use if needed.

The therapist ensures the child's success by laughing after the child does something. The therapist does not hold out for long in the early stages of playing this game. The game alternates back and forth quickly. If the child maintains the straight face for over 30 to 60 seconds, the therapist concedes a "win" for that round to the child. Any scoring system can be used to add reinforcement to the game.

After each player has been in the straight face role about four times, the game can be ended.

APPLICATION

Make Me Laugh is a quick intervention that can be used with children who, for any number of reasons, rarely smile or laugh. It is a useful technique for children who believe that experiencing or showing humor is unacceptable or who are unable to play for fear they will be judged. Make Me Laugh can be used for brief periods over several sessions. At no time should children be forced to play, but resistance to this game can be reduced if the therapist maintains a lighthearted and nonjudgmental atmosphere. Therapists must use caution with this technique and avoid any impression that they are making fun of the child.

Case Example

Josh, 9 years old, was referred by his teacher because he seemed isolated from his classmates. He was intellectually gifted and did extremely well academically, but he rarely interacted with his peers. His teacher described his behavior with classmates as superior and condescending. Early assessment revealed considerable anxiety and strong perfectionistic tendencies. He described himself as being more grown-up than his peers, but revealed a desire to be more accepted by them. When the therapist discovered Josh enjoyed Clint Eastwood movies, she decided that Make Me Laugh could be an ideal intervention with this seemingly joyless boy. At first, when Josh was in the straight-face role, he did not smile or laugh at all. The therapist praised his ability to keep a straight face. Josh's initial attempts to make the therapist laugh were stiff and tentative. With encouragement, primarily in the form of the therapist's smiling (and "losing" that round), Josh became bolder from session to session. After playing this game for four weeks (along with other play therapy interventions), Josh was able to stand up and do a silly monkey dance to get the therapist to laugh. As he loosened up and became more accepting of humor and playfulness, his relationships with peers improved.

47

Holding You in My Mind: An Approach for Working with Traumatized and Attachment-Disordered Children

Cynthia A. Langevin

INTRODUCTION

A common dilemma in working with children is treating those who have an attachment disturbance in combination with a history of traumatic stressors. The availability of diagnostic-specific play therapy techniques that address these complexities has been lacking. To work within the context of play therapy, a specialized technique that enhances the therapist–child relationship has been developed. It provides a creative structure, and by its cognitive therapy and relational enhancement design provides a much-needed mechanism for a corrective emotional experience to occur within the therapeutic relationship. Constancy becomes attainable with this technique.

Frequently children with attachment issues have difficulty maintaining a constant mental image of important adults, including the therapist. More than one child I have treated has greeted me in the waiting room with surprise that I was not dead and that I had reappeared. These children are often deficient in object constancy and self-constancy. Their play often is characterized by Hide and Seek, Peek-a-Boo, or Chase. As an alternative to those games, Holding You in My Mind was created. It places the therapist in the role of providing maternal preoccupation, an experience often lacking for attachment-disordered children. It also provides the additional linkage of reciprocity, whereby the child is encouraged to focus on the therapist. The interactional nature of this technique also serves to alter the internal working model.

Bowlby (1973, 1980) introduced and then expanded the concept of an internal working model and the role it plays in personality development and psychological functioning. The internal working model is a mental representation developed during childhood based on early experiences with significant caregivers. Bowlby suggested that a young child's early experiences of coping with caregiver unavailability may later come to generate cognitive rules or expectations about the availability and emotional supportiveness of others, including peers, teachers, and therapists. The child's developing self-concept may then be affected in that the child begins to view himself in terms of the caregiver's level of responsiveness. Some children develop a belief about themselves that they are unworthy of love or unlovable. Some children in attempting to navigate and adapt to an unresponsive caregiver develop provocative and oppositional behaviors as a means of ensuring some level of response. This oppositional stance can then become incorporated into the development of the child's self-concept and become a part of a self-fulfilling prophecy.

RATIONALE

These working models and the interrelated beliefs that are attributed to the self may be realigned or reworked through corrective interpersonal relationships. This play method is one tool to help in the reworking process. It also addresses the needs of children who continue throughout life to undergo transformations, including the task of renegotiating attachment, at each new developmental phase. The struggle to balance autonomy and being connected is compounded for the attachment-disordered or traumatized child. This challenge can be supported from a coordinated therapeutic support that assists the child in integrating often conflicting drives.

Disturbances in early attachment relationships may result in children who are more vulnerable to depression because they are left with very low internalized feelings of felt security. Such children have fewer resources for coping with stress and are thus more susceptible to reduced self-esteem, greater feelings of insecurity, and depressed affect or its corollary—acting-out behaviors. The depressive cognitions that develop are thus connected.

DESCRIPTION

Holding You in My Mind is a delightful yet simple technique introduced in the initial stage of treatment. It begins with an invitation to the child to create his/her own special Holding You in My Mind container. Many examples of other container creations labeled with first names are prominently displayed in the office. These examples act as an enticement, and they help overcome the child's initial discomfort, anxiety, and/or uncertainty by giving him a specific task to complete. The act of creation and ownership immediately brings satisfaction by its mere accomplishment. Materials to have on hand include plastic containers with lids, and an assortment of craft material such as tissue paper, glue, glitter, popsicle sticks, sequins, and pompoms.

Together, the therapist and child create their own containers with their names prominently displayed. Forming glue into letters and covering it with glitter is an attractive method. Any other creative uses of the materials are encouraged.

The task is explained in words: "In these boxes, we're going to write and collect the special things that we hear each other say. For instance, I'm often told that I say, 'Can you think of a time when something different happened?' Maybe you say, 'That really bugs me.' What I say will go in your box and what you say will go in my box. You will take your box home and bring it back each session and yours will stay here with me."

The process of collecting and writing messages on small fortune cookie–like strips of paper begins immediately. Since one aspect of treatment with attachment-disordered children focuses on providing nurturant experiences, the beginning dialogue from the therapist takes a prescribed shape. Focusing on, for example, counting the child's freckles and commenting on how they so attractively bring attention to that cute face would be written on the strip of paper. It would read, "I'm counting

19, 20, 21 freckles on the right side of your face. They're like a perfect frame for those big brown eyes."

Other statements that provide the kind of attention that is ideally present in the early mother–infant bonding process where each attribute of the child is commented upon and cherished could be used for the phrase collection. To start the child listening to the therapist, the therapist will often have to provide the impetus: "Oops, I think I just caught myself saying the same thing. Did you hear me say, 'Jonathan, you're a really good player,' again? Let's put that down on paper for your box." With that, the therapist either writes the sentence or helps the child write it.

With the cooperation of the adult caregiver, the child takes his box home and is instructed to read through the notes at any time. The importance of bringing the box back for each session is stressed. Just in case it's forgotten, a running tally of all the sayings in each box are kept in the child's file. Each session begins with a review of how the Holding You in My Mind system works. During subsequent sessions, if the therapist hears the child repeat a phrase that is already documented, the therapist searches it out and makes special reference to it. The same process is repeated if the therapist says something already captured in the child's box.

This process is incorporated into every session as the other work continues. It provides the cohesion and continuity that this type of child has often lacked. It also provides positive messages about the child in an attempt to rework former negative messages that have developed through neglectful or inadequate parenting. At the end of treatment, the child is able to leave treatment with his internalized object of the therapist well used, and the ability to capture and retain the therapist's presence well established in the child's routing.

APPLICATION

In addition to using this technique with children who have experienced disrupted or insecure attachments, or in parent–child relationships damaged through trauma, I have used it with families who are going on vacation or will have a planned separation from their child. Familiar and captivating phrases of endearment are placed inside the Holding You in

My Mind box for the child to review or have reviewed by his caregiver during the absence. It has been reported numerous times that this has been a source of enjoyment for the family to create, and a source of comfort and soothing for the child who is experiencing a separation from his parent(s).

References

Bowlby, J. (1973). *Attachment and Loss, Vol. 2: Separation, Anxiety and Anger.* London: Hogarth. New York: Basic Books.

———. (1980). *Attachment and Loss, Vol. 3: Loss, Sadness and Depression.* London: Hogarth. New York: Basic Books.

48

Feelings Dice

Mary Ann Valentino

INTRODUCTION

Increasing the child client's ability to label, differentiate, express, and manage affect are common goals of therapy regardless of the therapeutic orientation of the therapist. Through the use of interpretation, the therapist can aid the child in his understanding of emotional experience by reflecting affect and motive attached to play behavior; however, as the child develops cognitively, encouraging the child to verbalize his emotional experiences becomes increasingly important (Harter 1983).

RATIONALE

O'Connor (1983) identifies three subskills involved in managing emotions: (1) awareness of the range of feeling states, (2) ability to conect feeling states with the situations in which they occur, and (3) ability to appropriately express feelings verbally. There are a variety of educational-play techniques available to the play therapist for the labeling and expression of feeling states (e.g., "Feelings Charades" and "Silly Stories" in Kondracki 1993, "Color-Your-Life" in O'Connor 1983). Harter (1983) points out, however, that of particular interest to the child therapist is the acknowledgment and integration by the child of seemingly contradictory feelings occurring simultaneously regarding a single event or person. She describes a drawing technique that she developed and a new doll as a means of facilitating this acknowledgment. The Feelings Dice technique was developed to address the following goals:

1. Increase the child's awareness of various feelings states.

2. Encourage the child to talk about life events on an affective level.

3. Assess the child's ability to conceptualize the simultaneous occurrence of two feeling states.

4. Enhance the child's awareness of the simultaneous occurrence of two feeling states.

DESCRIPTION

Materials

Any four-inch cubed box can be used to make the die. Bennett and Bennett (1991) describe a method for making giant dice from half-gallon milk cartons, by cutting off the lower portion of two cartons, slipping one inside the other, and covering the cube tightly with white wrapping paper. To make a more durable die, the cube can be wrapped in strong shipping tape. Markers can then be used to label the sides of the die with feeling words.

Technique

Once the dice have been made, the feeling states chosen to label the sides of each die may vary depending on the specific problems that the child is facing and the developmental level of the child. For example, each die may be labeled similarly with the words *sad, angry, happy, afraid, disgusted,* and *surprised.* The dice are simply rolled and the game begins by having the child tell about either a hypothetical time when those two feelings may occur or a particular time in the child's life when those two feelings have occurred.

APPLICATION

The Feelings Dice technique may be used by a variety of individuals who work with children. The level of training required depends on the desired depth and content of discussion. Parents and teachers may wish to use Feelings Dice as a means for discussing labeling and expression of affect, whereas child therapists may wish to use Feelings Dice as a means of discussing contradictory feelings toward an abusive parent.

According to Harter (1983), the ability to acknowledge the occurrence of two feelings simultaneously follows a developmental sequence that coincides with the cognitive development of the child. The preoperational child appears to be limited to understanding only one emotion at a time; thus, this technique is inappropriate. As children enter concrete operations, Harter (1983) suggests a fourfold developmental sequence in the conceptualization of simultaneous feelings states: (1) feelings of similar valence regarding a single event or person; (2) feelings of similar valence regarding different events or persons; (3) feelings of different valence regarding different events or persons; and (4) feelings of different valence regarding a single event or person. Keeping this developmental sequence in mind, Feelings Dice may be used to assess the child's capacity to acknowledge simultaneous feeling states. However, a child who is able to demonstrate all four levels of the sequence when discussing hypothetical or relatively neutral events or persons, may have a great amount of difficulty when discussing highly emotional situations.

The Feelings Dice technique was used with a 9-year-old boy who had been physically abused by his stepfather and subsequently removed from his stepfather's and biologic mother's home and placed with his maternal grandmother. After several sessions, it became clear to the therapist that the child was having a great amount of difficulty acknowledging and expressing his many contradictory feelings toward his biologic father who lived nearby with his new wife and was expecting their first child.

He was angry and sad that his father did not take him to live with him, and he was happy to see his father on visits. These contradictory feelings often caused problems during visits with his father, because the child would end up sabotaging the visits by behaving in a passive-aggressive manner. The Feelings Dice were used to address the many different feelings people can have at the same time regarding the same event or person. Twelve feelings were chosen to label the dice: die one included *joyful, happy, excited, jealous, angry,* and *afraid*; die two included *proud, loved, hopeful, lonely, sad,* and *disappointed*. The feeling states were chosen to address the needs of the client; three comfortable and three uncomfortable feeling states were on each die, so that feelings of similar valence could come up together, thus allowing for easier and less threatening events to be generated. The Feelings Dice were presented as a game, and the first few stories generated were kept hypothetical and at times silly to keep his interest and to titrate his anxiety level. For example, the first time he rolled "disappointed" and "excited," he became visibly very anxious and was having trouble coming up with a situation. With the help of the therapist, he was able to come up with, "I might feel excited about traveling to the moon but disappointed that there isn't a McDonald's up there to eat at." However, later he was able to acknowledge, "I feel excited when I get to go to my dad's and disappointed that he doesn't want me to live with him." With the help of this technique, he was able to discover and understand why his visits to his father's often ended badly because of his contradictory feelings.

References

Bennett, S., and Bennett, R. (1991). *365 TV-Free Activities You Can Do with Your Child*. Holbrook, MA: Bob Adams.

Harter, S. (1983). Cognitive-developmental considerations in the conduct of play therapy. In *Handbook of Play Therapy*, ed. C. E. Schaefer and K. J. O'Connor, pp. 95–127. New York: Wiley.

Kondracki, L. (1993). *All My Feelings Are Okay: An Innovative 6-Step Program Using Stories, Skits, and Games to Help Families Identify and Express Their Feelings*. Grand Rapids, MI: Fleming H. Revell.

O'Connor, K. J. (1983). The color-your-life technique. In *Handbook of Play Therapy*, ed. C. E. Schaefer and K. J. O'Connor, pp. 251–258. New York: Wiley.

49

Up or Down: It's Up to Me

Donna Cangelosi

INTRODUCTION

Children commonly do not see how their behaviors affect either positive or negative outcomes, but instead tend to feel that good or bad things merely happen to them. This is particularly true with young children and those who tend to externalize difficulties such as those with impulse problems and other conduct and behavioral disorders. This technique was developed to help children see the connection between their behaviors and the situations, be they positive or negative, that arise in their lives.

RATIONALE

The primary goal in working with children who tend to externalize difficulties is to help them adapt more of an internal locus of control. This is achieved by enhancing their ability to self-reflect and by helping them identify connections between thoughts, feelings, actions, and consequences.

"Chutes and Ladders"™ (Milton Bradley Co., 1979) is a popular, non-threatening game that children tend to gravitate to in the playroom. It was designed by its creators to teach the "rewards of good deeds and the consequences of naughty ones." The game can easily be adapted to teach the importance of thinking before acting, identifying problematic thoughts or behaviors, highlighting positive decision-making skills, and taking pride in accomplishments.

DESCRIPTION

The child and therapist take turns progressing up the board by spinning the number dial until someone reaches the top square (#100). Each time a ladder is landed on, the player (child or therapist) discusses a time that he or she did something positive, productive, or helpful that resulted in a reward or sense of personal pride or accomplishment. Conversely, each time a chute is landed on, the player is asked to discuss a time when he or she may have been careless, not thinking before acting, or mischievous, which consequently resulted in a disappointment.

Each time the therapist takes a turn and lands on a chute or ladder, it is important to build upon the child's example/situation in order to highlight relevant points, to model taking pride in accomplishments, to stress the importance of thinking before acting, and to accentuate ways to effectively handle situations in the future.

APPLICATION

This technique is very useful for elementary-school children who have difficulties making connections between their behaviors and the situations or outcomes that arise in their lives. While this is commonly seen with acting out, impulsive, and behavior-disordered youngsters, it can also be prevalent among children with low self-esteem, who have difficulty seeing or internalizing their accomplishments, skills, or assets. As such, the technique is equally useful for both populations. It can also be used in a more general way to help children who are in the early stages of treatment to openly discuss life's ups and downs, thereby enhancing communication and reducing resistance.

This technique can be used in individual, group, or family therapy. When used with a group of children or with family members, ideas for effective coping are solicited from all participants.

50

When Life Turns Upside Down

Donna Cangelosi

INTRODUCTION

Children brought for play therapy often present with histories and problems related to losses, separations, and major life changes including, but not limited to, death, parental divorce, illness and hospitalizations, relocation, and the birth of a new sibling (Cangelosi 1997). Each of these very influential events is determined by forces outside of the child's control.

The lack of involvement in decision making regarding major changes and losses often leaves children with feelings of vulnerability, helplessness, anger, sadness, and a sense of being out of control. This technique was developed to help children communicate and gain mastery over these emotions and experiences.

RATIONALE

Effective clinical work with any population requires that the therapist find a way to make treatment safe for the client. Children with histories involving loss, separation, and major changes generally do not find it safe to talk about feelings openly due to loyalty conflicts, confusion, and a sense that it is not okay to feel what they are feeling. Like all children, these youngsters do not have the ability to put words to feeling states. Segal (1984) noted that their inability to discuss feelings prolongs the grieving process. Therefore, he recommends the use of therapeutic techniques that rely on symbolic communication.

Young children enjoy playing "Don't Spill the Beans"™ (Milton Bradley Co., 1984) and tend to find the game exciting and nonthreatening. While involved in the game they are freer to discuss situations and feelings because the process of play tends to loosen their defenses.

DESCRIPTION

The game's beans are first divided evenly among up to four players. Each player places one bean at a time on the top of the pot. As the beans accumulate, the therapist highlights how smoothly everything is going and might even offer examples or engage the child in conversation about how it feels when things go smoothly in life. Each time one of the players spills the beans, he or she is asked to talk about a time when something happened that made it feel like life was turned upside down and then adds the spilled beans to his or her pile. If necessary, the therapist can offer examples of situations that might cause someone to feel like life is turned upside down (e.g., a major change, loss, disappointment, etc.), focusing on the aspect of not having control. Each time the therapist spills the beans he or she uses the opportunity to highlight key points about what experiences the child has shared, to provide empathy, to support the child's efforts at coping, and to provide information about options for handling the situation.

APPLICATION

This technique was originally developed for elementary-school youngsters from divorced and separated families. Over time, I have expanded its use for any child who has undergone a major life change, separation, or loss. I've also found the technique useful in helping all children discuss everyday disappointments such as a baseball game being rained out, failing a test, or not getting a desired part in a play. Often older children gravitate to the game to discuss such issues. This technique can also be used in group or family sessions.

Regardless of what population this technique is used with, it is always important to allow children to discuss major losses and separations at their own pace so that they do not become overwhelmed. As such, it may be helpful to start the game talking about less traumatic experiences while simultaneously gathering diagnostic information about the child's overall functioning and his or her readiness and capacity to discuss major losses, separations, and changes.

References

Cangelosi, D. (1997). Play therapy with children from divorced and separated families. In *The Playing Cure*, ed. H. Kaduson, D. Cangelosi, and C. E. Schaefer, pp. 119–142. Northvale, NJ: Jason Aronson.

Segal, R. M. (1984). Helping children express grief through symbolic communication. *Social Casework* 65:590–599.

51

The Fishing for Feelings Card Game

Michael Kantrowitz

INTRODUCTION

One of the most difficult tasks to achieve in using any game in therapy is making sure that children will want to play. Many therapists spend hundreds of dollars on games that are just not interesting to children. Card games, however, have always been popular with children. Card games and play go well together, and they are easily adaptable for play therapy. Go Fish is played with a regular deck of playing cards. It can be adapted to make it both fun and therapeutic by facilitating the sharing of feelings and facilitating communication.

RATIONALE

The learning and expression of emotions is a process that is essential to mental health. Children often are unwilling to talk about how they feel especially when an adult is asking questions and probing delicate areas. Children may feel overwhelmed. But putting them in control of the sharing—what to share and how to share it—creates feelings of safety. I believe that if we can teach young children about feelings and how to

222

appropriately express them, we set the stage for a healthier adulthood for them. This is the concept behind "Fishing for Feelings," a game that helps children express emotions connected with any issues they may be experiencing, and to feel safe as they determine what to share and how to share it. Fishing for Feelings accomplishes these goals with fun and interactive sharing. Learning about and expressing emotions while playing leads children down the path that heals. It not only helps children survive but also allows them to thrive.

DESCRIPTION

Fishing for Feelings is played just like Go Fish. The major difference is that each card has a feeling and an animated face that matches the feeling (fifty-two cards with thirteen different feelings), so even if the child forgets what the feeling means, the matching face allows the child to understand and relate to the feeling.

Each player is dealt seven cards. The remaining cards are placed face down and spread out between the players and is called the fishing pond. Play begins with one player asking another if he has any "happiness," "sadness," or "fear" cards or any other feeling that the player who is asking must have at least one of in her hand. If the other player has one or more of the cards just asked for, he must give all of those cards to the asking player and it remains that player's turn; if the player being asked does not have any of the cards asked for, he says, "Go fish." The asking player then selects one card from the fishing pond. If she selected the card she asked for it remains her turn, if not it is now the other player's turn. When a player collects all four cards with the same feeling he puts them face up and, in order to keep the cards, must report a situation when he felt that feeling. Play continues until all cards have been collected and all feelings have been verbalized. The player at the end with the most feelings wins.

APPLICATION

Fishing for Feelings has multiple applications. It may be played by children ages 5 and up, and by adults of any age. It may be used as a way to teach individuals about feelings and how to express them, therefore improving communication in a relaxed, nonthreatening way. Its uses are only limited by one's imagination. Fishing for Feelings may be used in a group format by combining two or more decks. Since Fishing for Feelings contains feelings that children might not yet understand, they have an opportunity to learn a new feeling and match it to feelings they have already experienced, thus increasing their emotional "IQ."

In many cases I have used Fishing for Feelings to open up a child who had significant difficulty verbalizing feelings related to parents, school, or siblings.

One such case involved a 7-year-old boy who was getting into physical fights at school. He was also in the middle of his parents' divorce, which was now in its sixth month. As we played Fishing for Feelings, he lay on his back looking up at the ceiling talking about missing his father (related to the sadness cards) and feeling angry about his parents' arguing so much—sometimes about him and visitation rights—and being mad at each other. As he started to release these pent-up emotions the healing process began.

It is very important that the therapist not ask questions regarding any feelings the child has expressed while playing the game, so as to maintain the safe and trusting environment. To pull children out of a play modality by questioning them regarding feelings they have just verbalized can instantly create an unsafe environment. Therapists must trust that the child's expression of feelings and the subsequent relating to emotions facilitate the healing and growth processes, and improve communication and the child's relating to the external world.

Resource

The Fishing for Feelings card game is available from The Feelings Company. Go to www.feelingscompany.com for an on-line catalog. Mail Order: 30101 Town Center Dr., Suite 110, Laguna Niguel, CA 92677, phone (949) 363-0202; fax (949) 363-0206.

52

The Preschool Play Geno-Game

Paris Goodyear-Brown

INTRODUCTION

In my work with preschool children, I am continually looking for ways to adapt existing techniques to the unique conceptual, attentional, and communication needs of this age group. This technique is inspired by Eliana Gil's work with the family play genogram. However, this adaptation sets up the creation of the genogram as a game with incentives, a built-in token economy system, and a follow-up storytelling technique. Moreover, it is not a group endeavor as it is in the family play genogram, but a one-on-one assessment tool.

RATIONALE

The genogram has long been a tool to help clinicians conceptualize, visualize, and organize information regarding family systems. Usually, the information used to construct the genogram is gathered from adult members of the family. It is clear to me, however, that my young clients have deeply entrenched perceptions of their family dynamics that must

225

be addressed. Most of these children do not yet have the words to articulate even the behaviors that they observe in their family members, much less how their observations have shaped their idealization of each member of the family. The addition of play figures to represent each family member offers an outlet through which these children can give clear descriptions in their own language. The additional incentive of gathering stones to exchange for prizes helps to focus even the most severe attention-deficit/hyperactivity disorder (ADHD) children. I have been amazed by how quickly and easily children have understood both the rules and the symbolic essence of the game. As they play, I am gathering a wealth of assessment and diagnostic information to guide my future clinical interventions.

DESCRIPTION

In this technique, the child is invited to help the therapist make a "map" of his family. While the therapist draws the circles, squares, and connecting lines that form the genogram, the child is invited to give names and ages of family members. The therapist then puts a colored stone (or other token) on each circle and square, gives the child a cup and explains the rules of the game: "This is a game in which you get to pick any toy in the whole room to be your mom. You go get the toy and when you bring it back and put it on the paper you get to take the stone and put it in your cup. When you have gathered all five stones [this number will vary with the number of family members] you can trade in the stones for a treasure. Ready? Go find any toy that you want to be your mom." The youngest children may need a prompt for each family member. When the child is completely finished, then the therapist invites the client to tell a story about the symbols on the "map."

APPLICATION

I have used this technique with children ages 3 to 5, and have had only one client refuse to participate. More than one who has asked to play it again. Most children love the empowerment that they feel as they get to choose any toy in the room to be Mom. They are further reinforced by receiving a colored stone after each new figure is placed. In terms of assessment, it is important to look not only at the symbols that are chosen, but at how the child chooses. For example, one client immediately picked up my scary alien figure to be his dad, but then put it back and chose a superhero (the first choice seemed too close to reality for the child). Children may reveal themselves symbolically, or you may see their defenses at work in that they may create a "model" family when you have documentation of abuse.

Children speak volumes in their choice of symbols.

A 4-year-old chose three different figures to be Dad and placed them all on the genogram together. One figure was a large, very aggressive looking wrestling man, another was a small generic male figure that could not stand up, and the third was a Phoebus, the kindly prince from the Disney movie *The Hunchback of Notre Dame*. This child had witnessed domestic violence for four years and although he did not have the words, he portrayed the domestic violence cycle by his choice of three dads: "Dad is violent, then becomes small and says he's sorry, then is wonderfully nice for a while, then becomes violent again."

This preschooler's ability to express his understanding of his dad's changeability astonished me.

The follow-up storytelling is also an important place to gain insight into the child's belief system. Another 4-year-old boy chose Spiderman to represent Dad, a police car to represent Mom, and Batman to represent himself. The child was reluctant to tell a story, so the therapist began it.

Therapist: Once upon a time, there was a police car and Spiderman and they lived together for a long time, until one day . . .

Carlos: . . . they fight.

Therapist: They began to fight. (To Carlos) Show me.

Carlos: (Picks up both objects, makes them struggle, and then ends up turning the police car upside down.) It wrecked.

Therapist: The car gets wrecked. Then, Batman decides to do some-
                thing.

Carlos: He fixes the car. (Turns the police car back over.)

In addition to metaphorically describing the violence done to Mom, Carlos also portrays a belief system in which he is responsible for keeping his mother safe—a weighty responsibility for a 4-year-old. It is useful to take a picture of the play geno-game that is created, for your own records and to refer back to with the child at a time when it might help to further the therapy or assess change.

Lastly, the client is choosing a self-object when he chooses a symbol to represent himself on the genogram. The therapist is encouraged to track the client's treatment of this self-object in future sessions and to respond to the object in nurturing ways during the course of therapy.

Section Four

Puppet Play Techniques

53

Balloon People

Heidi Gerard Kaduson

INTRODUCTION

Many children harbor angry feelings toward others without being able to release these feelings in an appropriate fashion. These children may be teased on a regular basis or have to deal with dysfunctional homes where anger and yelling are a part of their lives. Not being able to appropriately release anger can cause children to have somatic complaints (headaches, stomachaches, etc.) or produce a discomfort that the child is incapable of living with without explosion. Through the use of balloon people, children can release their anger and feel relief in channeling the bad feelings associated with it.

RATIONALE

Anger is used as a shield to help children deal with uncomfortable emotions such as frustration, sadness, and disappointment. To deal effectively with the underlying feelings, children must first be able to release the anger in a safe, nurturing environment without having negative consequences. The release of anger is therapeutic in that it allows the child to feel "lighter" about particular situations, and also empowers the child to deal with the anger without the threat of punishment.

DESCRIPTION

Materials Needed

> 2 or more 11" balloons
>
> Outlines of mouths, noses, and eyes (Figure 53–1)
>
> Outlines of feet (Figure 53–2)

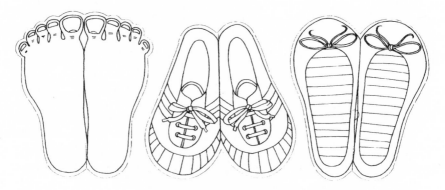

Figure 53–2. Outlines of feet.

> Markers to color on balloons
>
> Glue sticks or Scotch tape
>
> Safety scissors

Process

The balloon-people technique is introduced as an arts activity. The child and the therapist will both make balloon people who may or may not be like people in their lives. The therapist can suggest to the child that

Figure 53–1. Outlines of mouths, noses, and eyes.

he make a person who resembles a family member, a classmate, or himself in order to begin the process. The directive quality of the therapy guides the child to focus on a particular problem between two or more people. The child is told to blow up one or two balloons to make his balloon people. If the child has trouble doing so, the therapist can blow up the balloons and tie them off. Then the child is asked to pick from the pictures of eyes, noses, and mouths the features that he wants to use on the person. The child colors the features and cuts them out to paste on his balloon. The therapist follows the child and does the same thing, always being sure to replicate a person the child or the parents of the child have indicated has caused difficulty for the child. After the features are put on the balloons, the child picks the feet of choice and colors and cuts them out to attach to the bottom of the balloon through the knot. The therapist follows using whatever feet are left. When the child is done making his balloon people, the therapist should be finished as well (even though the therapist starts after the child).

The therapist then shows the child how to hold the balloon (with the knot between the forefinger and middle finger). Following the proper handling of the balloon, the therapist initiates a story about an incident that the child might have experienced (being teased, having a controlling sibling or parent, etc.). The therapist lightly hits the child's balloon with the therapist's balloon while showing the anger that probably developed during the true incident being portrayed. The therapist continues to do this while telling the child's balloon to show his own anger about the situation. Within a short period of time, the child lets go and begins the balloon fight between the two balloon people. Most children end up laughing about this as the eyes, nose, or mouth may fly off, the feet fly in different directions, and the anger the child is holding releases. The child is permitted to take the balloons home if desired and told to fight between the balloons whenever anger begins to develop again.

APPLICATION

The balloon-people technique can be used with children of all ages. It may be necessary for the therapist to cut out the features if the child has fine-motor difficulties. This technique allows for the release of anger for children with impulse control problems, behavioral problems, anxiety, and selective mutism. Children inevitably find themselves laughing about a previously anger-provoking situation.

Molly, 7 years old, was having social problems in school. She was very bright, yet found herself being teased a lot by the girls in her class. When the balloon-people technique was used, she made her balloon with small eyes, nose, and mouth, and the therapist made the other balloon to have a big mouth and look fierce. The balloon fight began by the therapist telling Molly that they were going to replay a day at school when Molly was being teased. She told the therapist what to say to the balloon ("Hey four eyes, you're so stupid you need glasses to see"). As the therapist copied the behavior as Molly scripted it, Molly began hitting the "teaser" balloon with all her force and laughing as the parts of the face fell off. Then Molly yelled, "Okay, you big mouth, now it's time for your mouth to go" and she hit the balloon until it flew off. Molly laughed so hard that she rolled on the floor. She had released so much pent-up anger with that moment that she went home more relaxed than her parents had seen her all year. She began to use some other cognitive techniques to deal with the bullies in her class, but felt much better about herself by all reports.

54

Big Bears

Linda B. Hunter

INTRODUCTION

Big bears, or other animals 3 to 4 feet tall, are extremely important group members for play therapy. They are repeatedly abused and nurtured, kicked and hugged by children from 3 to 13. Their role is central to the expression of feelings, which it is our goal to facilitate. They allow full-body interaction, and are both cuddly soft and insensitive to the pain of the most aggressive of acts.

Many child clients are struggling with angry feelings and aggressive behaviors. Many parents and teachers who refer children for therapy complain that they (usually) won't express their feelings, which means talking about them. Play therapists know that children are expressing their feelings all too accurately and dramatically by their aggressive behavior. Working with these children in the play room, we have two, sometimes conflicting, needs: (1) to permit full expression of feelings so that they can come to understand and control the behaviors they promote; and (2) to keep everybody safe from harm—other group members, ourselves, and the aggressors themselves, so that they won't feel guilty about hurting someone.

The use of large stuffed animals to redirect the aggressive behavior generated by angry feelings allows both full expression and safety.

RATIONALE

Bears fill the necessary role of substitute when children are told that "people are not for hitting/kicking or any other form of hurting." After having been punched, kicked, or thrown against the wall, bears have the decency to lie there and look hurt as opposed to some bop bags, sold for this purpose, that pop back up with a painted-on smile, as if being hit is fun, which every child knows is not true.

While extremely useful in individual play therapy settings, bears are essential to nondirective small group sessions. Bears provide a safe receptor for the kicks and punches of a raging child until the feelings are sufficiently released so that self-control can manifest and contain behavior. Using the soft bear to protect everyone from harm while reflections of feelings, limit setting, and choices are stated, provides the opportunity for children to develop empathy for others and to resolve their own conflicts.

Current awareness of the prevalence of violence by children has generated much useful discussion about positive prevention methods. Some therapists, parents, and teachers express concern that any form of hitting might actually encourage the violence we hope to prevent. But the use of large stuffed animals as punching bags can be described from a behavioral standpoint by the term *shaping*. For children who are aggressive toward others, it is a large and positive step to redirect their hitting toward an inanimate object that does not hurt them back or in any way feed into their anger. This, combined with a nonjudgmental attitude and empathic comments from the therapist, allows the child to ultimately come to accept his angry feelings and choose a less hurtful and more appropriate means of expressing them. The goal is positive self-control and assertive verbalization of feelings.

Large stuffed animals also fulfill other important roles in the playroom. After beating the bear to a pulp, jumping on its head, and kicking it repeatedly in the stomach, when the inner rage is released for the moment, the bear gracefully accepts being healed (with the equipment in the doctor kit), nurtured (fed, dressed, put to bed, carried tenderly), and loved (with kind strokes, words, and hugs). Small children proudly feel their own strength when they manage to lift, carry, and even throw something larger than they are.

In addition to aggressive, angry, hostile feelings, bears permit the expression of other difficult-to-deal-with-and-acknowledge emotions and concerns. The confusion generated by the bombardment by sexual images and messages even young children receive from TV can be acted out in a safe way with the bear with no reinforcement by adult reactions of shock or criticism. Thus, children find their own inner controls to temper these demanding impulses, which perhaps in the long run prevents premature and/or hurtful sexual activity toward peers or younger children.

DESCRIPTION

Large stuffed animals are an integral part of play therapy equipment even if they need to be carried to each weekly meeting. Before play therapy starts, they are placed conspicuously and invitingly in the room for whatever use the children want to make of them. When a conflict starts to erupt between two children wanting the same toy or disrupting each other's play or in any other form, the therapist moves to be near those involved, taking the bear with her. Reflection of feelings on both sides of the issue is the first intervention: "Two group members both want the same toy." "You got it first and are still playing with it." "It doesn't seem fair that he's keeping it so long." "You're both feeling really angry." "It's hard to work this out." When the conflict turns from verbal to physical, when one grabs the toy and the other starts to hit or kick or push, it's time for limits and for the bear to step in. The therapist uses the three-step limit-setting model known by the acronym ACT:

Acknowledge the feeling: "You're really mad that he took it away."

Communicate the limit: "But people are not for hitting/kicking."

Target an alternative: "The bear is for hitting/kicking."

The bear is calmly placed between the two children in such a way as to intercept the blows, while reflections continue. Often the angry child will proceed to vent his feelings on the bear. Sometimes all that is needed is the reminder and the opportunity for the children to come up with a positive resolution, mutual apologies, cooperative play, and so on.

In an individual session, when aggression is being directed toward the therapist, the room, or breakable toys, the bear can be brought in as a buffer and substitute in the same way, usually held in front of the child by the therapist or given to the child, placed on the floor or against the wall while reflections and limits continue: "You're so mad at me. But I'm not for hitting. The bear is for hitting."

APPLICATION

Large stuffed animals are useful across the range of presenting problems and ages, not just for the aggressive child, but also for withdrawn, sad, and fearful children.

A 5-year-old in preschool who was big for his age and subject to out-of-control explosions in class, was having a difficult time leaving his first group session at the ending time. He became enraged and began attacking the therapist, who picked up the large stuffed animal that happened to be a gorilla and held it in front of her for him to hit. Having the gorilla's protection so she did not fear being hurt allowed her to remain calm and reflect his feelings. After 10 minutes of beating up the gorilla, he said it was "totally out of control" and was able to take it in his arms, stab it with plastic swords, tie it up with ties and a rubber snake, pile things on top of it to make it stay down, and give it plastic pegs as "medicine" to make it better. After a few more minutes of expressive play, he hugged the gorilla, said "I'm sorry" to it and "Bye gorilla, see you next time," and returned calmly to his classroom.

While it is easy to understand why young children would use bears in this way, examples abound of the value of this medium for older children as well. For instance, the fifth-grade, sweet, verbal, bright girl who, while yelling "Kill the bear," tried every means to do just that, week after week for months in group, safely released the kind of accumulated rage that she never could have dealt with verbally in a lifetime of talking groups. When she had finally completed her work, not only could she kindly hold the bear, but she could relate much more positively and peacefully in class and at home.

The most creative and daring use of bears in our program was initiated by a young male counselor faced with the most challenging of groups, middle-school boys. Week after week he carried large stuffed bears to the classroom where the group was held, giving these extremely active young teenagers an appropriate target to safely express not only the aggressive and sexual energies raging in their bodies, but also the often carefully hidden nurturing qualities boys of that age have such a hard time acknowledging. The positive changes seen in these boys and many others since have validated the importance of large stuffed animals in play therapy.

55

Reflective Listening
Using Puppets

Lois Theall

INTRODUCTION

Since play is a child's language and a mode of self-expression, it is also a language for a therapist to use to intervene in ways that will stimulate shifts in a child's thinking, feeling, and behaving. In psychotherapy with children, as with adults, it is important that the client feel heard by the therapist. One way therapists help adults feel heard is by using the process of reflective listening. Since children are talking to us and revealing themselves through their play, therapists might find it challenging to assure the child client that the therapist hears the play process, especially in nondirective play. Therapists may also find it challenging to remain engaged with children as they play in nondirective ways. Remaining engaged is important so that further appropriate interventions can be made through the play interaction at the appropriate times.

RATIONALE

The technique of reflective listening with puppets is therapeutic for three reasons: (1) it assures the child of being heard by the therapist, (2) it allows the therapist to remain effectively engaged in the play process, and (3) it allows the psychological distancing often needed to create the right amount of safety for the child's self-expression. I have found this technique to be especially valuable in the following circumstances:

1. Play therapy with reluctant children: Sometimes, especially in the beginning of therapy, a child may be reluctant to play. By the therapist's use of a puppet, the child can become engaged with the puppet, and so the ice is broken and the child enters more easily into play.

2. Nondirective play therapy: When a child is thoroughly engaged in nondirective play, he or she is usually completely focused on the activity. When the therapist uses his or her own voice to talk with the child in these moments, the therapist can take the child away from the play mode and into the present moment with the therapist. By using one of the means of play, such as puppetry, to communicate with a child, the therapist will more likely allow the child to remain in the focus of his or her play and, at the same time, the child will know that the therapist is present and paying attention.

DESCRIPTION

The therapist chooses a neutral-looking puppet to use, something that looks friendly. An animal puppet is better than a human-looking puppet since friendly animals may stir fewer associations than human puppets might. A puppet with a "paw" to shake is best because it offers further possibilities to connect.

When a Child Is Reluctant to Play

If, after a period of exploration of the playroom, the child continues to be reluctant to enter into non-directive play, the therapist may quietly take the chosen puppet, keep some distance from the child while being at the child's eye level, and begin talking with the puppet:

Puppet to therapist:	I'm glad you picked me up. I see someone is here.
Therapist to puppet:	Yes. Someone came in a while ago.
Puppet to therapist	(audibly whispering): Who is it?
Therapist to puppet:	It's [child's name].
Puppet to therapist:	Oh, boy! Do you think I could say "Hi"?
Therapist to puppet:	I don't see why not.
Puppet to child	(very shyly and hiding under therapist's arm): Hi, [child's name].

The child may respond at this point. If the child does not respond, this is a moment for reflective listening with the puppet:

Puppet to therapist:	[Name of child] didn't say "Hi." Maybe he is shy like me.
Therapist to puppet:	Maybe so.

This part of the process of reflective listening, that is, commenting on the behavior observed and suggesting a feeling that may be present.

If the child says "Hi," the puppet can playfully become excited:

Puppet to therapist:	[Name of child] said "Hi." Do you think he would shake my paw?
Therapist to puppet:	Maybe so.

The puppet then extends a paw to shake the child's hand and asks, "May I shake your hand and will you shake my paw?" If the child chooses not to, this is to be respected, and the puppet may say to the therapist: "[Child's name] didn't want to. Maybe he is not ready. I wonder what [child's name] will choose to play with." If the child continues to be reticent, the puppet may turn to the therapist and say: "I'll bet [child's name] doesn't know what I like to play with best. Do you?" The therapist responds, "No." The puppet then whispers inaudibly into the therapist's ear.

In the above example, the therapist is using reflective listening through play. By talking with the therapist, the puppet has observed that the child has not started playing yet and/or has chosen not to shake a paw and names a feeling (being shy) or a circumstance (not being ready) that might be motivating the reluctance to connect or play. This reflective listening opens the door for the puppet to intervene by giving a suggestion about playing through play itself: "I wonder what [child's name] will choose to play with." This is done without the pressure of direct confrontation regarding play. When the puppet says to the therapist that the puppet is shy, too, that is an intervention intended to create identity with the child, build the connection, and increase the safety for the child to proceed. The puppet's whispering is a technique to pique the curiosity of the child and engage him even further.

The sequence can proceed as necessary:

Puppet to therapist: Some people think it is not polite to whisper to someone in front of someone else. Maybe [name of child] didn't like that. But I'm too shy to say out loud what I told you. I'd like to tell [name of child], but I'm too shy.

Therapist to puppet: Oh, I see.

This intervention puts the child in a power position that someone in the room should be shy in front of him and shows that the puppet trusts the therapist by admitting to being shy. It is reflective listening in that it cites the possibility that the child didn't like this move by the puppet and opens the door for another intervention:

Puppet to therapist: I wonder if [name of child] would whisper to me what he likes to play best. Would that be OK if he did that?

Therapist to puppet: It would be OK with me.

Puppet to child   (audibly whispering in child's ear): Would you whisper to me what you like to play best?

Using whispering as a technique is one of the less threatening ways to communicate with a child. In using puppets to engage reticent children, it is important that the puppet remain playful without having its energy be so exuberant as to overwhelm the child. The puppet's energy should complement the child's energy; it should not be so low as to further lower the energy level, but it should not be so high as to overwhelm.

When a Child Is Immersed in Nondirective Play

When a child begins nondirective play, it is important that the therapist stay in contact with the child so that the child feels heard and so that the therapist can intervene at the appropriate times. While a child is immersed in nondirective play, the therapist may quietly slip on the chosen puppet and, at a distance from the child but at the eye level of the child, begin to reflect:

Puppet to therapist: I see that [child's name] has chosen to play with the dinosaurs. I wonder what is going to happen next.

Therapist to puppet: I wonder.

Puppet to therapist: Look, they're starting to fight.

These occasional comments between the puppet and therapist are parts of the process of reflective listening in that the comments report what is observed. Further interventions may be made later at the right time:

Puppet to therapist: Look, the alligator keeps taking bites of the dinosaur. I wonder if it is hungry or angry.

This is reflective listening in that the puppet reports the observation and suggests a feeling. The child may answer at this point. If the child says, "Hungry," the therapist can intervene metaphorically:

Puppet to therapist: I wonder what it is hungry for.

The child may answer, "Hungry for dinosaurs!"

Using the puppet, the therapist can continue intervening metaphorically:

Puppet to therapist: I wonder how many dinosaurs the alligator is hungry for.

If the child seems very angry but not admitting it, the puppet may continue:

Puppet to therapist: Sometimes when I feel like biting, I'm really, really angry.

This intervention would give permission for the child to acknowledge anger to himself while identifying with the puppet. The child may answer softly, "Me, too," or simply nod.

Using reflective listening and other interventions whereby the puppet addresses the therapist rather than the child offers another layer of safety for a child who may be guarded. Having the puppet talk first to the therapist gradually brings into the child's play focus another character to which the child can tell his story. The puppet becomes the therapist for the child and can intervene as needed.

Later, the child may be addressed more directly by having the puppet talk to one of the characters the child is playing with, such as the alligator in the above case. The following is an example of what may be said after more rapport and safety have been established:

Puppet to alligator: I wonder if you ever feel so angry you want to bite the dinosaurs.

Here the alligator propelled by the child may attack the puppet. This is a sign that the puppet therapist is on the right track. If the child propels the alligator toward the therapist rather than the puppet, the alligator can be redirected to the puppet rather than the therapist. This keeps the therapist in charge of the session and shows a child a safe way of expressing anger rather than hurting himself or someone else.

Puppet to therapist: Wow! That surely looks like an angry alligator to me.

Here the child may say, "It is!" And so the anger is declared.

This is reflective listening in that the puppet suggests the feeling manifested, but still keeps the psychological distance by saying that the alligator is angry, not the child.

Since children are capable of healing through the metaphors provided by play, it is not always necessary to explicitly and directly have a child declare his feelings. However, sometimes it can be helpful to do so, especially if child play therapy is integrated into family therapy and the child's feelings can be admitted, discussed, and accepted by the family. If a therapist chooses to intervene in order to have a child explicitly declare a feeling, this intervention may also be done in play at an appropriate time:

Puppet to child (whispering):   Do you ever feel as angry as the alligator?

If the child says "Yes," this opens the door to further interventions. If the child says "No," but those around the child have witnessed the angry outbursts, it may be that it is too early for the child to acknowledge it and his pace has to be respected.

As in good reflective listening with adults, timing is very important. If a therapist pushes a child to a feeling level too quickly, the child will usually feel threatened and close down to the feelings, even while sometimes telling the therapist what he thinks the therapist wants to hear. This is especially true for children who have been in counseling before.

If a child becomes excessively agitated in the beginning by having a puppet watch him play, it may be best to stop using the puppet. However, this agitation could be noted, and the puppet might later be used to therapeutically stir up the agitation, discover the source, and promote healing. For example, a child who feels watched all the time outside of therapy could be agitated by the puppet watching him.

APPLICATION

I have found this technique to be especially helpful with reticent children. However, I have used it often with other children, and have found it to be helpful with most since it assures that the child is heard and that the therapist remains engaged in the play, and it creates distancing for the child's safety in self-expression. This technique can be used also in directive therapy. For example, a puppet may be used to engage a reticent child in a structured game or, as directed activities proceed, a puppet can reflect on the child's reactions and choices.

56

Puppet Characters with Feeling Names

Marijane Fall

INTRODUCTION

The process of counseling can take many different paths. Most young people who come to my school counseling office come because of wanting someone, or some situation, to change. Most young people who come to my private practice come because parents have decided that their children need to change. Both groups appear to have in common a lack of congruency between two opposing ideas, beliefs, or situations. My job as a therapist is to assist children in personal change that often exposes the incongruency with which they are grappling. However, I frequently find that uncovering the thoughts and actions is the easy part. Feelings may be less accessible. The technique of designing sock puppets, naming them with feeling words, and putting on a puppet show for the therapist has proven to be of great benefit in unraveling the mystery of feelings, naming them, and, in turn, beginning the process of change that can come with clarity.

RATIONALE

Adults in therapy wrestle for clarity and for congruency between thoughts, feelings, and actions. The process of obtaining this congruency often means uncovering the feelings that are attached to events, beliefs, or actions. Children have even less access to feelings since they (1) lack words for description, (2) are often in the concrete developmental stage, and (3) have an orientation to the present moment. The challenge for the therapist is to assist the child in the acquisition of a feeling vocabulary, to use concrete techniques that are developmentally appropriate, and to bring issues to the forefront to be dealt with. This sock puppet technique meets all of these challenges.

DESCRIPTION

This technique calls for a box of materials for making puppets:

Socks in a variety of colors (I get mine from second-hand stores for a nickel a pair)

Some yarns, fake fur, or other hair-like materials

Buttons, beads, googley eyes (in packages in the yard-goods stores)

Double-sided sticky tape

Magic markers

The child is invited to make a sock puppet that fits over the hand. The counselor may demonstrate putting the sock on the hand and attaching hair, eyes, and mouth. The counselor states only one condition: that the puppets must be "feeling" puppets, and must be given "feeling" names. As the child makes the puppet, the therapist can reflect the process and the child's interaction with the materials. When the child finishes, the therapist invites the child to put on a puppet show. Again, the condition remains that the puppets are named with feeling words. The counselor then becomes an appreciative audience, following the show's conclusion with a discussion about the show's content.

APPLICATION

The sock puppet technique could be used for most children in play therapy. It is especially beneficial for children who are exhibiting signs of confusion. The example below demonstrates how one child used this technique to make a decision.

Subsequent to making two sock puppets named "Confusion" (CFN) and "Make Up Your Mind" (MUYM), the child proceeded to form a stage out of the plastic shoebox that contained puppet-making materials. The puppets ducked down behind this box when not in conversation and jumped up to the stage when talking.

CFN:	My name is Confusion. What's yours?
MUYM:	Make Up Your Mind.
CFN:	Huh? I said what's your name?
MUYM:	Make Up Your Mind!
CFN:	Boy, are you stupid. What is your name, stupid?
MUYM:	Am not stupid. You're stupid.
CFN (loud):	Am not! You're so stupid you don't even know your name!
MUYM (hollering):	I said Make Up Your Mind, stupid.
CFN:	Oh, I'm so confused I'm just going to faint. Goodbye. (Faints.)
MUYM:	Oh, brother. She can't even decide to talk. (Loud) Goodbye.
CFN:	(Lifts head) Goodbye. (Faints again.)
Child:	The end.

On the surface, one might think that not much was accomplished. However, on that day the child had 24 hours to decide if she would prefer to live with Dad or with Mom. At 7, the child was too young to make such decisions and acted out the confusion of this decision. Within 5 minutes of putting on the show, she spontaneously announced that she would tell her parents to make the decision. "I feel like fainting," she announced. "They'll have to decide." The puppet show had released her from the state of confusion she was in. She made a decision, went back to the classroom, and finished her work for the first time in a week.

57

The Toy Theater

A. J. Palumbo

INTRODUCTION

Puppetry is widely used by professionals who treat children. Therapists, court psychologists, teachers, and nurses who work with children under stress are integrating puppet play and craft into their treatment process. I have been using puppets in treatment for 20 years, and I am also a professional puppeteer by the name of Dr. Silly. Thus, I understand the use of puppets from an artistic and entertainment point of view, and I see their value in child and family practice.

Puppetry can be adapted to suit the constraints of therapy, such as limited resources and the restricted parameters of managed care regulations. Workplace circumstances can reduce the therapeutic effectiveness of puppet play in several ways: (1) noise control often blunts vocal expression, creating less opportunity to observe qualitative data about children's anger, depression, imagination, and defenses; (2) available play space is often limited, constricting the ability to extend the large muscles in play or to establish associations between episodes of expressive play; (3) puppetry equipment is limited and stages are inadequate, causing interruptions in the flow of creative behavior and truncating the child's imagination.

Thus, it is difficult to create an adequate context of meaning in office-based puppet play, especially the emotional and ideational frames that encompass the puppet play and help relate its content to the child's life.

I use puppets in treating special populations: physically challenged children, and children in hospitals, orphanages, family shelters, clinics, special education programs, and refugee centers. I have found ways to reduce the limitations of resources and space and to increase therapeutic communication, using the classical "toy theater."

RATIONALE

Children who are diagnosed as attention-deficit/hyperactivity disorder (ADHD) or posttraumatic stress disorder (PTSD), who are stressed by poverty, homelessness, depression, abuse, and neglect, or who are unable to adjust to schooling or foster care often have low self-esteem, poor school adjustment and grades, a history of familial dysfunction, and are isolated or aggressive. Helping these highly defensive children participate in such a "baby" thing as puppet play requires that the activity entail (1) a low skills requirement but a high level of output, (2) unpredictability, (3) frequent opportunities for therapeutic commentary, and (4) sufficient silliness to create a relaxed and nonthreatening setting. Playing with paper puppets, taped to sticks, integrated with numerous related figures, objects, and settings in a small, well-lighted box is a play therapy intervention that adapts well to a variety of child therapy goals.

DESCRIPTION

Puppetry uses "toy theaters," simple tri-part, wooden screens with crudely painted and decorated panels that can be set up on a table. These toy theaters adapt easily to a wide range of talents, temperaments, limited play space, low budgets, and puppetry skills to produce dramatic and imaginative puppet play from even indifferent children. They reduce patient anxiety about performance, something that is often observed in traumatized children. The stages are small, so children can more easily project their feelings into these controllable spaces. Larger puppet booths can create panic in many children; smaller toy theaters offer no unwanted challenges or threats.

Toy theaters help children with underdeveloped imaginations more easily create spontaneous play. These theaters have a quick way to change scenes—simply dropping them from above. This quick background change process fits the rapid attention shifts that characterize many children in treatment.

APPLICATION

In addition to being a useful therapy tool with at-risk and traumatized children, toy theaters can be helpful in presenting health and prevention information.

Children with mild to moderate visual handicaps like to use toy theaters because they can be close to the puppets, usually only a few inches away. The stages can be highly illuminated with small lamps equipped with a spot. This intensity of illumination helps direct eye movement toward the stage and reduces the effects of extraneous stimuli. Other sources of light can be integrated into the lighting pattern of these toy theaters. Small flashlights are very useful in segregating background, emphasizing a main character, and allowing even very young participants, in sibling and family play, for example, to be part of the play.

Paper puppets can be easily created from cutouts. They work their magic, and the child engages in the intimate communication process that puppet play consists of. All of this therapeutic process seems to occur more easily and expand when the play is simple and safe.

Resource

For additional information about the therapeutic use of toy theaters, go to www.drsilly.com or Puppettherapyinstitute.org.

58

Balloon Twisting

Diane E. Frey and Douglas J. Griffin

INTRODUCTION

Have you ever been to a festival or craft show and seen all the children crowded around the vendor who is selling helium balloons? Or have you ever experienced the joy in the air as a clown twists an animal from a balloon and presents it to an eager child? Balloons can elicit positive emotions. Thus, it makes sense that balloons, and in particular balloon twisting, can be used in play therapy.

RATIONALE

The therapist can choose balloon animals or objects to incorporate into play therapy techniques. Examples of techniques that could use balloon sculptures include the "two-house" technique (Kuhli 1983), puppetry, and the mutual storytelling technique (Gardner 1986). In these techniques balloon sculptures can be used to enhance the therapeutic value of the technique.

New techniques can also be used and can focus on letting the balloon sculptures signify different traits, problems, and stereotypes that the client associates with the animal or object. Questions related to the balloon sculpture can be designed to aid the communication and diagnostic process in therapy, and also offer the many advantages of balloon sculptures in a play therapy setting.

DESCRIPTION

Balloon twisting (also referred to as balloon sculpturing) is the art of making recognizable animals (such as a dog, bird, or mouse) or objects (such as a sword) by twisting balloons. A good balloon for twisting measures approximately 2″ in diameter and 60″ in length (referred to as a 260 balloon) and is usually twisted to form smaller bubbles and designs to make the animal or object. Figure 58–1 shows several typical examples of balloon sculptures.

Target Population

The primary target population for using balloon twisting in therapy is children. However, the child must be able to comprehend the safety hazard and risk associated with swallowing a balloon. The child also must have developed the ability for symbolic or pretend play, which typically occurs between the ages of 2 and 6 (O'Connor and Schaefer 1983).

The technique can also be used with adolescents and adults, with the client actually making or helping to make the balloon figure. This process, therefore, has an added benefit of a feeling of accomplishment for the client. Another application of balloon twisting is for family or group play therapy since an entire family or group can participate in developing the balloon characters.

APPLICATION

Balloon sculptures have many distinct advantages for play therapy. Children are entertained by balloon sculpting, thus allowing the therapist

Figure 58–1. Examples of balloon animals: a swan, a rubber ducky, a hummingbird, and a bear (Visual 1996).

to quickly gain rapport with the client. Next, it is flexible, as there are many different figures that can be tailored specifically to the needs of the client. Also, it is effective since it integrates verbal, emotional, and cognitive responses in the same therapeutic technique.

Balloon twisting can aid in self-esteem by giving a feeling of accomplishment if the client makes or helps to make the balloon sculpture. Thus, this can be an excellent "ice breaker" to pave the way for more therapeutic discussions. In additional to improving self-esteem, fine motor skills can be improved by having the client make the figure. Also by letting the client create the sculpture, it becomes an art activity in play therapy. The concept of balloons as art can be further emphasized by

letting the client decorate the sculptures with different-colored permanent markers.

Another advantage is that it encourages the therapeutic power of
self-expression in cases where the therapist provides an incentive to a
child for storytelling with balloons. As an example, the therapist tells the
clients that if they tell a story about the balloon, they get to keep the
balloon.

Balloon twisting can be used for many different types of problem
clients since it is very adaptable, as well as entertaining. Balloons can also
be used as a benchmark to judge progress for clients by seeing if the client
progresses to other balloon sculptures or continues to focus on the same
ones each time. The therapist can ascertain if themes associated with the
balloon change over time.

The technique has a built-in intrinsic advantage in that it is very
portable. All that is required are balloons and a hand pump. Also, it
provides an object metaphor for the client to take home as a remembrance
of the session and as a reminder to perform whatever activities were
discussed with the therapist. It encourages parental involvement as it
provides an immediate focus for dialogue between the child and parents,
or the therapist and parents. Lastly, it creates positive anticipatory
feelings about future sessions, since the child looks forward to returning
to play with more balloons.

Training

The time required to master balloon twisting is several hours for basic
animal figures and 50 to 100 hours to master twenty or more figures. The
usual training approach is to teach yourself by utilizing video instruction
tapes, how-to books (Myers 1998), and Internet Web sites (Moss 1998). At
minimum, the tools required are an introductory balloon twisting video
tape (about $30), one gross of type 260 balloons (about $8), and several
hand pumps (about $5 apiece).

A 10-year-old nongifted girl in a family of profoundly gifted individuals (parents, two brothers, and one sister) told the following story to the
therapist during the termination phase of play therapy, using a variety of
balloons (bear, swan, poodle, frog, turtle, and duck):

Once there was a teddy bear who was really good at almost everything but swimming. He went to the swan to ask her to teach him to swim. She tried but couldn't teach him. She did not know how to teach. He went to the barber and he couldn't teach him because he did not know how to swim. Cutting hair was his thing. He only knew how to do that, so he gave him a haircut. A poodle came by and told him he knew how to swim very well, so well that they named a type of swimming after him—the doggie paddle. The bear could not do the doggie paddle though. He went to the cat, but the cat was afraid of the water. He went to the frog, but the frog just jumped in the water. He went to the turtle, and the turtle taught him how to float, but the bear still couldn't swim. The bear went to the duck and the duck said, "You are fantastic at all you do. Just be happy that you can do so many things well and forget about swimming."

It is of note that the client chose a total of six balloons, and there are six people in her family. The unique personalities of each family member are reflected in each balloon animal (she, of course, being the bear).

The theme of the story seems to be self-acceptance, rather than trying to be gifted or to be other traits one is not. This was a major goal of therapy—improving self-esteem and self-acceptance by reducing comparison to others. The interpretation of the story to the parents through the balloons was less threatening than interpretation through traditional therapy (which had previously been tried) and more poignant and effective.

It has been said that "You can tell more about a person by what he says about others, than you can by what others say about him" (Gregory 1990, p. 89). When this concept is applied to balloons in play therapy, it becomes: You can tell more about children by what they say about balloons, than you can by what others say about them. The creativity and versatility of balloons in play therapy can be adapted and used easily as an effective tool for children to express their world. Expression through balloons thus becomes more powerful and accurate than anything anyone can say about a child.

References

Gardner, R. A. (1986). The talking, feeling, and doing game. In *Game Play, Therapeutic Use of Childhood Games*, ed. S. E. Reid and C. E. Schaefer, pp. 41–72. New York: Wiley.

Gregory, M. (1990). *100 Inspirational Quotations for Enhancing Self-Esteem*, ed. D. E. Frey, p. 89. Los Alamitos, CA: Educo.

Kuhli, L. (1983). The diagnostic and therapeutic use of pretend play. In *Handbook of Play Therapy*, ed. K. J. O'Connor and C. E. Schaefer, pp. 274–280. New York: Wiley.

Moss, L. (1998). Balloon headquarters. Available at http://www.balloonhq.com/.

Myers, T. (1998). T. Myers balloon twisters catalog. Available by phone: T. Myers Magic, 1-800-648-6221.

O'Connor, K. J., and Schaefer, C. E. (1983). *Handbook of Play Therapy*. New York: Wiley.

Visual, C. (1996). *Captain Visual's Big Book of Balloon Art*. New York: Carol.

59

Clay Play Therapy: Making an "Oogly"

Myrna Minnis

INTRODUCTION

Making an "oogly"™ is a fun, creative way to build intimacy and trust with children. They often feel a visit to the counselor's office means they are in trouble. Making an oogly is a technique using clay to create a safe, calm environment and relationship with the child. Humor is a factor in play therapy. It works beautifully in this technique for reaching all children, young or old. The clay is wonderful, unique, nondrying, and clean, it has no odor, it can be left out, and it requires no clean-up. Oogly is nonthreatening; there is no wrong way to make an oogly. Each creation is an opportunity to experience success.

RATIONALE

Children love playing with clay. Creating a character called an oogly can quickly build trust and facilitate the sharing of sadness, personal conflicts, or pain. The holding, manipulating, and caressing of clay quickly releases our emotional body through our hands and fingers.

Working with clay serves to "ground" an individual. It functions some-what like the popular seed-filled "stress-balls," with the expanded opportunity to create something from the stress.

As a humanized character, the nonverbal communication created by the oogly's expression or body language can be an introduction to an individual's feelings. Children tend to tell you everything about their oogly. They may have the oogly character become the "bad" person that they can then hurt in order to release their feelings toward the perpetrator. In this way, the child can release emotions in a nonthreatening situation.

DESCRIPTION

Oogly is a clay character created with nonhardening clay (available as an oogly kit). One cannot fail when making one, for only its creator knows the significance or life of the oogly. The clay can be used repeatedly. There are many therapists who are still using the clay they purchased several years ago. The clay is an earth tone—a noncolor—to eliminate rejection of the clay due to color preferences or negative associations. The tools included are simple: an oogly stick for making eyes (a pencil), and a hair-raiser (a special garlic press). Simplicity is the key. It eliminates confusion and offers inhibited expression through working with the clay. The individual can smash the oogly and begin again.

I recommend giving the child a small amount of clay to begin massaging. It tends to soothe and comfort. As children work with their clay, I tell them we are going to make an oogly. They usually ask, "What's an oogly?" I reply, without much detail or direction, "Oh, it's this funny character, you'll see." I begin to make a pinch pot (flatten ball into a pancake about one-fourth inch thick, then raise the edges to make a pot). I then hand them enough clay to also begin a pinch pot. When the clay is of sufficient thickness and looks like a little pot, I have them place it on its side. The opening becomes the mouth of the oogly. I then say, "I'm going to put on a nose, any size will do." I roll some clay for a nose and suggest they do the same. "Now we're going to make eyes. How many eyes is your oogly going to have? Two? Three? One? Six?" With this suggestion they automatically get the idea that this is *their* piece; they get to create what they want it to look like. I then proceed with my oogly and give basic instructions along the way. I suggest horns, ears, warts, tongues with taste buds, teeth—whatever sparks the imagination. They see me playing along with them and it helps them relax. This focus on the oogly as we laugh and create often leads to stories shared and the beginning of trust between us.

As we add features, we open new doors for communication. The legs are coils rolled out like a snake and U-shaped; the ends are turned up to represent feet. Some children will not put on legs, a clue that perhaps they are stuck, and not going anywhere. Then arms are added. Some children do not attach arms. Perhaps they can't receive or are unwilling to reach out to anyone. I really try to emphasize that they add the arms and legs (especially the arms) because we give oogly emotions with the arms. We communicate with the positions and use or our arms and legs. I provide examples with the oogly I am making.

For instance, when the client first attaches the arms, they are raised above the head. This can signify that the oogly has just been born, or he just got up, and he feels pretty good about everything in his world. The arms extended with palms up mean "I give up." The arms extended with hands in the "stop" position mean "go away, get out of here, don't touch me." The arms out mean oogly wants a hug. If the eyes are covered, that may mean "Leave me alone." One eye covered and the other partially peeking out might indicate pouting.

Oogly has so many ways to tell how it feels, which in turn opens the door for the client and therapist to explore feelings.

APPLICATION

The primary application of this technique is in play therapy with children. It can also be used as an ice breaker with adults and families. It is indicated with attention-deficit/hyperactivity disorder (ADHD) and attention-deficit disorder (ADD) children, where it has been seen to calm and focus the child's attention. A disabled person with some hand dexterity can manipulate the clay and benefit from the opportunity to create a unique and special oogly.

Resource

Order an oogly kit or video, or request information by writing to
Myrna Minnis at Myrin Enterprises, P.O. Box 6211, Leawood, KS 66206 or
phone 913-649-1185.

60

Sleeping Bear

Sandra Foster

INTRODUCTION

Children often have difficulties talking about their fears. Going to bed as well as waking up during the night can bring out many fears in children. This technique can be used to help children process their fears and to give them something tangible to take home with them to alleviate fears when they arise. Sleeping bear fits under a pillow and a child's hand can be inserted inside. The bear is made of furry or soft fabric and some children choose to sleep directly on the bear, which gives them added comfort.

RATIONALE

This is a concrete exercise that helps children bring their fears and concerns out in the open. The technique enables children to verbalize fears and provides them the opportunity to talk in a safe way about what they are afraid of. Many children have difficulty talking about their fears, and as they are creating something they are able to express more openly what they are feeling. Feelings and attitudes that can be threatening for children to express directly can safely be projected through the bear and helps them feel less insecure. The bear, since it is a tangible object that they have made to take with them, provides a safe way to express feelings and provides for ongoing work in future sessions with the therapist as well as at home with the family.

I have also found this technique to be useful with children who are dealing with grief and loss. Since this is a tangible object, clients can use it as a concrete tool to express their feelings. Instead of their fears, children can deal with their grief and pain using the bear. Children grieve differently than adults and I have found that some children need a more concrete way of dealing with a loss.

DESCRIPTION

Materials

You will need pattern pieces, which can be photocopied (Fig. 60–1), pieces of furry fabric or felt in the child's color choice, and a needle and thread. Also a small music disk can be purchased very inexpensively in the craft section of a department store; it can be put in one of the bear's ears. Pushing gently on the disk activates the music. This often helps comfort a child.

Process

To make the bear, put the wrong sides of the fabric together and pin on the pattern pieces. Have the child cut out the pattern. The ears are sewn first and then turned right-side out. Once these are sewn, pin them in place with the ears facing inward. Sew around the head, leaving the bottom open and then turn right-side out.

When children are busy creating something in a playful manner, they are more easily able to express their feelings. As the child cuts out and sews the bear together, the therapist and child can make up a story about what frightens the child. Other feelings that the child may have can be incorporated into the story. The bear becomes the focal point in the story,

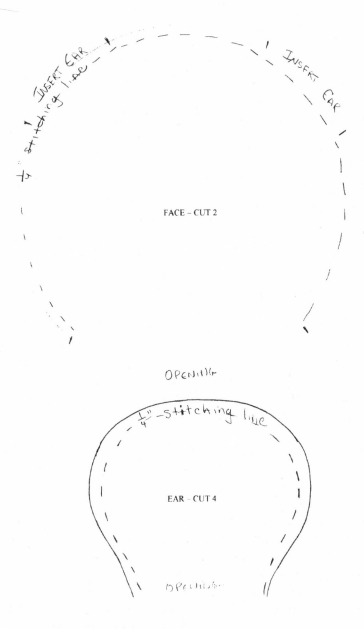

FACE – CUT 2

INSERT EAR

stitching line

INSERT EAR

OPENING

$\frac{1}{4}''$-stitching line

EAR – CUT 4

OPENING

Figure 60–1. The sleeping-bear pattern.

helping the child in whatever way the child deems best. The bear can be decorated with ribbon or buttons, but it is usually best to keep it plain since most of the children I have used this with tend to sleep on the bear.

As children are telling their story, I tape record it (with their permission), and before their next session I type it up with spaces appropriately left for illustrations. This story becomes another tool in the process. A cover is made and the book is bound in some way. Many of the children use their books to help them at bedtime.

APPLICATION

This technique is very helpful for children with bedtime fears. It can also be used with children with diverse problems. The bear can be used as a puppet to talk about any issues the child is having. Children have used it as a transitory object when their parents separate and they travel from house to house. It has also been useful for children dealing with the death of someone they love. The story changes with each individual situation yet allows the child to work through the necessary feelings.

Adolescents who are dealing with issues of fear and loss have also made these bears, but they fill the bear with pictures, letters, and things that give them comfort. They sew the bear closed and often sleep with it under their pillow as a comfort bear.

An 8-year-old client had lost her older brother in a car accident the year before and was unable to adjust. She came to see me and I suggested she make a bear. The process took four sessions. She began talking about how she was missing her brother as she was working on the bear. She insisted on sewing the bear by herself with little help from me. She was sometimes verbally open about her feelings; other times she was reflective and often she was quiet as she worked. She then told me about all the things she was missing about him and she suddenly decided that she needed to fill the bear with things that reminded her of his special qualities. She then scoured my room and put together her "treasures": a glow-in-the-dark bead so he would never be afraid, a rose-colored stone to remind her of how much she loved him, a picture of their family, and many other objects that made sense to her. When she finished she sewed the bear closed and stated that we had to take it to his grave. With the permission of her parents we went together and she was able to place it on his grave. The whole process was validation for her own experience, and she was able to work through her grief.

61

Psychodrama with Puppets

Douglas G. Sprague

INTRODUCTION

This technique is derived from psychodrama, the therapeutic process in the course of which clients act out their inner dramas spontaneously in a group setting. The psychodrama with puppets approach applies the principles and techniques of psychodrama to individual children, using puppets or stuffed animals.

In traditional psychodrama the therapist acts as the director. The director starts off the drama by choosing a client from the group to be the beginning character, called the protagonist. This client is instructed to talk as himself or herself or as some other character suggested by the therapist or other group members. The director then brings on more people to play different roles in the drama, usually important people in the protagonist's life, such as mother, father, sibling, teacher, spouse, or friend. Two of the techniques used by therapists/directors in directing the drama, which can be used with children and puppets, are role reversal and doubling.

In *role reversal* the director stops the drama and asks two players to switch roles and continue the conversation; for example, a person talking to someone playing her father would switch and continue the conversation as the father. In *doubling* the director stops the drama and asks another person to play one of the characters but with a different style or personality; for example, the director may bring another person into the drama to play a sad character or an angry character.

For psychodrama with puppets, the child and therapists use various puppets or stuffed animals to play the different characters. With this approach the therapist acts as both the director and one of the characters.

RATIONALE

The first value of this modified approach to psychodrama is in helping clients become more aware of their less obvious internal conflicts and emotions. By playing out various roles in a spontaneous way in a safe place, children are more likely to reveal a variety of emotions and personality styles. They can act out anger or anxiety that was previously hidden. They can act out various conflicting parts of their inner drama, such as wimpy versus assertive styles. This self-awareness information is very helpful to the therapist in assessing the child, and it is very helpful to children to discover more about themselves and to become more comfortable with that self. A second value of this approach is to give children a better chance to see the world from another's point of view, which will increase their ability to deal with the world by viewing it from the perspective of a mother or sister or friend. A final value of the psychodrama with puppets approach is to give children the chance to rehearse actions that they would like to try out later. A passive girl may find herself more likely and better able to ask her mother for some alone time if she had practiced it in a psychodrama.

Certainly any client could benefit from the increased self-awareness and increased repertoire of behavior and emotions this technique encourages.

DESCRIPTION

The technique requires a collection of ten or more puppets or stuffed animals. Although most of them would be around six to fifteen inches in height, some children like huge stuffed animals, because they can play the role while hiding behind the toy—an added degree of safety and comfort.

Warm-Up

1. Have the child choose a puppet to be him or her: "Choose a puppet that can be you."

2. Have the child make the puppet talk and act like him or her: "Now, play yourself. Make the puppet talk and act like you."

3. If the child has trouble thinking of things to say, offer some suggestions: "Why don't you tell what you like or who is in your family or what you like to do?"

4. After the child talks a while by her/himself, have the child pick another puppet to be a family member: "Okay, pick one of the puppets to be someone in your family, like your mother or father or sister or brother."

5. The therapist plays the family member and has a conversation with the child: "Let me play the _____ [family member] and you and I will talk for a while."

6. After a bit the therapist checks to see if she/he is playing the family member accurately: "How am I doing? Is this like your _____ [family member]?"

7. The therapist plays the family member adjusting to the child's input. Have another conversation and after a bit check in again: "How am I doing?"

Role Reversal

8. Have the child and therapist change roles, so the therapist is playing the child and the child is playing the family member. Continue the conversation: "Let's switch. You be _____ [family member] and I will be you."

9. After a little time switch back again and talk some more: "Okay. Let's switch again. You be yourself again."

10. Check in with the child: "How is this going?" "Do you like this?" "What was it like to play your _____ [family member]?"

Doubling

11. Have the child pick another puppet to be her/his twin: "Let's stop a minute. Pick out another puppet to be your twin."

12. Have the child play the twin, only with a different personality, such as the happy twin, the sad twin, the mad twin, the scared twin. Have the twin in conversation with the family member played by you: "You play the twin and I will play the _____ [family member]. Let's make the twin different from you. Make the twin very _____ [personality trait]. Have the twin talk to your _____ [family member]."

13. Have the child and the therapist change roles, so the therapist is playing the twin and the child is playing the original child. Then, continue the conversation: "Let's switch. You be _____ [family member] and I will be the twin."

14. After a little time switch back again and talk some more: "Okay. Let's switch again. You be yourself again."

15. Check in with the child. If the child is willing to talk, continue: "How is this going? What do you like about the twin you?"

16. A further step is to have the child play both her/himself and the twin and have them talk to each other: "Now let's have the twins talk to each other. Put one in one hand and the other in the other and have them get acquainted. Let's have the twins start talking."

17. Check in with the child. If the child is willing to talk, continue: "How is this going? Are the twins starting to like each other?"

18. Continue trying this with more role reversal and doubling and with other family members or other significant people in the

child's life. If the child starts talking about important issues at any point, be sure to stop the drama and continue the conversation. Go back to the drama when the child is finished.

APPLICATION

This technique could be effective with the following types of children:

Emotionally restricted children: Children who do not have access to all their emotions as a result of trauma, temperament, or training would have a chance to experience a fuller range of feelings.

Behaviorally one-sided children: Children who overemphasize one part of their personality such as acting out or inhibition can learn to behave in a variety of ways.

Overanxious children: Children who are anxious and worried about most things in life will be able to experience fearful situations in a safe play situation and, often, reduce their anxiety in real life.

Egotistical children: This technique allows children who lack normal empathy and are overconcerned about their own needs to better appreciate another's point of view.

Children with few social skills: This technique offers an opportunity for children with limited social skills to try out and practice new and effective ways of dealing with people.

Section Five

Toy and Play Object Techniques

62

Therapeutic Use of Block Play

Charles E. Schaefer

INTRODUCTION

Few toys are as durable and versatile as blocks. Highly popular as stacking toys for babies and toddlers, they become, in the hands of preschoolers and school-age children, sophisticated building tools that offer infinite construction possibilities: skyscraper, zoo, highway, airport, bridge, castle, or dinosaur house. Construction play provides children with a real sense of accomplishment, which boosts their egos and satisfies their drive toward mastery of the environment.

RATIONALE

For many years educators have used block play to foster the physical, social, cognitive, and emotional development of young children (Cartwright 1974). Indeed, blocks are reported to be the most widely available play object in early childhood classrooms (Hartley et al. 1952, Kinsman and Berk 1979).

Block play appeals to both boys and girls. For boys, tall is better—they tend to build tall structures. Girls, on the other hand, are more likely to build horizontally. They enjoy building enclosures for dolls and animals and are more focused on creating pretend scenes with blocks.

DESCRIPTION

While simple wooden unit blocks in a range of shapes and sizes will satisfy most preschoolers, more unusual construction materials—empty shoe or cereal boxes, plastic or fabric blocks, milk cartons, and foam bricks—can also stimulate creativity. One can further enhance block play by introducing simple props: toys animals to live in a zoo, flags for a castle, little people to inhabit a house, vehicles for tunnels and bridges.

APPLICATION

The use of block play as a psychotherapeutic technique has been a relatively neglected topic in the play therapy literature. Block play has application to two childhood disorders: social withdrawal and attention-deficit/hyperactivity disorder.

Social Withdrawal

Block play creates a foundation for friendship development because it provides children with the stimulus to engage in positive social inter-action with others (Rogers 1985). Cartwright (1974) noted that block building invites children to work together, and that when the children are interested and intent on creating a building together they tend to seek each other's help and learn to tolerate differences. Rogers (1985) found that during block play, prosocial behaviors, such as smiling, taking turns, helping, and asking (as opposed to commanding), occurred more fre-quently than antisocial behaviors, such as grabbing someone else's blocks, hitting, threatening, and throwing blocks.

However, individual children differ in their ability to engage in successful block play. The developmental theory of social co-construction offers an explanation as to why some children are better social negotiators than others (Ross and Rogers 1990). Co-constructivist theory suggests that children who have a good understanding of how to act during a specific play situation are more successful in their social interactions than children without a clear understanding of the play situation. Ross and Roger (1990) state:

> Children were successful players because of their ability to understand the language and actions of others and respond with appropriate language and action themselves in the context of the immediate play situation. In order words, to be successful in one's play interactions, a child must enter the play situation with a similar understanding of how to act and what to say in this situation as his/her playmate and be able to adapt his/her language to the continuous changes in the physical and social situation as the interaction occurs between peers. Thus, the conventions and procedures of block play are both intra- and interindividually co-constructed. [p. 18]

Children who are unable to negotiate play interactions on their own will need to be taught this skill by a therapist. The therapist, acting as a play tutor, instructs, models, prompts, and reinforces appropriate interaction in block play. The therapist works with the socially withdrawn child individually until the child is ready to handle peer interaction.

Attention-Deficit/Hyperactivity Disorder (ADHD)

Block play may also be useful as a therapeutic technique for children with ADHD. The essential feature of ADHD is a continual pattern of inattention and/or hyperactivity-impulsivity. Children with this disorder typically have difficulty sustaining attention to a task and difficulty in delaying responses and awaiting one's turn.

A specific therapeutic task for children with ADHD is to teach them to be reflective, that is, to stop, think, plan ahead, and weigh alternatives and consequences before acting. Construction play with blocks, by definition, requires that children plan ahead so that they may build a desired structure. Children must also carefully place each block so that the structure does not collapse. In this manner, ADHD children practice being reflective and less impulsive.

Initially, the therapist spreads out a variety of blocks on the floor of the playroom and suggests to the child, "Let's use our imaginations to build something really great!" Then, to boost deliberate (stop and think) thinking in an impulsive child, the therapist should ask a few questions before the child starts the construction play: "What would you like to build?" If the child responds "a house," the therapist would then ask, "How big do you want the house to be? How high? How many rooms? Will there be doors and windows? What's my job in helping you?"

To further promote reflective thinking in the child during the construction, the therapist models thinking out loud by asking, "What would happen if we did this? What could we do to keep the tower from falling?"

In addition to reflective thinking, block play can be used to develop an ADHD child's attention span. Since blocks are a highly preferred play material among young children (Kinsman and Berk 1979), block play is likely to encourage ADHD children to persist at the task until they complete a structure (sustained attention).

By age 4, a child is capable of seeing a construction project through to the end of a 30-minute session and may work on the project over several sessions. This helps develop persistence—the ability to attend to a task over an extended period. The therapist can facilitate persistence in the child by showing great interest in the building project and by occasionally offering suggestions for improving or expanding the structure. At times the child is encouraged to continue developing the complexity of the structure by working on it over two or more sessions. If a "Do not disturb" sign will not ensure the safety of the construction, a photograph of it is taken to facilitate reassembly at subsequent sessions.

References

Cartwright, S. (1974). Blocks and learning. *Young Children* 15:141–146.

Hartley, R. E., Frank, L. R., and Goldenson, R. M. (1952). *Understanding Children's Play*. New York: Columbia University Press.

Kinsman, C. A., and Berk, L. E. (1979). Joining the block and housekeeping areas: changes in play and social behavior. *Young Children* 20:66–75.

Rogers, D. L. (1985). Relationships between block play and the social development of young children. *Early Child Development and Care* 20:245–261.

Ross, D. D., and Rogers, D. L. (1990). Social competence in kindergarten: analysis of social negotiations during peer play. *Early Child Development and Care* 25:15–26.

63

Anger Management: Bottle Rockets

Neil Cabe

INTRODUCTION

Anger, and its accompanying behaviors, are perhaps the most commonly encountered symptoms in children who present for therapy. Most children are able to identify the fact of their anger, but few are able to deal with it constructively, and fewer still are able to vent it appropriately. Teaching a child to release anger in appropriate ways, and to acknowledge the dangers of keeping it inside, are primary issues in anger management.

RATIONALE

To some degree, a child's anger serves as a defense mechanism for integrity and self-identity. As such, it must be dealt with as a power and control issue, which allows children to avoid personal responsibility for their actions, to avoid the true feelings that underlie it, and to reinforce the poor communications that perpetuate the family or personal dysfunction allowing the anger to arise. They must first identify the fact that anger held in leads to explosions, and anger released slowly and appropriately brings relief. The bottle-rocket technique can be used for this purpose.

The bottle-rocket technique provides a release for the child that is safe and noninjurious. Most children do not like their own anger, and want to be rid of it, but have no way to deal with such a powerful emotion constructively. This technique moves from the conscious present into long-term memory through contact with a number of stimuli, through the use of sound, touch, smell, sight, and occasionally taste, and through the explanation by the therapist of the affectively laden content of the experiment.

DESCRIPTION

Get a few 35mm film canisters from a store that processes film. (The stores recycle the canisters.) Translucent white FUJI canisters, with tightly fitting lids, work best. Then buy a quantity of white vinegar and a box of plain baking soda. These are the only required materials, though I often use a drop or two of food coloring of the child's choice for added effect. While best done outside, the activity may be accomplished indoors on a table covered with plastic or newspaper.

With the child, fill the film canister about half-full of white vinegar. Fill the indentation in the lid of the canister with baking soda, place the lid firmly on the canister, and quickly place it in the middle of the table. In two or three seconds, the canister will explode as the mixture forms gas and builds pressure. Outside, the film canister lid will "launch" as much as thirty feet in the air. Inside, it hits the ceiling.

CAUTION
**The film canister will explode with some force.
Keep the mixture and the canister
away from eyes and faces!**

Especially with younger children, I often use safety glasses, and the mixture itself is totally nontoxic. In the several years I have been using this technique, no child has ever been injured; however, I use the technique only with children who are able to follow my instructions, and I do not use it with children under school age.

The child will request to try the bottle rocket several times. In a subsequent "launch," without the knowledge of the child, I use a paper clip to poke a hole in the lid of one of the canisters, and perform the experiment with the child. In this case, the mixture from my canister squirts a wonderful geyser of foamy liquid into the air, while the child's canister explodes again.

Immediately after, I ask the child why my canister did not explode. Invariably, I'm told my lid had a hole in it and that let the pressure out slowly. At that point, I insist the child look me in the eyes, and I explain to him or her that whenever we let anger build up inside, it causes an explosion, but when we let the anger out a little at a time, the explosion never happens. No one ever forgets the experience. Following this, I explore with the children the roots of their own anger, what lies underneath it, and ways that they can release anger slowly without "exploding."

APPLICATION

This is an appropriate technique for most angry children. I have used it successfully with most age groups, in both individual and group sessions, and have found it to be particularly effective with latency-aged and adolescent clients. Oppositional-defiant and conduct-disordered clients love the noise, the action, and the mess. I have also let the children choose colors to represent particular feelings (blue for sad, red for angry, yellow for anxious, green for envy or jealousy), complete the exercise again, and discover with the child how he or she can release these other powerful emotions in more constructive ways. Many children who have never addressed their own deep and powerful emotions have done so using the bottle-rocket technique.

64

Play-Mates:
The Use of Dolls
in the Therapeutic Setting

Cynthia Caparosa Sniscak

INTRODUCTION

The inclusion of therapeutic dolls in my child therapy setting has been very helpful. The dolls offer a multitude of unlimited and creative options to the therapeutic process. Most often, in our work with children, our humanity is one of our most powerful therapeutic tools, but on occasion the fact that we are real, live human beings seems to create problems for our child clients. There are many times in my psychotherapy practice that my attentiveness, focus, and empathic responses are not sufficient and hamper the client's process. It occurred to me that I could use some outside support from sources that were not as responsive as I. I was looking for something that would offer my clients a safe and comfortable opportunity for expressing feelings, and offer me an opportunity to better assess their issues and needs. E. C. Hanson, a soft sculpture artist from Colorado, was asked to develop a few therapeutic dolls to assist with these needs. The result of this inquiry led to the development of Play-Mates. My clients and I now have a whole community of therapeutic support available and ready to help.

Play-Mates are soft fabric dolls, stuffed with polyfill. They average 30 inches in height. They are durable, washable, very tactile, and engaging. Part of their appeal seems to be the variety of facial expressions and special features that each doll has. These dolls are handmade and no two are alike. They reflect many feeling states and moods. Some of the dolls look safe and comforting, others look anxious or worried. Other expressions suggest anger, fear, boredom, surprise, or delight. Play-Mates also offer diversity in terms of age, race, gender, ethnicity, group affiliations, and style. They can look like a grandmother, a baby, or a teenage punker, skater, prep, or jock. They can be moms, dads, siblings, or extended family members. They have been assigned the roles of perpetrators, teacher, police officer, friends, or bullies.

Therapeutic dolls are useful in both child-centered play and in directive or therapist-initiated play. They are appropriate for use with individuals and with families. The uses of the dolls are limitless. Clients have spontaneously and creatively engaged the dolls in many ways. The dolls have proven helpful with a variety of populations and problems. I have used them with children who have survived trauma or have a history of victimization. They have been helpful with impulsive children or with children who have suffered loss. Play-Mates have been used by children who have difficulty managing anger or aggression and by children who have difficulty expressing feelings. They have helped children with social skills and communication difficulties and they have been used with anxious and fearful children. Children who have attachment issues or whose families are going through transition have also engaged them in their therapeutic work. Sometimes clients, especially adolescents, choose a doll and hold it for comfort throughout the session.

RATIONALE

Therapeutic dolls offer support for clients while they work on issues, problems, or skills by practicing, through play, fantasy, or dramatization. They act as props for clients as they do their therapeutic work. Communications regarding emotionally laden material is difficult for children and adolescents. They are more comfortable with play and fantasy than with talk therapy. The dolls are useful for reenacting historical happenings or for creating new realities. Children can develop their own setting and act out the roles in their own stories. The child becomes the director in scenes of their own choosing, engaging dolls as characters in their stories. Dolls can play any parts that the children assign, and the therapist can join in if invited. This child-centered play therapy approach is very empowering for children. The dolls promote many opportunities for children to feel strong, powerful, and in control.

The dolls also help with the development of mastery, exploration, and interaction, and they are available for experimenting with different or new behavioral choices. They have been useful for very impulsive children who struggle with their behavioral choices and their judgment. Often children will put the dolls in the same situations that they find themselves in when they make bad choices and must cope and adjust to the consequences of their actions. Therapists can assist by joining the play and demonstrating more appropriate behavioral choices. Play-Mates offer children opportunities for problem-solving and practicing new skills, while discharging feelings. The dolls have frequently been used for practicing assertiveness or working on difficult social behaviors.

Many children who have been victimized, who have survived trauma, or who are experiencing broken or disrupted attachments are emotionally constricted. These children may not be in touch with their feelings or they may be afraid to feel them or express them. Therapeutic dolls offer them the opportunity to do projective work. Child clients may give the dolls roles, attitudes, voices, and moods. Themes may be related to anger, safety, protection, aggression, power, and control. Clients frequently play out themes related to good and evil. The dolls provide children with the safety and distance they may need to work on difficult or overwhelming feelings. They are able to say things they may not be able to say in the real world. Child clients can get away with anger and aggression directed at the person of their choosing, without the risks associated in their real world. Many children have expressed strong affect toward perpetrators or family members after having assigned the dolls those roles. Sometimes these are particularly useful opportunities for families to witness. It provides parents and caregivers with an opportunity to see the intensity of affect their children may have in these situations, and gives children an opportunity to involve their parents in some of their therapeutic work. Fearful and anxious children have also found the dolls to be particularly useful. Children can work on their fears by creating fantasy situations and confronting their anxieties. They can practice being courageous and assertive and standing up for themselves.

Play-Mates are very compliant. They will be whomever the client decides they will be. They don't try to control, talk back, or threaten with punishment when feelings are expressed or directed at them. They allow the child to take charge. They are substantial enough to be manipulated and they are of appropriate size. These dolls have assisted clients in expressing anger, hurt, loneliness, embarrassment, and jealousy. They have been beaten, cuddled, yelled at, danced with, kissed, and put in handcuffs.

DESCRIPTION

Children with social skills and communication difficulties have used the dolls as characters in a story that is developed together by the client and the therapist. The therapist invites the child to create a setting for a story. If the child has difficulty coming up with a setting, the therapist can offer suggestions. If it is appropriate, a story line may be offered that may be a metaphor for the significant issues in the child's life. Often, after the therapist makes several plot suggestions, children will jump in with their own ideas. Then the dolls are chosen as characters in the story and their roles are assigned. The children decide which characters they will play and which the therapist will play. The therapist and the child develop the story together through the improvised conversations of the characters. The therapist can respond to the child's characters based on the child's therapeutic issues. The therapist's characters can model appropriate behaviors, express feelings, suggest helpful coping behaviors, and use appropriate communication and social behavior styles that the child is struggling with. This intervention was useful with two children diagnosed with Asperger's disorder.

Children who have been victimized often feel angry, fearful, and powerless. It can be helpful to stage a mock trial for their perpetrator. The child usually likes to play the part of the sentencing judge or the police officer. Props can be added such as a gavel, robe, and handcuffs. The dolls act as perpetrators, jurors, witnesses, other court officials, and significant others. Play-Mates have been sentenced, sent to jail, beaten up, stomped on, yelled at, and sentenced to life in prison or to death. Often they are made to publicly apologize for their heinous acts against the client. While these issues are quite serious, the dolls enable children to relieve their emotional distress. There is usually a lot of laughter while children play out these scenes, and it is very empowering for them.

For children who are either figuratively or literally separated from their parents, the dolls can serve as the absent parent. Children usually have a lot of feelings in relation to this situation and often have little opportunity to address them. Child clients will put the dolls in the empty chair and share their feelings with them. The dolls allow for a hands-on tactile experience in which the child can express what he or she is feeling. This technique not only helps with the discharge of the affect but also offers children the opportunity to problem solve.

Sometimes children fantasize about being famous and they wish for an audience. These dolls make a wonderful audience. They do not interrupt. Children fantasize about the dolls' adoration and appreciation and positive regard for them. They give the dolls the self-esteem–enhancing language the child is craving. This audience provides the opportunity to practice singing and dancing. Children can work on self-esteem, mastery, and developmental issues. They also offer the therapist insight into additional issues for further therapeutic work. Sometimes, this practice helps to reduce embarrassment and self-consciousness.

Another child put the dolls in the roles of a few schoolmates who had teased him. He was anxious, fearful, and angry. He practiced being powerful and assertive and told those bullies how it felt to be treated so unkindly. He also told them how it would be from now on. After discharging the strong affect, he was able to engage in a discussion of real and appropriate alternatives to his dilemma.

APPLICATION

The addition of therapeutic dolls into the playroom and office offer the opportunity to work on issues of conflict resolution, anger management, affective expression, communication and social skill development, creativity, problem solving, victim and perpetrator issues, relationships, and mastery. They assist with the treatment of posttraumatic stress disorder, depression, oppositional defiant disorder, attention-deficit/hyperactivity disorder (ADHD), parent–child and peer relational problems, grief and loss issues, low self-esteem, and anxiety and developmental issues. These dolls can be used in both a directive and nondirective sessions. They allow the therapist to identify affect and assist with insight.

Resource

For inquiries about Play-Mates, call (888) 909-0644 or visit the Web site at www.echanson.com.

65

Finding One's Balance— on the Rolling Balance Board

Sally Kondziolka

INTRODUCTION

Many traumatized children are in need of active, physically engaging play. Other children need a variety of body-oriented activities to master in order to build self-esteem or develop an internal locus of control. Some children have sensory and motor difficulties or poor body image, or somatic issues secondary to physical or sexual abuse. These children often require activities to help incorporate and integrate all their body parts or the upper body with the lower body. Those children with attention problems often need to cultivate focus through the use of a body-level task. Still other children need a prop or game through which they can elicit, clarify, and channel their nervous or high energy. All children can benefit from developing trust—in themselves as well as in others. All of these issues and more can be addressed through the use of the rolling balance board (sometimes known as a bongo board) as a prop in active play. The origins of these balance-related props and devices come from physical and occupational therapies. These props are often used by dance and movement therapists but with psychotherapeutic, not physical, goals in mind.

RATIONALE

Active, physical play engages children concurrently in cognitive, emotional, social, and somatic realms. Expressive movement and active physical, nonverbal play elicits immediate and sometimes more authentic (or less defended) communications. It can also be of help in formulating concrete goals to work toward that involve both emotional growth as well as physical accomplishment; it can become a metaphor for the child's personal style and/or process.

DESCRIPTION

The flat board is placed on top of the roller (cylinder) piece. The therapist may first wish to demonstrate balancing on the rolling balance board (Figure 65–1). The child can then begin by placing his or her

Figure 65–1. Balancing on the rolling balance board.

feet on the grips. The therapist acts as the "spotter" to keep it safe: "I'm here to catch you if you fall, but it won't work properly if you lean all your weight on me at first. If you do that, your own body cannot learn to find its center." The therapist should coach and guide children with confidence-building statements. Encourage them as they try to find their balance point; spot them all the while yet not so closely that their independence is undermined. Allow them to keep trying as long as they wish. Remind them that it is hard to balance; many new things that people try to master will at first require some practicing. Additionally, trying to find one's physical balance can help begin to introduce concepts of grounding, centering, and learning about staying calm no matter what comes our way and throws us off-center.

Advanced balancers (such as teenagers and those children who like challenges) can try doing additional tricks. These might include doing slow deep knee bends or juggling objects while maintaining their balance on the board. One could role-play challenging aspects of life and toss nerf balls at the children while they try to "keep their cool," "hang on to their own power," and try to stay centered no matter what comes their way. This is also a great point of departure for the child's imagination. The therapist may also spontaneously find parallels or additional metaphors that are specifically meaningful for the individual client.

APPLICATION

This prop is useful for adolescents (particularly those engaged in competitive and/or resistive behaviors) but can be used successfully by children as young as 4 years. It can additionally have a diagnostic use: it allows the play therapist to observe children's physical integration, self-confidence, self-esteem, ability to take moderate risks, drive to mastery, locus of control, sense of kinesphere (personal space), and ability to trust. The play therapist may leave it out visibly in the therapy room so that a child might initiate exploring with it. It may also be offered as a suggested activity: "Do you feel like trying something new and different today?" It also offers an opportunity for a child to work on learning to accept support—literally—from an adult.

Resource

The rolling balance board and other active and interaction-oriented props are available from SPORTIME, 1 Sportime Way, Atlanta, GA 30340, 800-283-5700, or www.sportime.com.

66

The Parent Adaptive Doll Play Technique

Carol A. Brennan

INTRODUCTION

Parents of children in distress are often at a loss for what to do to help their children feel better. The need exists for specific, age-appropriate techniques that parents can successfully implement under such circumstances. The parent adaptive doll play technique was originally designed for use by parents of young children experiencing emotional symptoms during transitions or changes in their lives. Under the direction of Dr. Garry Landreth, the author developed the technique as the focus of a dissertation study that examined its effectiveness when used by parents of young children to ease the stresses of parental separation and/or divorce. Most often the child's reactions while in distress resemble fear or anxiety. The purpose of the technique is to alleviate a child's observable stress during a particular situation so that future experience in the same or a similar situation will be more positively experienced. The technique has been quite useful to many children in a variety of situations. It has also evolved into the adaptive doll play technique, which the creative clinician will find not only easily adaptable to a variety of situations involving young children but also easily taught to and implemented by parents and other significant adults in children's lives.

RATIONALE

Children are active beings. When not sleeping most children are moving, learning about themselves and their world through play. According to the research of Jean Piaget in the area of cognitive development, young children are concrete thinkers and learners. More specifically, young children learn best by actual experience. Spoken words, therefore, are often insufficient for a young child's understanding and learning. The most optimal learning situation for a young child may best be accomplished through a combination of words and concrete objects.

Parenting is a complex task that most undertake with little or no preparation. Unintentionally, parents may mishandle situations with their children only to find that their efforts are futile. Discouragement may follow and as children become more troubled, parents seem likely to experience feelings of incompetence. For example, in their efforts to help when their children are tearful or distressed, most parents will often try calm reassurance, logic, or passive support. If these prove unsuccessful parents may then resort to bargaining, threatening, or loss of privileges as they become increasingly exasperated. It is believed that parents are in perhaps the best position to positively impact their children's emotional distress. Most parents seem motivated to help their children if they know what to do when the usual interventions are unsuccessful. ·

Storytelling has long been a popular form of entertainment as well as a form of learning for children. Stories can be read directly from a book, told from memory, or made up. Some stories take the form of plays, using dialogue and characters. The parent adaptive doll play technique combines a simple story with concrete objects or figures. Its intended use is that of presenting a child with a verbal explanation as well as with a simple but concrete representation of the situation presented through the story.

DESCRIPTION

The parent adaptive doll play technique is recommended for use with a child who is 7 years old or younger and who exhibits distress during a particular situation. It is an adult-directed technique that begins with a parent's formulating a relevant scenario for a story that will be told to the child. It should be simple, concise, and have a clear beginning, middle, and end. The story should focus on one situation and depict a positive version of a situation that has previously been difficult for the child. The parent should then choose dolls, toy figures, or stuffed toys to represent the main characters in the story. Most often the characters will be the child, the parent, and possibly one other person. As the story is told to the child, the parent acts out the most important elements using the preselected characters. A relaxed, comfortable setting for telling the story is recommended, and timing should be appropriate for the parent as well as for the child. In order for the technique to be most effective, a parent should plan to tell the same story at least two or three times to a child before any change in the child's behavior is expected. If desired, a story can be repeated within the same day but it is recommended that repetitions be at least a few hours apart.

The technique is designed to help decrease a child's stress or anxiety associated with a troublesome transition or situation. Examples of such situations might include a child's difficulty going to bed alone, worry regarding a change in child-care arrangements, or fear of going away overnight without a parent. The following story is divided into three paragraphs to illustrate a clear beginning, middle, and end and can be used in helping a child having trouble transitioning to bed at night.

> I want to tell you a story about going to bed and waking up in the morning. Here's the Abby doll and here's the Mommy doll. They've had their dinner and Mommy said, "Abby, it's time for you to get ready for bed." Abby replies, "Okay Mommy, I'll go put my pajamas on." (Move child figure away.) And while Abby gets her pajamas on over here, Mommy picks out a story to read to her. Then Mommy helps Abby brush her teeth (add sound effects) and helps her into bed. (Lay child figure down.) Then Mommy sits on the side of Abby's bed and reads the story to her. After the story is over, Mommy gives Abby a big hug and kiss goodnight (add sound effects) and says, "Goodnight, Abby, have a good night's rest and I'll see you in the morning. I love you." And Abby says, "G'nite, Mommy, I love you, too."
>
> Then Mommy goes out to the kitchen (move parent figure away from child figure as if out of sight) and fixes the coffee pot

for the next morning. Then Mommy goes to her room and gets ready for bed. She brushes her teeth (add sound effects), puts on her pajamas, gets into bed (lay parent figure down), and turns off the light (add sound effects).

And so, while Abby is in her bed sleeping and Mommy is in her bed sleeping, the house is very quiet and they're both getting a good rest. Soon it's morning. Abby wakes up in her bed, rubs her eyes, and wonders if Mommy's awake yet. She gets out of her bed and goes to Mommy's room (move child figure toward Mommy figure). She leans over Mommy and says, "Hi, Mommy!" And Mommy opens her eyes, smiles at Abby, and says "G'morning, sweetie, I'm glad to see you." Then they hug each other for a minute before getting up to start their day, and that's the end of the story.

The story explains through the combination of words and concrete objects that the child and parent are together prior to bedtime when they then separate to sleep before being reunited again in the morning. The positive "picture" the child sees as the story is told in this manner is thought to be easier for the child to retain and therefore more comforting than a verbal explanation.

Clinicians teaching this technique to parents should encourage them to add real elements of their daily routines to the stories they formulate. This helps keep the child's attention as does the addition of sound effects and movement of the figures as the story is told. Parents should also be discouraged from using a story to lecture, warn, or otherwise criticize the child's previous behavior in a scenario similar or identical to the one represented in the story. The story should be upbeat, positive, and focused on "planting a seed" in the child's mind that the situation depicted can be comfortably and successfully experienced. When possible the technique is most effective when told to one child at a time.

APPLICATION

The parent adaptive doll play technique was originally designed for use by parents of young children who were experiencing parental separation/divorce-related stresses. Since that time the technique has been successfully used by adults in many roles to help children experiencing distress in a broad variety of situations. Some examples include, but are not limited to, children in foster care or who've lost parents through any number of circumstances, children in treatment settings, children in the process of being adopted, children changing schools, children fearful of going out to play in their own backyard alone, and children worrying that they will be forgotten and left at their day-care center at the end of the day. Use of the technique has been found not only to be useful in helping decrease children's anxieties in many situations but also to increase feelings of competence in caregivers.

67

Nesting Doll Depictions

Jo Ann L. Cook

INTRODUCTION

The initial inspiration for the use of nesting dolls (Figure 67–1) in play therapy evolved from the use of commercially painted dolls and figures. Their incremental sizes represented growth, and the combination of dolls nested within one another was symbolic of the internalization of previous states of development. The analogy and symbolism were easily understood by children, who grasped that with physical growth there was also the associated opportunity for mental, emotional, and behavioral growth and for their internalization. With unpainted sets of wooden nesting dolls, issues of personal development, self-esteem, and increased personal awareness can be illustrated and addressed. Children can use their dolls as they describe their life stories and future plans. They can combine the dolls to represent an integration of the self. The technique has been of interest to boys as well as girls and to a wide age range of children and adolescents.

Figure 67–1. The nesting dolls.

RATIONALE

The concept of individual personal growth is abstract and more easily understood by children by using specific recollections. Involvement in the development of materials to be used during sessions allows the child greater control and opportunity to recall experiences, situations, and issues. Children may illustrate and decorate a particular figure to enable them to more clearly define a period of their growing up that was significant as positive or negative or difficult. Additionally, the technique points to future ages or stages of development, and provides a situation in which problems may be reworked and reframed. Similarly, when the child identifies periods of particular strength or success, the analogy is that these remain internalized within succeeding stages and can be drawn upon in the future. Since time, sequence, and emotions are abstract concepts, the actual creation and development of a personal sequence of growth provide the opportunity to engage recollections and associations that may not have otherwise been captured in a single technique or application.

DESCRIPTION

Children are introduced to a set of unpainted nesting dolls, initially as a single figure. Then they are shown that the figure can be disassembled to reveal a sequence of figures of increasing size. These figures can be discussed with reference to a variety of issues, including one's individual growth at different ages or stages, one's talents and skills and their relative proportions or strengths, and one's identity and subsumed roles and interests. The children are encouraged to identify a series of ages, events, strengths, talents, or roles that they wish to address or depict. During discussion, children begin to determine which figures will illustrate their choices. The illustrations can be completed with a variety of media including markers, crayons, paints, ink, and pencil. As they do the illustration, some children offer a great deal of related information and associations. Others may be engrossed in the process and become verbal only when they have completed their illustration, and their figures are available for use in play activities, discussion, and storytelling.

APPLICATION

The applications of the nesting dolls depictions have been numerous and are a means of engaging children actively in a process in which they develop associations and understanding regarding their present behavior in relation to their history or to the potential for change in the future. The technique has served well for children who could benefit from self-esteem strengthening. Their talents, strengths, and accomplishments become internalized and serve as foundations for future successes. Children who are immature or anxious similarly benefit from a concrete and personalized illustration that the process of maturation involves emotional as well as physical growth, and risk-taking and change can lead to growth, which results in strengths with which they continue to move forward. The fact that the nesting dolls allow for illustrations and applications/drawings/

annotations reflects the ongoing conception of a child's growth and learning. Using these figures, children are easily engaged in storytelling or drama related to their experiences and memories.

The issues of overcoming adversity and preparing to deal with the future have been seen in numerous enactments. These issues are encouraged by probing for information and experiences that children may have understood at later stages but not during periods of difficulty when they were younger. The content can be framed to enable children to understand that they may not have been able to address certain issues at a younger age, but now they have the knowledge and strengths to do so. Children with multiple talents and creativity can use the technique to come to an increased understanding of making choices and setting goals in which they can apply their multiple abilities with a view toward an increased integration of their differing interests and abilities. For some children the figures represent personal goals that they were striving to attain, such as becoming involved in certain activities or sports in which there was a progression of stages of preparation, leading to involvement and success, such as practicing for and attaining a specific goal/belt in martial arts, or becoming a safety patrol member.

The most interesting application was by a girl with trichotillomania, which had been a problem of long standing. Her series of figures displayed her earlier years when her hair was plentiful and undamaged, followed by a period in which her problems were obvious and notable and masked by hair coloring and wigs. Finally, the last figure was completed when she had overcome her problem; her appearance was normal and the affect she displayed was also markedly changed, depicting her accomplishment of control and personal growth in the process.

Resource

Unpainted nesting dolls can be ordered from FLAX art and design (1-800-343-3529 or visit Web site flaxart.com).

68

Tin of Trinkets Technique

Jo Ann L. Cook

INTRODUCTION

The Tin of Trinkets play technique (Figure 68–1) was initially improvised as an adaptation of Dr. Richard Gardner's (1986) bag-of-toys game to provide portable, interesting, and stimulating material that would engage reluctant youngsters in investigating and expressing interests and associations. These trinkets were a childhood collection placed on a desk to draw the attention and involvement of withdrawn children, and over the years they have been used for a variety of applications and responses. More recently, Gardner (1994) developed the Pick-and-Tell games, which include the bag of toys (trinkets) as well as other bags of stimulus materials, such as emotion pictures, words, and actions. The reader is referred to Gardner (1994) for some initial ideas with which to begin a collection. Miniature toys can become inspirations for one's own unique collection. The tin of trinkets technique has been observed to stimulate interest, participation, and expression in children from preschool through adolescence and has also been used with children and their families. Engagement has been highly consistent through the use of the technique. Portability has been beneficial, as materials may be used at a desk, on the floor, or as markers for personal movers in games.

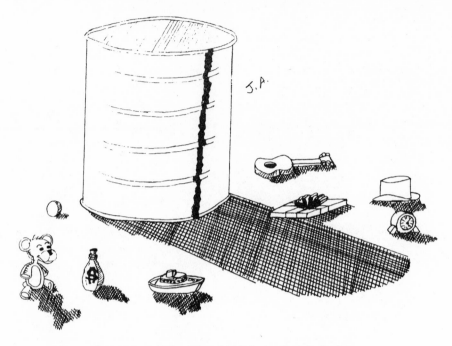

Figure 68–1. The Tin of Trinkets play technique.

RATIONALE

Initially it is often difficult for children to verbally express their thoughts and emotions. Representational objects and toys enable them to communicate through associations and actions as they begin to integrate verbal communication with active self-expression. The choices made by children, and their illustrations and associations with these choices promote participation and expression without requiring initial verbal communication. The open-ended presentation allows children to choose to reveal as much as or as little as they desire as well as to return to the initial symbolic toys during later work as they may expand and clarify their initial choices.

DESCRIPTION

The technique is presented by introducing the tin of trinkets, display-
ing the collection on a surface, and allowing the children to explore the
trinkets, choose the ones they would like to work with, and arrange them
in any way they would like. The therapist also models exploring, if
needed, and can participate if the children request. When there is
sufficient time and the children indicate they have chosen several, they
are asked to tell about what they have chosen, why, and to describe their
particular arrangement. The presented material facilitates observation of
the exploration and choices in decision making; the descriptions and
personal associations; the order of arrangement, whether by preference,
temporal order, or sequence; and an enactment as a tiny play, story, or
other actual or metaphorical expression. When the children have completed their play, description, or demonstration, they are encouraged to
consider if they can identify with any of the trinkets, for example, if they
have a favorite toy or favorite memory, or conversely, if there is one they
would like to discard from the group and why. The trinkets can then be
used to superimpose on a drawing as a backdrop, and can be moved by
the children or used in the playroom, in the playhouse, or sand tray as
they move forward in their therapy.

APPLICATION

Other applications have included having a group of children use the
tin of trinkets technique during introductory sessions to stimulate sharing
of individual information and identification of commonalities. The technique is useful with families where sharing can include history and
particularly evoke childhood memories. The technique has been used
effectively with groups and with families that are involved in play
therapy by requesting them to choose items that help them relate to or
communicate with the other persons or in choosing symbolic gifts and
meanings to share with other members. The trinkets can also be used as
markers in games. The choice to change representational trinkets during
sequential board games or activities is allowed, with discussion of a

characteristic or memory that the use of the mover allows the children to express. For example, one quiet child continually chose a white mouse as a mover in games but with increased confidence later changed to a "white rabbit that just jumped out of a hat."

References

Gardner, R. A. (1986). *The Psychotherapeutic Techniques of Richard A. Gardner.* Cresskill, NJ: Creative Therapeutics.

———. (1994). *Dr. Gardner's Pick-and-Tell Games.* Cresskill, NJ: Creative Therapeutics and the Center for Applied Psychology.

69

Lenses

Celia Linden

INTRODUCTION

One of the common challenges in treating young children is how to make information concrete enough for them to use in their everyday world. Techniques learned in the playroom need to be practical enough and well rehearsed in order for the child to use them in other milieus in which the child functions. This is the foundation of effective treatment.

Cognitive-behavioral theory has much to offer children within the playroom. Often, however, the therapist struggles with making this information understandable. Techniques that can make the theory come alive in play are extremely valuable resources for clinicians to have at their fingertips. Children will often be more verbal and open with their feelings when they are immersed in a playful activity that provides a safe place to express themselves. Experiential activities offer the child the opportunity to engage in learning important constructs in a playful and nonthreatening manner.

RATIONALE

Play therapy is founded on the notion that through play children can experience novel situations and learn new behaviors outside the realm they currently negotiate. Using props is an effective manner to engage children in the journey of gaining perspective and expanding their vision.

DESCRIPTION

To use this technique you will need several pairs of sunglasses with different colored lenses. You can also use colored saran wrap or any material that when looked through will change the color of what you see.

The therapist introduces the activity by explaining the word *perspective* and how it applies to the child's individual position. In this part of the introduction the therapist tailors the activity to the exact goals she is trying to achieve. If the child is depressed, the therapist can talk about the different lenses as the rosy and gloomy way to see things. If the child is conduct disordered, the therapist can discuss the different lenses as people's views of a specific situation.

The child then tries on the different glasses. The therapist will ask the child to describe what he sees and how things look to him. If the child is depressed, the therapist would use only two different colored glasses (one dark and one light) and focus on the difference between the lenses as the difference between seeing the rosy or gloomy view of things, illustrating the notion that the reality is colored by the "lens" the child looks through. The glasses can be worn outside of the office as well to generalize the idea that the child's view of home, school, and community is affected by the lens the child chooses to use. Homework assignments can be given, for example, to wear the rosy glasses in a place where the child feels very negative as a physical prompt that the child's feelings can change by altering the lens. The child can then report back to the therapist how different the view was with the different lenses, and subsequent discussion can focus on the cognitive-behavioral theory behind the notion that how we think affects how we feel.

If the child is conduct disordered or has oppositional defiant disorder, the therapist would have several different pairs of glasses for the child to use. After the child has worn them and has had an opportunity to describe what he sees, the therapist would focus the discussion on how each pair made the room look different and that the reality was changed by the lenses the child looked through. The discussion would illustrate that although the views were different, they were each valid, depending on the lens the child was looking through. These glasses could be sent with the child to use when a situation occurs outside of the play therapy session. During a conflict at home, for instance, the child and parent can use the glasses as a way to "see" one another's perspective about a situation. They would first wear their own glasses and discuss the situation. Then they would switch glasses and try to "see" differently. They can report on the outcome of their experience during the next session. The following is an example of using this technique with a depressed adolescent:

Therapist: Today we are going to use these different glasses to help us look at the things that are bugging you. You will notice I have two different pairs—dark and light. First we will use these dark glasses and I want you to think all your negative thoughts about something bothersome. Then we will use these light rosy-colored ones to let your positive thoughts talk. Let's pick a subject from the "Things That Upset Me" list.

Child: I'll start with percussion.

Therapist: Great. Put these dark glasses on and let's hear your gloomy negative side talk about playing the drums and your teacher.

Child: It stinks!

Therapist: Well, that's pretty negative!

Child: And I have a bad teacher and everyone else is better than me and it's not fun.

Therapist: Anything else?

Child: No . . . that's it.

Therapist: OK. Now let's switch glasses and put on these rosy-colored ones. Now we are going to take those thoughts and see them differently. You said you have a bad teacher. I know you don't like him or the way he treats you in class. How can we change that thought and look at that with a positive perspective?

Child: Well, I get rid of him next year!!!

Therapist: So he's your teacher for now but not forever.

Child: Yeah.

Therapist: Are you still learning?

Child: Yeah.

Therapist: Okay. There's one more piece to the negative thoughts that we need to try to see differently. You said everyone else is better than you are. That's a very negative way to look at your performance. How can we put a positive spin on that so that you don't feel bad based on what everyone else does?

Child: Um . . . (pause) . . . it doesn't matter how everyone else plays because I shouldn't compare myself to them.

Therapist: Your skills are individual to you and you are a capable player. Your negative side doesn't want you to feel good about what you do. Remember these thoughts like you to feel unhappy and see things dark and gloomy. Let yourself enjoy the music and have fun in the process of making it. You don't need to focus on the product.

Child: Yeah, but I'm still not as good as the rest of the kids.

Therapist: Hey!! You are in the wrong-color glasses for that statement!

Child: Oh yeah. I forgot.

Therapist: The negative thoughts are what you are used to letting rule your thinking. It takes practice to change them! Let's see if we can make a summary statement from the positive side to combat your gloomy talk.

Child: Well, even though I don't like my teacher now, I'm still learning and I can have fun when I am playing (child rolls her eyes).

Therapist: It sounds strange to hear yourself talk this way, but in time it will sound more natural! I promise!

The therapist and child went on to discuss different subjects using the same technique until the list was exhausted.

APPLICATION

This activity is useful with most children to illustrate the notion of perspective and the idea that differences in opinion are valid and honorable. This is especially valuable, however, with those children who have a great deal of difficulty tolerating someone else's position and need their own perspective to be the only perspective on a subject. Children with depression also benefit from this activity when structured slightly differently to illustrate negative and positive cognitions.

70

Using Anatomical Dolls in Psychotherapy with Sexualized Children

Jamshid A. Marvasti

INTRODUCTION

Anatomical dolls, also known as natural dolls, are constructed with genitalia, body cavities, and pubic hair. They usually consist of an adult male and female and prepubertal boy and girl, ideally in both brown and white. These dolls have been used for a number of years in the evaluation and validation of sexual abuse in children, are generally used in forensic evaluations of child sexual abuse, and have been a controversial subject among some defense attorneys. It is felt that a naked anatomical doll is sexually suggestive to a child and may contaminate and bias the process of evaluation and validation of incest and sexual abuse. These dolls are considered tools rather than toys in forensic evaluations, and are introduced only after a child verbalizes sexual victimization, in order to facilitate communication.

There are other ways to utilize the dolls, such as in the treatment of sexualized children. In this instance, I have used them as toys, not tools. Sexualized children have been sexually abused or overstimulated. They have already gone through the process of forensic validation and the legal system, and have subsequently been referred for treatment. These children not only need therapy for the trauma of abuse, they need further intervention for sexualized behavior, for example, doing to others what was done to them—touching others' genital area, or asking and provoking others to engage with them in a sexual way.

Sexualized children, also labeled as sexually reactive children, may be sexually aggressive toward their peers, are preoccupied by erotic and sexual acts, and may excessively masturbate or sex play in a compulsive way, with complete disregard for its inappropriateness (Marvasti 2000).

RATIONALE

The sexually abused child may present a variety of pathological and unwanted behaviors, and many times play therapy is the treatment of choice (Marvasti 1989, 1993). Anatomical dolls are used as toys for the following purposes:

1. Giving the child an opportunity to repeat the sexual abuse act with the doll rather than with people.

2. Ventilating the trauma, for example, striking the male doll's penis.

3. Providing sex education.

4. Enhancing the child's memory of traumatic events. Memory is a "state-dependent" phenomenon, which means memory is enhanced when the person is exposed to the state and circumstances that registered the original event. These dolls, with explicit genital areas, may trigger the child's memory in regard to the circumstances and details of sexual abuse.

5. Allowing the child to desensitize herself and prepare for a gynecological exam or reenact it, if it was perceived previously as discomforting.

6. Substituting for the therapist's body when a child wants to touch the therapist's genital area (Marvasti 1994).

Child: Can I touch your pee-pee? (pointing toward the male therapist's genital area).

Therapist: I don't like to be touched by children, but I can give you this special doll, and you may pretend it is me and do whatever you want with it.

Child: Is your pee-pee just like this one? (pointing toward the doll's penis).

Therapist: Yes, I have a boy's and man's pee-pee. Girls also have something called a vagina. You may see it by looking at the other doll (hands the child the female anatomical doll).

DESCRIPTION

Clothed anatomical dolls are introduced whenever the therapist feels it is indicated. He/she may explain to the child that the dolls have body parts similar to a real person and the child may, if desired, remove the clothing and play with them in any way she wishes. The child may then:

1. Reenact a sexual activity between male and female dolls (if she was exposed to parental intercourse and was overstimulated).

2. Repeat the sexual abuse incident if it was perceived as traumatic. The therapist, or the therapist's doll, may participate in play and give solutions, suggestions, clarification, and interpretation or change the helplessness/powerlessness and negative outcome of the event; for example, the girl doll can fight the offender or call the police. Police dolls can enter the doll house and arrest the offender, or when the offender doll tells the victim, "This is a game and you should keep it secret," the therapist doll, or puppet, can jump in and say, "Tell someone about it now because this is not a game."

Children who were sexually overstimulated may have the need to repeat the sexual act with others in a compulsive way for the purpose of decreasing the internal tension and achieving ego mastery over the trauma. These children are helpless in controlling their anger and preoccupation, which is in the category of obsession and compulsion. Anatomical dolls may be used in therapy for the purpose of repeating the trauma in displacement, with the assumption that it may decrease the child's need to reenact it in reality with others. The therapist may offer the child just the anatomical dolls to play with during the session, and the child may play out what he/she wants to do to other children. Sometimes it may take three sessions weekly during the first couple of weeks, especially if the child was expelled multiple times from different day-care centers or schools due to the indiscriminate and frequent sexual play with nonconsenting peers. These children generally don't respond to punishment.

APPLICATION

This technique is helpful for overtly sexualized children who are acting out and possibly victimizing other children. Some traumatized children with the diagnosis of posttraumatic stress disorder (PTSD) may react negatively to seeing a naked anatomical doll, by having a flashback of the victimization. They may throw the doll or run screaming from the therapist's office.

The therapist may need an informed consent form from the parents that explains the benefits and side effects of utilizing the doll. If, in the future, the child is sexually abused again, the anatomical doll cannot be used for forensic evaluation, as some defense attorneys may comment that the child's experience with these dolls invalidates anything elicited in a forensic evaluation. Thus, anatomical dolls should not be introduced in play therapy if the child is still in the process of forensic evaluation and/or may need to testify in court in regard to the sexual abuse allegations. The therapist also should feel confident that using naked dolls in therapy is not against the parents' value system and religion.

References

Marvasti, J. A. (1989). Play therapy with sexually abused children. In *Vulnerable Population*, vol. 2, ed. S. Sgroi, pp. 1–41. Lexington, MA: Lexington.

———. (1993). Please hurt me again: posttraumatic play therapy with an abused child. In *Play Therapy in Action*, ed. T. Kottman and C. Schaefer, pp. 485–525. Northvale, NJ: Jason Aronson.

————. (1994). Play diagnosis and play therapy with child victim of incest. In *Handbook of Play Therapy*, vol. 2, ed. C. Schaefer and K. O'Connor, pp. 319–348. New York: Wiley.

————. (2000). Child suffering in the abusive and dysfunctional communities and families in the U.S.A. In *Child Suffering in the World*, ed. J. Marvasti, pp. 326–360. Manchester, CT: Sexual Trauma Center.

71

Family Sandplay Therapy

Lois Carey

INTRODUCTION

Sandplay has become a respected therapeutic technique for children in the last few years and, more recently, its value has been expanded and enriched through its use with families. Sandplay is a modality that uses a sand tray and a broad collection of miniatures with which a child or a family can construct a scene that immediately can illustrate the psychological issues of the child or the family. There are significant differences between therapy with an individual or with a family, but this chapter addresses this technique's use with families. For further information, see the bibliography.

Families today experience stress related to the needs of two-career parents, divorced parents, single parents, grandparents raising grandchildren, teenaged parents, and alcohol and drug addicted parents. One of the major issues for these families is that children become the symptom bearers. Families believe that if the child is healed, everything will be all right. As we all know, this is not the case. Busy parents may often mean emotionally neglected children who live in families with poor basic communication skills and who do not know how to handle problems effectively when they arise. Family sandplay therapy is designed to enhance the ability of families to improve their communication patterns as well as to foster relationship building and to support the symptom bearer. These issues can be addressed through the use of a playful modality, one that can be nonverbal as well as fun.

RATIONALE

Play is the way that children communicate their thoughts, hopes, feelings, and concerns. Parents are not trained to look at play as a therapeutic technique or as a possible avenue of communication with their children, and they question its value. Play therapists know otherwise. Therapists who use sandplay as one element in the treatment of children often exclude parents, except in parent consultations. Family therapists who are trained to see families as a system often exclude young children from the sessions, and refer the younger members to a play therapist. Family sandplay is a method that can engage both the children and the parents almost immediately. Families can learn about their children's issues (and their own) through an understanding and use of metaphors that become visible in the sandplay process and that are often nonverbal. For example, I once treated an 8-year-old girl who wanted to show her mother the sand picture that she had just completed. The picture had an island in the center of the tray, surrounded by a moat. A large dragon perched atop a castle, while on the opposite shore sat a girl and her dog. The mother's reaction was immediate. She gasped and said, "Is that the way she sees me?" Since this was the girl's first session and I didn't want her to feel judged, I responded by telling the mother that it was too early to make that kind of an assumption. My dodging the issue was purely to alleviate the anxiety of both mother and daughter so that the work could proceed. If this had occurred at a later stage of treatment, I would have handled it in a different way, probably by having the pair role play the issue that was illustrated.

DESCRIPTION

Families who are referred for therapy for one or several of their children are always apprehensive as to what the experience will be. The therapist's role is critical to help families understand play therapy as a first step. This is followed by helping them to see the value of family play therapy and the benefits that are inherent when the whole family is included. This is best done with a description of systemic family therapy, especially related to communication issues. Families need to be assured that this technique will aid their overall communication patterns and will help them to see their dilemma in a different way and to possibly find different solutions. After this kind of introduction, and acceptance by the family that they are willing to try this unfamiliar form of therapy, they are introduced to the sandplay room. The family members are encouraged to touch both the wet and dry sand in order to begin to make a beginning connection with this unknown modality. Then it is suggested that they look at the collection of miniatures that are displayed on shelves lining the walls. The final instruction is that they will each have an opportunity to talk about the scene at the conclusion of the session. The therapist's role at this stage is that of observer, especially to note how each person behaves with respect to the feel of the sand and to each other. All of the interactions, verbal as well as nonverbal, are important as the family prepares to use this unknown therapeutic technique.

Mom, Dad, Billy, age 10, and Joan, age 8, are in therapy for Billy's encopresis and Joan's depression. They have been apprised of family sandplay therapy as described above, and have made a sand picture sometime during the first six weeks of treatment. The picture is made in wet sand, with all family members using one sand tray. (There are times when it may be beneficial to break the family into two teams and each team uses a separate tray.) Mom is uncomfortable with the wet sand and is allowed to be a participant/observer. The other family members select miniatures to use, occasionally fighting over who gets what. The therapist allows them to work it out among themselves in order to observe their problem-solving capacities. Dad tries to bring order; the therapist suggests he refrain. Billy has chosen several snakes, a dinosaur, a small and large hippo, and a tiger. He asks to add more water to the tray as he wants the hippos and the snakes to roll around in the mud. The selection of these miniatures is his way to engage with and to illustrate his anal issues. The tiger and the dinosaur are nearby and face each other. Mom, the observer, is appalled and states that she can't stand such a mess. Joan is also uncomfortable with the amount of water that Billy has added and takes one corner for herself that is damp, but not soaked. In that corner, she fences off a small area and makes a farm scene with a house, some cows, horses, pigs, and chickens. Then she places a small girl with her arms upraised on the roof of the house. This is of concern to the therapist because of the suicidal implications; however, nothing is said at the moment. Dad takes the center of the tray and adds a couple of large trucks, a bulldozer, some soldiers, and knights. He tries to make a road through Billy's wet mess, but Billy tells him to back off. (Billy is setting the boundary.) He next places the soldiers (with guns) aimed at Billy's hippos in the mud. (Dad's reaction to setting limits?) The knights on horseback face Joan's farm scene. (Protection?)

The family looks at the finished product and are encouraged to tell a story using the characters that they have chosen. Billy begins by saying that the animals all liked to roll around in the mud and get dirty. He said that the tiger was there to guard anyone from bothering the rest of the animals, but that the tiger and the dinosaur were enemies. Joan says, of her part, that the little girl is afraid of what the animals might do, and so she put her on the roof to protect her. (She seems to be referring to the farm animals, but could also mean Billy's ferocious ones.) Dad says that his soldiers are there to keep order. He says that the knights will rescue the little girl on the roof. Mom says nothing but looks helpless and quite upset; her eyes fill up.

The therapist now summarizes: "It seems as if the hippos and snakes are showing us how good it feels to be rolling around in the mud. The tiger, on the other hand, seems to be angry and to not know what to do. Maybe the tiger wants to attack the ones in the mud, but needs to fight off the dinosaur first?" (The therapist attempts to link Billy's symptom to his mixed feelings of pleasure and anger.) The therapist then turns to Joan and comments about how frightened the girl on the roof seems and that she is perhaps glad that the knights are near to rescue her. (Alludes to child's possible suicidal ideation along with the fact that the knights are there for protection. Links the parental presence as support.) Some comments are then made about the trucks being present to build a road (implies Dad's trying to assist) along with the soldiers being angry at the animals wallowing in the mud (Dad's anger about Billy's symptom). Next, attention is directed to Mom's nonverbal affect: "You seem as if this is quite uncomfortable for you to observe; but it seems as if some constructive work is being accomplished. Is there anything you would like to say?" Mom bursts into tears and is able to say how helpless and sad that this makes her feel.

A sand picture such as this enables a family to begin to open up their deepest fears and feelings through a playful, nonthreatening modality in which all can take part—even the participant/observer.

APPLICATION

Family sandplay therapy provides links between individual sandplay, play therapy, and family therapy. As such, the practitioner needs to have knowledge of all these various approaches and to feel comfortable in experimenting with a relatively new concept. Family sandplay therapy has as its theoretical base a family systems orientation. The technique is especially useful for families where communication issues are prevalent, when there has been a significant loss, such as in cases of death, divorce, remarriage (with children of one or both spouses), when children are the symptom bearers, or when substance abuse is an issue. The practitioner can think creatively about other situations where sandplay may be useful.

Bibliography

Bowen, M. (1966). The use of family theory in clinical practice. *Comprehensive Psychiatry* 9:345–374.

Bradway, K., ed. (1981). *Sandplay Studies*. San Francisco, CA: Jung Society.

Carey, L. (1990). Sand play therapy with a troubled child. *The Arts in Psychotherapy* 17:197–209.

———. (1991). Family sandplay therapy. *The Arts in Psychotherapy* 18:231–239.

————. (1992). A child-centered approach to family sandplay therapy. *Quaternio, Journal of the Brazilian Society of Jungian Psychotherapy* 1(3):6–11.

————. (1999). *Sandplay Therapy with Children and Families.* Northvale, NJ: Jason Aronson.

Gil, E. (1994). *Play in Family Therapy.* New York: Guilford.

Kalff, D. M. (1980). *Sandplay: A Psychotherapeutic Approach to the Psyche.* Santa Monica: Sigo.

Landgarten, H. (1987). *Family Art Psychotherapy: A Clinical Guide and Casebook.* New York: Brunner/Mazel.

Mitchell, R., and Friedman, H. 91994). *Sandplay: Past, Present and Future.* London and New York: Routledge.

Moustakas, C. (1959). *Psychotherapy with Children: The Living Relationship.* Carron.

Schaefer, C., and Carey, L., eds. (1994). *Family Play Therapy.* Northvale, NJ: Jason Aronson.

Wynne, L. (1965). Some indications and contraindications for exploratory family therapy. In *Intensive Family Therapy,* ed. I. Boszormenyi-Nagy and J. L. Framo, pp. 289–322. New York: Harper & Row.

72

Therapeutic Responses to the Bop Bag: Healing Anger and Aggression in Children

Victoria McGuinness

INTRODUCTION

Expression of anger and aggression is a critical intervention issue. This type of play is not fun for a child; it is both an expression and release of a painful reality. The therapist's response to a child's expression of aggression will either reinforce the aggressive feelings and behaviors or help to release and transform them. Correct utilization of aggressive play is essential for the reclaiming of true empowerment for the child. The therapist's responses are designed to break the connection between negative self-feelings held by the child and the aggressive behaviors. Therapeutic responses focus on the feelings the child has rather than on the acts of aggression.

There are many angry children today who are brought to therapy by frightened and desperate parents seeking to help their child. Children in general lack the cognitive and verbal skills to say, "My father hits my mother and that makes me so angry that I hurt my little sister." I receive calls from distraught parents who report, "She strangled someone at day care today because the child said he didn't like her picture," or "He doesn't know his boundaries; he's always poking other kids," or "He is mean and very aggressive at times; it scares me—that's the way his father was . . . he witnessed a lot of domestic violence."

Anger and aggression in children are two of the most common symptoms requiring therapy. Children appear unable to identify the deepest source of their anger, even if it appears obvious to us as adults. Perhaps the parents are divorcing or the child has been abused or feels unprotected in some way—there are a wide variety of environmental profiles that will cause angry and aggressive behavior in children. Parents are very frightened by their children's anger and are often embarrassed by it. A play therapist's responses to a child's anger is crucial to transforming the anger, which is generally the result of fear.

RATIONALE

The impact of violence on children has been entering into societal awareness since 1984 when the federal government officially recognized marital violence as a problem; at least 3.5 million children are exposed to marital violence annually. Witnessing domestic violence or being the direct recipient of abuse harms children in many ways that disrupt normal development. Using a bop bag is one way of expressing anger and hostility, and it is a very common choice for children. The internalized pressure within a child that externalizes as aggressive behavior must be transformed into an expression of the emotional energy being carried by the child and then redirected or released.

Many angry children discover that hitting the bop bag is a good way to release pent-up anger and aggression. The bop bag, when used for this kind of release, enables a child to show the therapist the level of emotional pain, anger, or violent experiences that the child has endured or witnessed. The first goal is to discharge negative feelings in the playroom. The neutral-looking bop bag can wear many faces during play therapy sessions. Discharging anger is an important first step, but redirecting the anger is critical. The therapist's responses to the bop bag will either increase or decrease the anger and aggression that a child feels. It is vitally important to reduce the connection between the child's negative feelings and experiences and the angry/aggressive behaviors that the child has learned to engage in. Careful responses to the discharge of anger at the bop bag will release the child's anger and reveal the fear and sadness that lurk behind the protective shield of anger. After all, it feels a lot more empowering to be angry than it does to feel sad or hurt.

DESCRIPTION

The therapist sits in a chair that puts the therapist on the child's level. The child pulls the bop bag out of the corner or confronts it in some way. As a child enters reenactment play, many negative feelings or experiences are projected onto the bop bag as well as the assigning of a negative identity to the bop bag itself. Neutrality of response to the bop bag, including its gender (until revealed), is important for the therapist to maintain, along with empathy for what the child has endured. Emphasis on the feeling or experience being conveyed by the child is critical to neutralizing the anger. Most children do not verbalize very much during this process. Sometimes I will ask the child, "Is there anything you want to tell this one?" Or "Is there anything you want this one to know?" If they remain silent, I let the question go.

When a child starts to hit, kick, or punch the bop bag, I start by providing feedback.

Therapist: You want this one to know you are angry. You would like this person to know what it feels like to be hurt. You want to tell them not to hurt you anymore.

Child: (Very angry but empowered; takes a sword or a gun or a baseball bat and puts a lot of energy into "hurting" the bop bag. The child spends a great deal of time beating it around the face—possible issues of identity—and the ears—perhaps indicates exposure to verbal abuse or violent arguments.)

Therapist: You want this one to know what it feels like to be hurt in the face . . . more than one time. . . . You want this one to know what it feels like to hear things that hurt. This one needs to learn a lesson. It needs to know what it feels like to get hurt a lot.

Child: Yeah, he needs to learn a lesson. I'm strong. (To the bop bag)
                  How do you like it? (The child continues to hit the bop bag.
                  As the child experiences the therapist's understanding of
                  the emotional events, the child goes deeper into his play.)

Therapist: You want this guy to know you are strong now. You have
                  some power over this guy now. Is there anything you want
                  to tell this guy?

At this point, it is the rare child who will talk directly to the bop bag.
Some children do; sometimes the bop bag symbolizes "God" or some
power that causes hard-to-understand things to happen. Sometimes it's a
person—an adult who has hurt them or the playground bully at school.
Sometimes it represents a force to be reckoned with. In any case, staying
with the feelings is crucial to healing. The most feedback I will provide is
in terms of the aggression: "That's gotta hurt." Children like to hear that,
and I will repeat it. Then I add: "You want this one to know what it feels
like to be hurt."

Child: His hands are stuck down; he can't use his hands.

Therapist: You want him to know what it feels like to be powerless. He
                  just has to take what you dish out. He just has to know what
                  it feels like to just take it.

Children are often in a position of powerlessness. This feedback is very
validating to the child's experience and feelings that are motivating the
aggressive behaviors. I have had very angry children hit the bop bag for
up to 45 minutes. It takes a lot of awareness and patience to continue to
"be" with a child and the angry feelings for a long period of time. My
experience is that as the child's feelings and experiences are validated by
appropriate responses to the bop bag, the need for aggression diminishes.

Therapist: We have five more minutes left to play for today. What
                  would you like this one to know before we leave for today?

Child: That he's going to jail (Metaphor for containment). I'm
                  putting him in jail! (Puts the bop bag in the corner, face to
                  the wall.) You don't look at me, you have to stay there.

Therapist: You feel safe now. He is in jail; he can't hurt you anymore.

You showed him how it feels to be hurt and how it feels to be in jail. He has to listen to you now.

It is very important for the therapist to know the child's environment and to make sure that the environment is safe for the child now. Children lose interest in beating up the bop bag the more their feelings are validated. If the aggression continues for more than about 10 sessions, sometimes I will say: "How else can you show this guy you're angry besides hitting him?" or I will remove the bop bag from the playroom and when asked where it is I reply: "Let's explore other ways of expressing angry feelings besides hitting, first, then you can tell that one all about it."

APPLICATION

Children exposed to violence often engage in internalized behaviors by exhibiting anxiety, depression, or withdrawal, or they engage in externalized behaviors such as aggression, delinquency, or hyperactivity. Sometimes the effects of violence on children will play out as social incompetence and lowered school performance as well as other problem behaviors. Research on the effects of violence on children show that these children are prone to suffer psychological damage in four general areas: (1) immediate trauma; (2) adverse effects on development; (3) living under high levels of stress, particularly fear of injury to themselves or their family; and (4) exposure to violent role models (Straus 1991). There are many techniques for helping children express and redirect their anger. Appropriate responses to aggression discharged with a bop bag in the playroom is only one avenue, but it is one that children choose often and therefore needs to be understood and utilized to effect positive change.

Reference

Straus, R. (1991). Children exposed to marital violence. In *Family Violence Across the Life Span: An Introduction*, ed. O. W. Barnett, C. L. Miller-Perrin, and K. V. Perrin. Los Angeles, CA: Thousand Oaks and Sage.

73

Disaster Dinosaurs

Risë VanFleet

INTRODUCTION

Disaster Dinosaurs are particularly useful for children who have experienced a trauma such as an accident or injury, lived through a disaster such as a hurricane or earthquake, or who have experienced family illness. This technique can be used individually or in groups. Disaster Dinosaurs creates a metaphor for injury and healing and provides children with an experience of mastery and control.

RATIONALE

When children are exposed to trauma or illness, they often feel helpless and frightened, just as adults do. Adults are able to talk about their experiences, but children do their "talking" through their play. Disaster Dinosaurs help children feel more in control when they are exposed to uncontrollable and anxiety-provoking events. They should be used as part of a comprehensive treatment plan.

DESCRIPTION

Materials needed for this play therapy technique are as follows:

1. Bendable dinosaurs (can be obtained inexpensively from Fun Express, phone 1-800-228-0122).

2. Plaster-cast, a mesh fabric coated with plaster powder (available from medical supply stores or craft stores, sometimes known as Rigid-Wrap).

3. Small bowl of warm water.

The therapist gives the child a dinosaur and uses one herself as well. The plaster mesh is cut into ½- to 1-inch strips, and several are provided for the child and therapist to use. The therapist begins by creating a brief story about the dinosaur:

> These dinosaurs have been in a disaster [or have had a really rough time, or have had something bad happen to them], and they've gotten hurt. What kind of disaster do you think it was? [This optional question can be posed to the child to involve them in the storytelling.] Well, they're hurt and in need of some help. I have some things here we can use to help them get better. We can put on some bandages and casts.

The therapist then shows the child how to dip the plaster mesh quickly in the water to soften it. Then the child applies the strips to whatever parts of the dinosaur's body that he feels needs a cast. The therapist puts some casts on her dinosaur as well, but lags behind the child so the child isn't influenced by the therapist's choices.

After the plaster strips are applied, the dinosaurs are set aside so the plaster can dry and harden (approximately 20 minutes). Another intervention can be used during this time. When the dinosaurs' casts are dry, the therapist can comment about how their dinosaurs are now going to be able to heal. The therapist can then briefly discuss with the child the various ways the dinosaur will be different: both negative ("It'll walk with a little limp") and positive ("It'll know how to help other dinosaurs who have been through similar disasters"). Ideas should be elicited from the child. This discussion should be kept very brief, lighthearted, and within the dinosaur metaphor.

It's important to let the child know that the dinosaurs' casts won't come off, but that people's casts do. This activity can include decorating the casts with markers, if desired.

APPLICATION

Disaster Dinosaurs can be used with children who have been hurt or injured, who have experienced traumatic events, or who have ill family members. This technique is best applied in the middle of the treatment process rather than at the beginning.

Chris, a 7-year-old boy, had been in a car accident with his family. No one was injured seriously, but the accident had been very frightening and everyone had some cuts and bruises. Following the accident, Chris experienced nightmares and a fear of riding in the car. Disaster Dinosaurs was used following release play therapy (Levy 1933) and concurrently with filial therapy (VanFleet 1994). Chris selected a black and blue dinosaur with a very long neck and tail. He wrapped plaster strips the entire length of the neck and at the tip of the tail. He asked to use more strips and then bandaged each of the dinosaur's legs. When the bandages had hardened, he colored two of the leg casts with markers. When finished, Chris said that the dinosaur was lucky to have someone "fix him up" and that he (the dinosaur) would eventually get all better.

References

Levy, D. M. (1933). The use of play technique as experimental procedure. *American Journal of Orthopsychiatry* 3:266–275.

VanFleet, R. (1994). *Filial Therapy: Strengthening Parent–Child Relationships Through Play*. Sarosota, FL: Professional Resource Exchange.

74

The Use of Toy Animals to Reveal Family Relationships

Dolores A. Mortimer

INTRODUCTION

Toy animals are listed among Axline's (1969) suggested playroom materials. According to Guerney (1983), "Axline's original list of toys is probably representative of what most therapists still use, in spite of the many recent innovations in toys" (p. 27). A basic premise of play therapy is that a child will reveal how he seems himself and his world through creative modalities and fantasy (Irwin and Rubin 1976). As therapists, we must learn to astutely observe, relate to, and decipher the messages the child is sending through the types of toys chosen, how they are used, the intensity of play, and the accompanying verbalizations.

The benefit of using play in family therapy is manifested many ways. It exposes underlying thoughts, feelings, and perceptions of each family member; engages family members in a pleasurable task; facilitates communication; and reveals the dynamics of how a particular family system is operating.

RATIONALE

Animals can take on a multitude of personality traits and have been used throughout the ages metaphorically to portray human strengths and weaknesses, emotions, value systems, and character development. Animals have been used in mythology, proverbs, fables, allegories, anecdotes, cartoons, poetry, and music to reveal a message, teach a lesson, or make a specific point. The therapist in turn can use play animals to gain insight into family relationships and facilitate a greater understanding among family members.

DESCRIPTION

Although it isn't necessary to have a multitude of play animals, it is desirable to have a few samples of wild animals, farm animals, some reptile or water animals, and a few dinosaurs. It is also advisable to include some animal families, or at least mother and baby combinations such as a cow and a calf or larger size cow and a small one. All the animals should be mixed together in a container in no particular order.

The technique can be used in a nondirective or directive mode, depending on the goal of the session, the developmental level of the child, and the information that is hoped to be acquired during the session. In the nondirective approach, the container is presented to the child: "Here is a box of different kinds of animals. You may want to look through the box and notice all the different kinds of animals. Then you can play with them in any way you would like."

In the directive approach, the therapist presents the container and says, "Here is a box of animals. Take each animal out of the box and carefully notice their size and the expression on their faces. Think about what each animal is like. For example, I think the deer is a quiet animal, very gentle like Bambi. You may think differently than I do about the deer, but that's okay. After you look at and think about the animals, and after they are all on the table, I'll give you your next direction." When the child has completed placing all the animals on the table say, "Now think about each person in your family. What does each person enjoy doing? How does each person behave? Choose one animal to be a person in your family. If everyone in your family, including yourself, were an animal, which one would each person be?" After the child chooses an animal for each person, you can process how each person is like the associated animal: "What are some things he or she does that is like the [animal]? Show me how the [animal] behaves. What does he/she say? What happens next?"

While most children find it difficult to express ambivalent feelings about family members or the chaos or conflicts in the family, using toy animals as a medium for expression removes any anxiety the children may experience. They are free to express their innermost thoughts, feelings, and perceptions of themselves and their world.

APPLICATION

This method has been used successfully with children who have experienced parental separation, divorce, or abandonment. It has also been used with children who demonstrate oppositional behavior, attention-deficit disorder (ADD), attention-deficit/hyperactivity disorder (ADHD), anxious or perfectionistic children, and children who are experiencing instability in family life due to a variety of reasons, including a parent who is chronically ill or one who is chemically dependent.

Billy, a 4-year-old, was described by his parents as very active. His parents had received several complaints by his preschool teachers of Billy's being physically aggressive toward other children. He had difficulties making and keeping friends because of his lack of social skills and his inability to appropriately interact with other children. Billy appeared to have a stable home environment. He enjoyed the luxury of a stay-at-home mom, and the stability of loving, caring parents who were both college graduates. Yet they were at a loss as to why their son demonstrated such aggressive tendencies.

I decided to use the nondirective approach to gain insight into Billy's behavior. He was given the box of animals, and he really delighted in playing with its contents. His play became very intense and there was much fighting among the animals. He played out a lot of conflict. I noticed that there was a fierce looking tiger, which fought with all the other animals and seemed to win all the time. Most of Billy's comments during the play were growls from the tiger and some screams and sighs from the animals that lost the battle with the tiger.

Toward the end of the session I asked questions.

Counselor: If you had to be one of these animals, which one would you be?

Billy   (Broad smile and great enthusiasm): This one, the tiger!

Counselor: How come you would choose to be the tiger?

Billy   (very proudly): Because he's active! I'm pretty active!

Counselor: Who says you are active?

Billy: Mom says so. But I am [active] because I want to be.

Counselor: What does active mean?

Billy: It means fight.

Counselor: Do you like being active?

Billy: Not fighting active.

Counselor: What kind of active do you like to be?

Billy: I just like to roar around!

It was quite obvious that Billy heard himself being labeled as active. This is not unusual. Many parents affectionately label their children as "active," "hyper," or, as I have seen on one toddler's T-shirt, "Here comes Trouble!" However, even young children begin to conceptualize what these labels mean. After hearing the word *active* associated so often with his name, Billy began to internalize his conception of it. Billy associated the word *active* with fighting. It was a self-fulfilling prophecy. Billy demonstrated being active with other children through physical aggression. He just thought he had to be active because that's what people said he was. But the statement, "I just like to roar around," meant "I just want to be heard; I just want to be noticed." This statement makes a lot of sense from a 4-year-old's perspective. Preschoolers are at a very egocentric stage of social development.

Mother was encouraged to refrain from using the "active" label, and to ask others who repeatedly communicated with Billy to do the same. Slowly, Billy began to learn appropriate ways to socialize as we began to positively reframe what the term *active* could mean.

Gerald, an 8-year-old, demonstrated an inability to focus at school. He was underachieving academically, and he was described by the teachers as a "behavior problem." At my first meeting with him I presented the box of animals. He enjoyed looking at the animals and taking them out of the box. He was very methodical about taking each animal out of the box and pairing it with a similar animal. I noticed all the like animals were standing next to each other (larger horse with the smaller horse, cow with calf; large bear, small bear, etc.). He was quiet while he worked and I was careful not to speak because I did not want to break his concentration. Once all the animals were paired, he laid the large pig down next to the small pig. The two were facing each other. Then he sighed, "There, all the Mommies are with their babies."

"Yes, I see all the Mommies are with their babies," I reflected.

"Mommies should never leave their babies," Gerald continued.

"You're right. I understand. Mommies should never leave their babies." I affirmed his beliefs and then questioned something I had observed:

"All the animals are standing up, but these two are lying down. How come they are lying down?"

"The Mommy is nursing the baby," Gerald explained.

The information gathered from this first session revealed to me much that I could work with in the sessions that followed. Gerald's mother suffered from mental illness, was hospitalized, and eventually became so distraught that she abandoned the family. His father could not cope with raising a child on his own, so Gerald's grandparents were raising him. Gerald felt abandoned and confused. Through his play he revealed his belief that mothers should be nurturing and he could not understand why his mother would leave him. In sessions following this initial session, nurturing themes were played out through art and nondirected play. We were able to process his feelings of abandonment, sadness, and loneliness. He was also able to eventually come to terms with the idea that his mother's leaving had nothing to do with him, his behavior, or her lack of love for him as her child. It had more to do with her inability to cope and to express her love for him because of her illness.

Play is powerful, energizing, soothing, and healing. Using play animals is a creative, nonthreatening, and effective way for children to reveal their innermost thoughts and feelings regarding their family relationships. It is a potent and masterful tool for the therapist.

References

Axline, V. (1969). *Play Therapy*. New York: Ballantine.

Guerney, L. (1983). Client-centered (non-directive) play therapy. In *Handbook of Play Therapy*, ed. C. E. Schaefer and K. J. O'Connor, pp. 21–64. New York: Wiley.

Irwin, E., and Rubin, J. (1976). Art and drama interviews: decoding symbolic messages. *Art Psychotherapy* 3:169–175.

75

Let-Out-Your-Anger Challenge

Erika L. Surkin

INTRODUCTION

Suppression of anger and lack of awareness of angry feelings are often the cause of children's behavioral difficulties as well as the root of many anxiety-related disorders. Expression rather than suppression is the goal of this technique. Children learn to experience active catharsis while the therapist gains insight into those issues that create problems for the client.

RATIONALE

Barry C. Ginsberg's (1993) exploration of catharsis indicates that emotional expression and release is an essential part of psychotherapy. Failure to express emotions causes maladaptive attitudes and behavior. Verbal expression of sources of anger paired with active emotional release moves the client toward a new integrative level by providing a source of self-expression and assertive behavior. Expression of anger in the presence of a therapist may help to achieve a sense of release, promoting self-acceptance. The therapist's validation by encouraging the vigorous release of anger is an important step in establishing the therapeutic alliance. When the client verbalizes the cause of anger, the therapist can then plan appropriate intervention in order to facilitate effective problem-solving skills.

DESCRIPTION

The required materials are round 10" or 12" light-colored balloons, a quick-drying ballpoint pen, and Snapper Hands, which may be found in toy and novelty stores. Balloons immediately create a sense of playfulness in the therapy room. Deep breathing is a beneficial side effect of blowing up the balloon, resulting in a state of relaxation. The child inflates the balloons to less-than-complete size so they don't pop during the drawing phase. Use one balloon to match each family member and instruct the child to draw a face on each balloon to represent each member of the family (including himself).

Snapper Hands are stretchy rubber-like toys made in the shape of a hand attached to a long, think handle. Some are sticky, which provide extra excitement. The child is encouraged to take the balloons one at a time, state why he is angry at that person (using an angry tone of voice), and then spank the balloon. As the child "spanks" the balloon, the therapist should join in, encouraging the child to hit it again in an excited tone of voice, mirroring the child's anger and affirming the right to feel the emotion. The amount of effort required to direct the stretchy toy, hit the balloon, and untangle the hand soon creates an atmosphere of fun as well as physical exercise. The more effort expended, the greater the emotional release. If possible, several reasons for anger may be expressed for each family member. Allow the child the freedom to choose the sequence of balloons.

APPLICATION

Expression of anger in an accepting and safe environment is an important step in the therapeutic process for anxious children as well as oppositional/defiant children. Achieving emotional release will move the child to the next step in the therapeutic process. Observe the artistic expression as the child draws each face, noting size of drawing, facial expression, and physical similarity or differences between family members. The order in which the choices proceed indicates the child's level of comfort in expressing reasons for anger. This is particularly informative with children of divorced families. Some children may not be able to admit to any anger toward a particular family member, which may be an important indicator of anxiety, feelings of lack of safety, and concern about loss of love. The child's stating the reasons for his anger in the therapist's presence, followed by the therapist's encouragement of the expression of anger, creates an atmosphere of acceptance. The livelier the encouragement, the freer the child will become in expressing feelings and thoughts. Buried issues may surface as children experience release by going through a list of grievances. This is particularly notable as the client "spanks" the balloon representing himself.

This technique is not intended to be a device for change, but rather a cathartic technique. Recording the child's statements will provide content for future therapeutic interventions. Vigorous use of the Snapper Hand will result in a tired, flushed, and relaxed client who has experienced emotional release.

Reference

Ginsberg, B. G. (1993). Catharsis. In *The Therapeutic Powers of Play*, ed. C. E. Schaefer, pp. 107–141. Northvale, NJ: Jason Aronson.

76

Joining with Symbolic and Metaphorical Play

Carol Whited

INTRODUCTION

In nondirective play therapy, the child is totally free to choose his medium, and the therapist should remain respectful of this principle. However, I have found a way to join with the child in whatever his choice may be, using a playful manner but one that incorporates meaningful underlying symbolic content.

Initially, the child will probably not be aware of the implications of his choice, but the therapist can choose to be intuitively aware of meanings in the context of the child's life. The nature of the therapist's symbolic/ metaphorical associations provides a unique connection with the child and his play.

This process must be approached with care, in order to be true to the symbolic meanings, without forcing the child into an artificial agenda, and/or breaking down important defensive barriers too soon.

RATIONALE

Even a very young child will quickly respond to symbolic play that enters his reality, without needing any explanation on a cognitive level. The therapist gives the play a frame of reference and if one is successful, the play seems to take off on its own, driven by the authentic quality of the moment. If the child does not appear receptive, you might wait for another opportune moment and try again.

This style of joining in play becomes therapeutic when the child, on some level, realizes that the therapist understands him in a way that goes deeper than anything he has ever experienced before. The child will return to it time and again, creatively expanding the play until he feels fulfilled.

At first, the child may not, on a conscious level, understand how the play is part of his own life. It is very important, particularly at the beginning, not to intellectualize, explain, or ask questions that may intrude on the metaphorical nature of communication between therapist and child. The therapist can simply put into words what is happening in the play.

DESCRIPTION

The child may choose the same toys or medium week after week, expanding his play but always including a particular toy or medium. This becomes a clue to what meanings he may unconsciously be putting on this item. At the same time, the therapist has knowledge of the total milieu in which the child has lived.

Using this awareness, the therapist begins to extrapolate some possibilities, and muses to herself, "I wonder if that big motorcycle could be Dad and the little motorcycle could be Johnny?" At this point, if Dad is incarcerated, for example, and Johnny has mentioned it often, the therapist might put some blocks in a square and say, "Hey, Big Motorcycle, you have to stay in here and can't get out!" (implying a jail). If the child understands, he might put the big motorcycle into the square and then knock down the blocks, saying in a loud, angry voice, "But I'm gonna get him out!"

He then plays "getting Dad out of jail" over and over, with his little motorcycle, finding relief in the play that fulfills his fantasy of rescuing and being reunited with Dad. At first, the therapist can merely acknowledge this wish: "That little motorcycle sure wants to help the big motorcycle." But in future sessions the therapist might be able to talk more directly about Johnny's feelings for his dad, feelings that might be more ambivalent than originally expressed.

APPLICATION

This style of therapeutic journey can be used in a number of ways and with the materials usually found in the playroom. The point is to connect with the child's chosen material and, with a few minor props, to modify the play slightly but continue to conform to the child's agenda. Thus, the therapist can help the child make an intuitive association. Here are a few examples:

Trees and beautiful rocks (resembling a cemetery) can be incorporated into a child's play of repetitive burying in the sand, when there has been a death in the family. A child's playing with two houses, little blocks, and fenced-in places may represent the child's worry about his divorced parents. The therapist might use an animal family, rather than human figures, to represent Mom, Dad, and a child. Putting Dad in one space and Mom in the other, the therapist can add a path of marbles to connect Mom and Dad and set the child animal on the path, perhaps playfully having him run back and forth from one house to another.

Rage or fear of angry feelings represented by wild animals can be handled by using little plastic fences to form safe places for the ferocious animals, where they can calm down and feel safe. Band-Aids placed on baby dolls, on the therapist, or on the child himself may denote repair of physical and emotional abuse. The therapist communicates her part in helping to make things better with her cooperation in the repair and with the doctor kit. She protests loudly over shots that hurt her, saying, perhaps, "No more hurting!"

This process can be applied to the kinds of distress children experience, such as acting-out behavior, past sexual trauma, domestic violence, bereavement, divorce, rage, and anxiety and fears.

The following vignette is an example of how I have used this creative technique with good results.

The mother of Scotty, a 4-year-old with severe temper tantrums and oppositional behavior, described his behavior as "out of control." In play group, Scotty began to drive his car all over the playroom, knocking toys off the shelves, and crashing wildly into other toys and into other children's play things. I grabbed another car and said, "Uh-oh, Mr. Car! You're out of control! You've got to go inside this safe garage until you're back in control!" I set up some large cardboard blocks and put a "roof" on them. Scotty immediately drove his car into the garage. With a sigh of relief, he said, "He has to stay there until he's back in control." Several times he checked to see if the car could manage safely. Sometimes it "escaped" and acted-up again, and each time Scotty put him back until the car could be "trusted." Eventually, the car could control himself from crashing into other toys and people. Each week, Scotty returned to this game on his own with great delight, starting with an out-of-control car, building a safe garage for it and teaching the car to have self-control. It even became a helping car, with a tow line, in case other cars got in trouble.

I never spoke to Scotty directly about his needing to improve his out of control behavior, but often during the play I would say, "You are really showing that car how to stay in control," or "You are teaching the car how to be helpful," thus validating his great success with that car. Scotty's own behavior improved at home and at school, and Scotty felt very good about himself.

77

Knock-Down Talk-Down

Richard Bromfield

INTRODUCTION

Though frustrating and angering experience torments many children, they often cannot speak of it directly. Though their distress is obvious to an onlooker, even with our inviting words they may deny that anyone or anything upsets them. Knock-Down Talk-Down offers these children a safe and pleasurable opportunity to broach the very subjects bothering them.

RATIONALE

When children are unable to express their frustration, they can develop all sorts of problems, including stomachaches and headaches, excessive guilt and self-hatred, and inhibition. In the course of this game children feel more willing to share pieces of their frustration, both in words and in action, and to experience that doing so results, not in disaster or punishment, but in relief and a freeing up.

344

DESCRIPTION

The therapist sets up dolls and action figures on a table top or platform of blocks. The child is given small nerf-type balls.

Therapist: Before you can knock these down, you need to tell me something, anything that your teacher does that you don't like.

Child: He doesn't call on me when I raise my hand.

Therapist: Okay. (Child will readily understand the cue to throw the balls to knock down the dolls.)

After setting up the dolls again, the therapist repeats asking the same question about other people in the child's life (siblings, parents, friends, relatives, classmates, and even the therapist). The therapist goes slowly, allowing plenty of time for the child to state her case, and refrains from probing every one of the complaints (for that would grow tiresome quickly). Also, it is important to ask for comments on a lot of people (not just the one or two persons the therapist thinks are most relevant). For the aggressive child it is particularly important to maintain the framework (i.e., no throwing without some kind of revelation).

As the game proceeds, children tend to grow more talkative, more delightedly aggressive and freer. Those with somatic discomfort often find that their pains fade or disappear while playing. If the therapist resists the temptation to pursue, the children will likely stop more frequently on their own and for longer periods to explore their feelings.

APPLICATION

This game is useful with a child who struggles with frustration and anger. It is especially helpful for children who experience undue anxiety, inhibition, undeserved guilt, and somatic complaints.

78

Relaxation Training: Bubble Breaths

Neil Cabe

INTRODUCTION

Most children are unaware of their own mind–body connections. That is, they do not realize that their emotional states produce physical reactions. From a clinical perspective, the physical reactions to both anger and anxiety may require relaxation training in order to help children over-come their problems. Anger may itself be a cover for anxiety in a child; effective relaxation training can help a young client manage both. The bubble breath is one tool the therapist can easily teach, and the child easily learn to implement.

RATIONALE

When children begin to feel anxious, or when anger threatens to overwhelm them, one necessary tool is an immediate technique to de-escalate the physical reactions of these two powerful emotions, before behaviors and acting out occur.

When children become anxious or angry, a series of physical reactions occur as a result of a complex set of physiological processes. Most prominently, the adrenaline "rush" children encounter, which may actually feel good to them, causes vasoconstriction, with blood vessels growing slightly smaller. This in turn causes an increase in both heart rate and shallow breathing, as the brain calls for more blood and greater amounts of oxygen. Teaching the child deep and controlled breathing can slow heart rate, increase oxygen, and send messages to the blood vessels to return to more normal conditions.

Teaching children simple ways to address these physical conditions not only helps to relieve the physical responses, but also helps to ease the emotional distress and, perhaps even more importantly, teaches them that they are empowered enough to begin to manage both emotions and behaviors. The bubble breath can effectively help to achieve these goals.

DESCRIPTION

Blowing bubbles engages several of the child's senses simultaneously, allows interactions between therapist and child in a nonthreatening way, and is an inexpensive activity that can be done in almost any setting. Commercial bubbles are available at any toy or department store. The activity can become even more interactive if the child and therapist make the concoction together (see below). I always perform this activity with the child.

Begin by simply filling the room with bubbles, blowing them with abandon. Most children will "pop" the bubbles as they fall, and some will even bite them. Flavored bubbles are available and grape is the favorite in my office.

After a few minutes of this, invite the child to try to blow only one bubble. It is harder than most children imagine, but easily done with some practice. The focus then becomes deep breathing and controlled exhaling. I try to teach the child to breathe from the tummy, using the deep breaths associated with meditation. Have children place their hand on their tummy and feel the hand rise and fall as they breathe. The calming effect on them is almost immediate.

At this point, I explain to children that when they get angry or anxious, the brain calls for more air, but the lungs are working too hard being anxious and can't send enough up to their heads. If they breathe deeply, their brain will tell their heart to slow, and their lungs to work more efficiently. I then make it clear by describing the physical reactions to anger or anxiety that they can keep angry behaviors from happening if they learn to take bubble breaths whenever they feel themselves becoming angry, nervous, or tense. One good example that seems to work with most children is how they feel before tests at school.

Practice the bubble breaths with the children until they can produce one single large bubble regularly. Then ask them to remember to take bubble breaths whenever they feel themselves becoming angry or nervous. I tell them that it takes three breaths—not two and not four—to accomplish this. The point in this instruction is to force the children to focus only on breathing. As they learn to breathe, they also learn to relax.

APPLICATION

I have used this technique successfully with children in all age ranges. Adolescents as well as younger children enjoy the activity, and I have used it with some adults who were sent to me for anger management treatment. For many clients, it is the first time they have ever been made aware of the mind–body connection involved with their anger and anxiety.

This is an excellent group activity, which I have used even in workshops I have done for groups of over 200. The sight, smell, tactility, and even occasionally taste of the bubbles seem to be healing almost by themselves. The technique is useful in treating anger, anxiety, tension, relaxation training, test phobia, and other anxiety-producing situations.

Variations

A number of variations allow greater client interaction. Instead of the small commercial bubble wand in each bottle of bubbles, try some of the following:

Bend a coat hanger into a large circle, wrap it with yarn, and dip it in a pie pan filled with bubble mixture.

Kitchen utensils will often produce bubbles: old time potato mashers, spatulas, wire whisks, funnels, straws, small pieces of hose or tubing, and strainers all make great bubble machines.

Bend pipe cleaners into interesting shapes.

Six-pack soft drink holders make multiple bubbles.

Put some food coloring in the bubble mixture, blow the bubbles into a pie pan, and lay a piece of paper over the bubbles for a "bubble print."

Use an empty and clean soft margarine container, put one hole in the lid for a straw, and put another on the other side. Blow in one side, and watch as the bubbles flow out the other.

Tie a long piece of yarn or twine, soak it in the bubble mixture, and with the child, wave it in the air making bubbles big enough to put him or her inside it.

Coat little hands with the bubble mixture, make a circle with the thumb and forefinger forming a loose fist, and blow hand bubbles.

Bubble Mixture Recipe

Thoroughly mix the following:

1 cup Joy Ultra or Dawn Ultra dish-washing liquid

10 cups water

½ cup Karo syrup (commercial glycerin may be used if no one is going to eat the bubbles)

Food coloring, if desired

You may also add flavoring if the children would like to bite their bubbles. The bubbles taste a little bit like soapy grapes, but in such small quantities no harm to the child is done. Increase or decrease the recipe measures depending on the quantity of bubble mixture desired.

79

Exclusive Use of a Dedicated Toy Box

Otto Weininger and Linda Perlis

INTRODUCTION

The use of a separate toy box for each child in treatment, containing toys and materials used exclusively by that child during the therapy, is both a technique as well as an essential component of the contemporary Kleinian approach to play psychotherapy—as essential as the use of toys themselves (Klein 1955)!

RATIONALE

Each child in play psychotherapy has a toy box that contains all of the toys, materials, creations, and productions of the treatment. The box and contents are unique and specific to each child and rapidly become an invaluable diagnostic aid and an essential component of treatment. This toy box becomes significant both as a symbol and container for the child's inner world and as a concrete representation of all aspects of the therapy, including the relationship with the therapist and the ongoing progress of treatment.

The use of materials dedicated to each child has its origins in the Kleinian tradition and is widely used in treatment centers such as the Tavistock Clinic in Great Britain. It remains one of the delineating features of the play therapy technique as pioneered by Melanie Klein. Its use and significance in play psychotherapy is derived from her emphasis on the importance of understanding the inner world of children and their fantasies, as they enact them repeatedly through their use of materials and toys, and in the relationship with the therapist. The boy box comes to represent all aspects of the therapeutic process as well as elements of the inner world of the child and the real and fantasied relationships to external figures.

DESCRIPTION

The box of toys and materials is assembled for each child by the therapist before the beginning of treatment, based on the needs and diagnosis of the child as determined during the assessment process. The box contains a variety of simple toys, for example, figures, cars, animals, and so on, as well as scissors, tape, glue, paper, plasticene, Play Doh, crayons/markers, one or more balls, and any other materials or items that the play therapist feels might be of specific use for that child. For example, children who are felt to be in need of the expression of aggression might have made available to them suitable toys for this purpose, such as balls and/or plasticene. Materials or toys may be added during the course of treatment, as are any items, drawings, or productions made in the sessions. Nevertheless, the box and its contents remain intact throughout the course of the entire treatment. The boxes are kept in a separate and secure storage space, perhaps a locked cabinet or room. The box is brought into the playroom prior to each session. A simple cardboard file box with a lid is sufficient, although at the Tavistock Clinic, and other locations, separate drawers are assigned to individual children.

The toy box, essential furniture, and perhaps a few large play items such as a doll house are the only materials available to the child and therapist in the playroom. Generic and/or shared toys are not present. Some therapists provide shared board games; however, it would appear to the child from session to session that only she uses these games. Other therapists have on hand basic art supplies, such as markers and paper, and bring them out at the start of sessions, rather than keeping duplicate sets in each child's box.

APPLICATION

The use of the box is seen as an essential component of the treatment and its significance for the therapeutic process and relationship emerges in the first session, when the box is produced and its contents and use are discussed with the child. In this first and important session, the child quickly understands that these toys, and by extension himself, are special. They will not be used, or shared, or even seen by anyone else, and will be available at each session. Through this communication the child is immediately able to begin to appreciate the private and confidential nature of the therapeutic relationship. The uniqueness of the setting and its difference from other situations in the child's life, such as the reality of sharing toys with siblings, or with other children in a classroom, is gradually understood by each child. When the child learns that the box will not even be shown to parents, this emphasizes the separateness of the treatment relationship. It is also discussed that the toys and materials belong to the child, and because of these aspects of control and ownership, the toys take on a symbolic importance to the child in his use and/or destruction of them. Whereas one might assume that children will want to take their toys home, in fact just the opposite occurs—children frequently bring things from home to keep safe or put in their box.

The fantasy or exclusivity, often so predominant and necessary, especially in the beginning phases of treatment, is enhanced through the presence of the toy box. It is always an important point in treatment when a child can relinquish her omnipotent control over the therapist and begin to ask about the boxes of other children, and show curiosity, envy, and other imaginings and feelings about other child and adult patients. For some children this emerges first in interest they might express in other boxes, or in anxiety they may express about other children seeing their box, touching their things, or stealing items from the box. Reactions to the presence or absence of any of the contents, including expressions of disappointment or demands for new toys, are important aspects to understand in the treatment.

The ongoing dialogue between child and therapist as to the nature and quantity of the contents throughout the course of treatment can reveal aspects of the child's feelings of sufficiency, need, greed, and/or impoverishment in his relationship to the therapist as well as to others in his life. The box records the progress of treatment and the work done as particular toys are ignored or discarded, only to be returned to in time of stress or regression, or when remembering previous sessions. It holds the shared understanding that the child and therapist have evolved, which, when internalized, helps the child carry the therapist into his home and school life and thereby function more effectively.

The manner in which a child approaches her box both initially, and throughout the course of treatment, reveals aspects about her feelings about herself in relation to important persons in her life, both as they exist in reality and as she imagines them to be in fantasy. Some children are very inhibited in approaching the box and it is almost as if they are frightened by its contents. Others behave in a wilder and more aggressive fashion, tossing the materials around the room or dumping the box upside down. In part, these actions can be used to assess a child's expression of aggression and/or other feelings of the moment.

In addition to unique and child-specific reactions to the contents of boxes, similar variations are quickly expressed with respect to the box itself. Some children crayon on the box, either in an effort to embellish it or decorate it, or in a seeming effort to destroy or deface it. These actions and expressions often reveal elements of the child's feelings about significant persons in his life.

Yet another use of the box and contents arises in the context of the central Kleinian concept of reparation, in which a child, through the use of the box and contents, can symbolically repair, or restore, important persons whom the child fears she may have damaged in fantasy, as a result of her aggressive and demanding thoughts and wishes. Through the destruction and subsequent repair and/or decoration of toys and box, and in the addition of toys and creations to the box, this important restorative element can be repetitively worked through by the child, in relation to both the parents and the therapist.

An aspect that often emerges in the use of the box is the drawing by a child of a part of himself, often a "bad" or frightening part, that he projects onto the box. For example a 4-year-old drew a picture of a zombie and insisted that he be helped to have this written on the box. A 7-year-old drew a picture of a monster on the box and printed his name underneath it. The box itself may be incorporated into the play, as it was by one child who carefully cut a handle into the top to use it as a shield. The box sometimes takes on a magical protective and safety function for children whose inner or real lives are chaotic or frightening.

The box and its contents stand in the place of the verbal communications and free associations of adult patients in therapy. The box records the ongoing nature of the communications between therapist and child, and many children will look into their box before beginning a session, as if searching for a concrete reminder of the content of previous sessions. All play therapists appreciate the remarkable ability of children to pick up where they left off from one session to the next and this is enhanced by the accessibility of the items in the box. Plasticene figures or art work in progress can be retrieved and play resumed. Of course this also speaks to the potency of the play therapy process, as well as to the use of the box, since children will do this even without a special box.

Children derive a sense of familiarity and comfort from the box, and from the ability they gradually believe their therapist has to hold them in his or her mind from session to session. The box functions literally and metaphorically as a container—a concrete but also psychic receptacle for the feelings, thoughts, ideas, imaginings, and enactments of the child in treatment. It is particularly useful as a symbolic holding space for a child's anxiety. Children speak to their boxes as if they were able to hear them and leave feelings and things behind for safekeeping or for self-protection and preservation from session to session. When apparently overcome by anxiety, children often go and look in their boxes for reassurance.

The box is kicked, raged at, sat on, ignored, ravaged, feared, and embraced. All aspects of the child's inner world are projected onto the box and contents, such as the relationship to the therapist and hence, through the transference, the relationship to significant others, usually the mother. It provides a link between the outer world left behind with the parent in the waiting room and the constructed reality of the playroom. The presence of the box affirms the continuity and reality of the therapeutic relationship while at the same time allowing for the free space in which a new emotional experience can be mutually constructed.

The box symbolically contains the therapeutic experience of the child and stands for the containing function of the therapist. It becomes an important part of the termination process, as a child and therapist remember times they experienced together, and select those toys or items that will be taken away, and those that will be left with the therapist as a reparative symbol of the enduring link between them.

Reference

Klein, M. (1955). The psycho-analytic play technique: its history and significance. In *Envy and Gratitude and Other Works, 1946–1963*, pp. 122–140. London: Hogarth, 1975.

Section Six

Group Play Techniques

80

Dynamic Dinosaurs

Risë VanFleet

INTRODUCTION

Dynamic Dinosaurs are an effective group ice-breaking technique. They permit children to express themselves without getting too personal, which is particularly useful for children who are uncomfortable with self-disclosure or with their involvement in a group. This technique has been used with children from preschool through high school, and even with adults. Needed for this technique are bendable dinosaurs. These can be obtained inexpensively in four different dinosaur styles from the Fun Express (phone 1-800-228-1002).

RATIONALE

Direct self-disclosure can be threatening, especially during the early stages of group therapy. On the other hand, when therapy time is limited, it's important for the therapist to move into relevant issues as quickly as possible. One of the great advantages of play therapy is its ability to provide sufficient distance for children to express themselves and work through their issues without risking their self-image or self-esteem. Dynamic Dinosaurs are designed to help children move quickly toward their therapeutic issues while learning more about each other in less direct ways. The dinosaurs used are appealing, yet somewhat neutral in appearance, so children can project many different feelings, interests, and issues with them.

DESCRIPTION

Each child is given a bendable dinosaur. The therapist asks each child in the group to spend a few minutes individually with his or her dinosaur, getting to know it. Then the children are asked to name their dinosaurs and to bend them into a position that expresses something about their dinosaurs' personalities. The therapist participates in this activity as well.

When everyone is ready, the therapist asks each child to introduce his or her dinosaur to the group. The therapist can bring this activity to a close by asking the children what they thought of meeting all the dinosaurs. It's advisable to keep the conversation within the metaphor.

The dinosaurs can be used in subsequent sessions as well. The therapist can give instructions such as the following:

"Bend your dinosaurs into a position that shows how they feel today."

"Bend your dinosaurs to show how they feel when they're mad."

"Bend your dinosaurs to show how they feel when they're sad."

"Bend them to show how they'd feel if the other dinosaurs teased them."

The therapist can then ask the children to show their dinosaurs and make some comments about their dinosaurs' feelings. The therapist need not prolong the discussions each time. The atmosphere needs to stay light and pleasant during this activity.

When using the dinosaurs for multiple sessions, it's important to permit the children to use the same dinosaur each time. A system such as keeping the dinosaurs in separate envelopes labeled with each child's name can be developed. When the dinosaurs are used for the last time, the children may take them home.

APPLICATION

Dynamic Dinosaurs can be used with a wide range of problems. They are particularly useful in group play therapy to help children begin to interact with each other, and subsequently to help them express various feelings. The therapist can describe a limitless number of situations to which the children's dinosaurs can react. The dinosaurs provide an imaginary context in which real-life problems can be tackled.

81

The "Good At" Play-Doh Figure

Paris Goodyear-Brown

INTRODUCTION

I have worked for the past two years exclusively with children ages 3 to 5 who have experienced severe trauma or who are categorized as severely emotionally disturbed. Some of these children are violent, all of them are regressed in at least one area of development, and many of them are stuck, developmentally, in the "terrible twos." This technique came intuitively out of a play session in which I was trying to find ways to engage a 3-year-old in the arduous work of positive self-examination.

RATIONALE

Preschoolers are egocentric by their very nature and believe that everything happens because of them. Thus, children internalize trauma and incorporate negative events and beliefs about these events into their already fragile self-esteem. One of the primary treatment goals for these children should be to increase their self-esteem. However, work with children of this age can be complicated by the limitations of their burgeoning linguistic abilities and the concreteness of their thinking. They have difficulty grasping the abstract concepts of self-esteem and positive self-talk and it is up to the therapist to invent ways of concretely engaging them in this process. This exercise begins with the widely used therapeutic medium of Play Doh and involves the use of colored stones that metaphorically represent the beautiful qualities in each of us. The children are engaged on a sensorimotor level and are distracted from the discomfort that can arise when they are asked to focus on their positive attributes. The same 3-year-old child who stared at me blankly when I asked him to tell me one nice thing about himself was able to make fifteen positive self-statements in a row while playing this game.

DESCRIPTION

This technique can be used whenever a child first chooses Play Doh in the playroom or can be introduced as early as the third session. The only materials needed are two containers of Play Doh and some colored stones (or beads, gems, marbles, etc.). The child and the therapist each choose a color of Play Doh. The client is invited to make whatever he likes while the therapist begins to form a deep cup-like formation with her Play Doh (set aside some Play Doh for the next step). The therapist then makes a flat circle (big enough to cover the base) and invites the child to make a face on the circle with some of the colored stones. While the child is doing this, the therapist fills up the hollow base with stones. The face is then put on top of the base and the therapist begins to talk about how people may all look the same from outside, but it's when you really get to look inside (take off the top) that you get to see all the neat things inside a person.

The therapist then says, "Let's pretend that this Play Doh person is me. I have lots of neat things inside me. For instance, I'm good at . . . playing [therapist picks one bead out of the Play Doh figure and hands it to the child], I'm good at . . . swinging on the playground [gives client a second bead]," and so on. The therapist's statements should model for the child the phrase "I'm good at . . ." followed by a simple behavior that is stated in age-appropriate language. The therapist can pretend to have trouble thinking of things and enlist the client's help in generating ideas. After the therapist has made one positive self-statement for each bead and the child is holding all the beads, the therapist can invite the client to pour them all back into the Play-Doh figure and put the lid back on. Then it's the child's turn! I thought that I would have to have a two-tiered token economy system for this technique to work (i.e., so many colored stones gets you a tattoo), but the act of picking out a stone with every "good at" statement and handing it to the therapist has been enough of an incentive for children in my own practice. Every client that I have tried this with has been able to make at least five positive self-statements and sometimes as many as twenty!

APPLICATION

This technique only takes five to ten minutes and is often helpful if used at the end of a session to build up clients before they are sent back to the home environment. Children as young as 3 years old are able to play this game and make simple "good at" statements. One application of this technique is to help clients create a hollow figure that will be permanent and represent themselves. After the initial game is played, each session can be ended by thinking up one or two new "good at" statements, attaching them to a stone, or rolling them up and putting them inside the figure. As part of the termination process, all the positive self-statements are reviewed and the client takes the figure full of "good at" statements home to combat future negative self-talk.

This technique can also be used in a group setting. In the beginning, group members can make their own figures full of stones and share their own "good at" statements with the group. If a child has trouble making positive self-statements, the group can help generate them based on positive attributes they see in the child. During termination, all group members can participate in making one large figure, filling it with stones, and then generating statements about what the group as a whole has been "good at." In closing, each member keeps a stone to remember the group experience and to transfer the therapeutic gains to other life arenas.

82

Chinese Jump Rope

Bernadette H. Beyer

INTRODUCTION

This activity offers flexibility in terms of the group focus. The basic structure of using a Chinese jump rope for the children to hold onto during the group session remains constant. The therapist selects the content of the discussion that is appropriate for the group based on the stage of the group and the issues that have surfaced. I discovered by accident that having a jump rope for the group members to grasp hold of has deepened the group experience. The jump rope becomes an object for the members to discharge some of their anxiety onto in a safe manner. Anxious or impulsive members will often twist or pull at the rope when their comfort level goes down. The jump rope is comparable to using a talking stick, stuffed animal, or squish ball that is passed around as members take their turn in the discussion. The rope also serves the purpose of maintaining interconnectedness between the group's members as the sharing unfolds. The circular form contributes to building group cohesion. The foundation for developing this technique is based on the work of Dr. Tom Smith (1996). My supervisee, Susan Wilson, first introduced me to Smith's work on challenge education activities. I have adapted Smith's work on challenge education activities to fit the needs of children engaged in play therapy.

RATIONALE

My play therapy groups are typically for girls and boys ages 7 to 12 with up to eight members per group. The Chinese jump rope technique helps lower the members' defenses and encourages the safe expression of emotionally charged issues in a nonthreatening manner. The exercise is an invitation to bring painful or uncomfortable issues into the group process. The children frequently choose to disclose their problems regarding low self-esteem, family conflicts, temper outbursts, sibling rivalry, and peer difficulties.

I am often able to perform an ongoing assessment of both the group as a whole as well as each child's progress based on what information is revealed during this activity. As the children hear the other group members disclosing secrets, fears, or wishes, they recognize they are not alone in their feelings. Resistant children will often take the risk to open up more fully to the group process as their anxiety is lowered through the play.

The Chinese jump rope technique is also effective to use for bringing closure to the group process. Frequently, the children have been focusing intensely on their internal dynamics during the session. It is important to help the children prepare to leave the world of play therapy and reenter their external reality. If the therapist does not assist the children in making this transition, the parents my report some acting-out behavior following the weekly group session. Through the Chinese jump rope activity, the child will have an opportunity to regroup, review gains, and/or integrate the emotions experienced during the session.

DESCRIPTION

Use a Chinese jump rope, tubular webbing (available in camping and sporting stores), or soft rope that is approximately 3 to 5 feet in length. Rope burns are avoided by using soft materials. I prefer the Chinese jump rope for several reasons. It is soft and stretches easily, it is inexpensive, it comes in a variety of colors and designs, and typically it has a manufacturer's tag sewn into the rope that can be used as a marker for the activity. If you use the webbing or a soft rope, tie a secure knot to use for the marker.

Ask the group members to take hold of the rope. The rope will be moved around the group as the children continue to grasp a hold.

The first example for the group discussion is instructing the members to identify a "high" (something that happened to them during the past week about which they are happy or excited) and a "low" (something about which they are mad, sad, or scared). After instructing the children to grasp the rope, the therapist says, "Go," and indicates whether to move the rope to the right or left. The therapist then starts the motion of sliding the rope toward the first person, with all members sliding in the same fashion. When the therapist says, "Stop," the person touching the marker or knot describes her/his high or low. For example, the child might say; "I scored a goal at my hockey game this week and I felt proud." Typically, the therapist will see to it that everyone has a chance to share at least one high and one low. When the therapist describes her/his high and low, it is an opportunity to model for the child the importance of each member focusing on her/his own issues rather than another person's issue (e.g., mom, brother, friend, etc.). Initially, the children will describe less threatening highs and lows. As the group progresses, the members will often disclose secrets during the process because they have an outlet for their anxiety and group trust has been built. Many times the group members will ask to describe more than one high and low because of the safety they are feeling within the experience. Other topics to use include the following: "Practice making an angry (sad, scared, etc.) face." "If you could change one thing about yourself, what would it be?" For a closing activity, the therapist could suggest: "The best thing that happened in group today was _____," or "As I leave tonight I feel _____."

APPLICATION

I have used this activity with all age groups and have adapted the content to fit the age and group issues that have emerged. Holding onto the jump rope has served the purpose of releasing the members' anxiety, connecting with each other, facilitating discussion of threatening material in a playful manner, increasing members' trust, and building group cohesion. I have found that children with impulse control problems were able to concentrate for longer periods of time when holding onto the jump rope. Often the group process and discussion will assist the children in improving their communication skills and learning the social skills of cooperation and bridging from self to community while accepting one another's feelings.

Reference

Smith, T. (1996). *Raccoon Circles*. Cazenovia, WI: Raccoon Institute.

83

The Magic Crayon

Bernadette H. Beyer

INTRODUCTION

To begin each play therapy group, whether the group is time-limited or ongoing, I start with a warm-up activity. The children look forward to the activity and often one of the first comments is, "What are we going to do today for our warm-up game?" A favorite game of the group members is the magic crayon. Warm-up activities are a wonderful way for group members to reconnect with each other as well as reconnect with themselves and become physically grounded. Often the children we meet in treatment have been taught to distance themselves from their feelings and/or disconnect from their bodies. One of our roles as a play therapist is to model behaviors that encourage children to integrate their mind and body and as a result become grounded. Particularly children who have been traumatized will defend against feeling their pain by shutting down their body. Within the safe environment of the playroom, the magic crayon activity will encourage the children to experience their bodies in a playful manner. Given clear guidelines and boundaries, the children can experiment with becoming more flexible and spontaneous through these playful body movements.

RATIONALE

Children are often anxious at the beginning of each group meeting. They are in the midst of making a transition from the stressors of their day to the safe environment of the playroom. One way children feel safe is with the use of rituals. Knowing that each group starts with a warm-up activity provides the space for the children to become less guarded and more present in the therapeutic experience. Often the warm-up activity will involve something physical. This provides a bridge for the children to get out of their heads from their school activities and get into their bodies. The magic crayon activity assists the children in releasing the body tensions that have built up during the day. As the children open up through the warm-up activity, they are more receptive to the deepening of the group experience. Another benefit of this activity is building group cohesion.

DESCRIPTION

This technique can be used with groups of children from the time they begin to learn to spell simple words. The therapist asks the children to stand and make believe they have a magic crayon between their teeth. The group members are then asked to write the word *play* in the air with their magic crayon. The therapist exaggerates the movement in order to encourage the children to move freely. Initially, the children will often be tight and timid in their movements. Encouraging the children to make "great big letters" may help them to become playful in their movements.

The therapist can then ask the group members to move their magic crayon to another body part, such as their forehead or nose. This time the group members write their name in the air. Frequently, a child will ask about writing their first and last name or printing versus cursive writing. The therapist encourages the child to proceed with the actions they are most comfortable doing.

Next, ask the group members to move their magic crayon to another body part (elbow, knee, and chin). A particularly helpful body part to use that involves the children moving their lower body is their belly button.

Typically there will be an increase of giggling with this position of writing!

Select words for the children to write that are appropriate for the group. With some groups it may be appropriate to have the children select a body part to use for writing with their magic crayon. The children often are also eager to make a suggestion of a word or phrase to write. When group members are working through problems with poor impulse control and/or sexual acting out, it would be best if the therapist makes the selection of body parts or words to be used for this technique. For certain groups this technique may not be an appropriate selection.

Children can easily participate in the magic crayon during the beginning stages of group since cooperation among members and/or physical contact between members is unnecessary. On more than one occasion I have seen that even the timid, rigid child, cannot help but let go and move her/his body. Since there is no right way to write with your elbow or knee, each child's choice of movement is acceptable. Frequently, the quiet child will be heard giggling along with the other group members. By the end of this activity, the anxiety level in the group has decreased considerably. It is as if everyone in the room has let out a big sigh and the anxiety starts visibly melting.

APPLICATION

This technique is helpful with most children, including the shy as well as the child with impulse control problems. The undercontrolled child will need to respond within the parameters the group establishes. The overcontrolled child will have an opportunity in a safe place to experiment with being flexible and open to experiencing her/his body. Since all group members including the therapist are moving their bodies, it will be less threatening for a timid child to join in the play. The magic crayon activity is a playful way to break the ice, build group cohesion, and/or assist each child to be more present in her/his body.

84

The Gallery of Goofy Art

Risë VanFleet

INTRODUCTION

The Gallery of Goofy Art is designed to help children become less self-conscious about drawing. This is useful because there are many play therapy techniques that involve drawing. Some children resist drawing or art interventions, saying, "I can't draw." Others expend excessive amounts of time trying to make their art perfect. The Gallery of Goofy Art is a play therapy technique that helps children get past these hurdles so that the therapist can use other art approaches more effectively.

RATIONALE

Children who resist art interventions often do so because they are self-conscious about their artwork. They may be perfectionistic and fear that others will criticize them. They may lack confidence and fear that their drawings don't measure up. The Gallery of Goofy Art is designed to counteract these notions about themselves and/or the production of artwork, thereby permitting them to be more spontaneous in their art expressions.

DESCRIPTION

The Gallery of Goofy art can be used individually, but is best with a small group of children. The therapist prepares the drawing paper with a simple frame border and a top or bottom label that says, "Goofy Art." The center of the paper remains a large blank. Each child is provided with the Goofy Art paper and some colored markers. The therapist explains that they all will making some very special artwork to be placed in the Gallery of Goofy Art. It's special because the gallery only wants artwork that is very silly, goofy, messy, or sloppy. The gallery does not wish to have neat, tidy, perfectly drawn artwork—there are other galleries that specialize in that.

The therapist explains that the children should draw the silliest, goofiest, messiest pictures they can. They should draw fast so their drawings are really sloppy. The therapist does a drawing as well, modeling for the children how to make goofy art. As the children draw, the therapist tries to create a fun and somewhat fast-paced (but not tense) climate, laughing and commenting on how goofy everyone's artwork is. Care must be exercised to avoid any impression that the therapist is criticizing the children's artwork. Great sensitivity is needed as the therapist reinforces the evolving drawings. Examples of appropriate comments are, "That'll look terrific in the Gallery of Goofy Art," or "Wow! There's a silly one—I'll bet the gallery will love to have that one."

After just one or two minutes, the therapist asks the children to show their goofy drawings and hangs them up for the remainder of the session. The group can walk around the room viewing the drawings as if they were at a real art gallery.

APPLICATION

Play therapy often uses art interventions to help children express themselves. Various play therapy activities use drawing to help children work through problems or learn new skills. When children resist drawing, a number of potentially helpful techniques may become inaccessible. The child's resistance to drawing can be the result of perfectionism, self-criticism, self-consciousness, or lack of self-esteem. The Gallery of Goofy Art technique can sometimes be used to help these children become less self-conscious about their artwork. This technique is useful with many different presenting problems, but is particularly applicable to anxious children.

Samantha was a perfectionistic 9-year-old who had difficulty trying new things because she was afraid of failing. She was in a play therapy/friendship-skills group. Whenever the therapist asked the group to draw something, Samantha and another girl would refuse, both saying they couldn't draw very well. The therapist had the entire group use the Gallery of Goofy Art technique during two separate sessions. Samantha became increasingly willing to use art in other contexts, especially when the therapist cued her to remember the Gallery of Goofy Art exercise.

85

The Anger Box

Heidi Gerard Kaduson

INTRODUCTION

Many children in group therapy have a lot of problems dealing with their anger. However, when asked about what makes them angry, or by doing straight cognitive-behavioral work, children do not seem to be able to focus on the real issues that bother them. When using the Anger Box, the entire group is able to listen to others having the same problems they are having, and also join in and validate the response given by the child who is speaking. Anger is a common phenomenon, but many children know only how to feel it, not how to manage it.

RATIONALE

Since anger is so common in children, it has become very important for us to work on ways and techniques to allow children to express their anger in a safe environment. Also, by the group process, the anger that is expressed can be validated by others, and the child does not feel alone in his or her experience. Through the use of the Anger Box, each member of

375

the group gets to say how he or she feels. There are no wrong answers, and only confirmation of others if they agree. This allows the children to express themselves about angry situations without repercussion or punishment.

DESCRIPTION

Materials Needed

Coffee tin decorated by the group with construction paper

Markers

Poker chips or bingo chips

Anger cards with sentence stems, as follows:

I get angry every time . . .

I get angry whenever somebody . . .

I get over being angry quickly when . . .

The next time I'll be angry will be when . . .

When I let my angry feelings out, I . . .

When I get angry my face . . .

You can tell I'm angry when I . . .

When I tell someone I am angry with them, I feel . . .

When I keep anger inside, I . . .

The best thing for me to do when I get angry is . . .

Some ways to get my anger out without hurting anyone are . . .

After I lose my temper, I . . .

A safe place to get angry is . . .

When I get angry at Mom or Dad, I feel like . . .

When I get angry at a friend, I feel like . . .

When someone is angry at me . . .

A time I was glad I controlled my temper was . . .

When I am angry and don't want anybody to know it, I . . .

Angry feelings always follow when I . . .

Dad lets you know he is angry when he . . .

Mom lets you know she is angry when she . . .

Process

The can is passed around the group so that the members can write an angry word on it. If they don't want to write, they can draw an angry symbol. After each person contributes to the making of the can, the therapist puts the anger cards in the can. All of the children are given twenty chips each. With the roll of the dice, the child with the highest number goes first. He picks a card out of the can and completes the sentence. Those members who agree with him put a chip in the middle of the table. The game continues until all of the cards are used. Each child gets at least one or two turns. A child can choose to pass.

APPLICATION

This Anger Box game is suitable for children who express anger in appropriate ways, as well as those who have trouble acknowledging that they have any anger. The mere verbalization of the anger statements helps the child release some of the anger, and the validation that the members of the group give the child makes him feel accepted and not wrong. The more chips that are put in the middle of the table, the more the children feel that what they are expressing is normal and at least understood by others.

A social skills training group of six 10- to 12-year-old boys was given the Anger Box game to play. The children wrote the following words of anger on the can: Angry, Mad, Furious, Really Mad, Pissed Off, and Red-faced Mad. The chips were dealt out, and with the roll of the dice Michael went first. Michael pulled the stem, "You can tell I'm angry when I . . ." and he responded, "Scream." John said, "Me, too," and added a chip to the center of the table. Paul did not add any, but commented that he gets in trouble if he does that. Stuart said, "Screaming feels good," and added a chip. Bobby said, "I agree," and added a chip, and Bill finished with "Not me." When it got back to Michael, he said, "Wow!" This continued for the entire fifty-minute session, with no one passing, although the members knew they were allowed to do so. The Anger Box can be used with ages 5 and older. It has also been successful in adult groups, when no one wanted to start to talk about anger and how they try to manage it.

86

Cooperative Creativity

Ellen M. Stickney

INTRODUCTION

The ability to form and maintain peer relationships is a developmental task crucial to a child's positive functioning in most areas of his life. This is an aspect of development that can easily be impaired by a wide variety of mental health or family problems, including depression, anxiety, attachment disorders, attention-deficit/hyperactivity disorder (ADHD), learning disorders, family chemical dependence issues, and inadequate parenting. The cooperative creativity game, used in a group setting, allows children to practice skills that will assist them in making friends, and to give and receive positive feedback on these prosocial behaviors.

RATIONALE

A play therapy group provides an excellent environment for children to develop the social skills necessary to establishing and maintaining positive peer relationships. One of these skills is cooperation. Since peer relationships in young children are formed in the context of play, teaching

this skill in the context of a play activity is most effective. The combination of this play with a preceding discussion about helpful things people
do and a follow-up discussion of observations of helpful things group
members did helps to reinforce and internalize these behaviors.

DESCRIPTION

The therapist and a group of four to six children sit around a table or
in a circle on the floor (uncarpeted). Materials needed are four to six cans
of Play Doh, each of a different color. For children able to read, a marker
and large sheet of newsprint to record discussion ideas would be useful.
The therapist explains:

Therapist: Today we are going to talk and play about something that's
                very important in being a good friend. That something is
                cooperation. Who wants to tell us what cooperation is?

Child: It's when you do what you're told.

Therapist: That is cooperation, when you do what your mom or your
                teacher asks you to do. What else is cooperation?

The discussion continues with the goal of getting a list of cooperative or
helpful behaviors such as sharing, taking turns, offering assistance,
listening, giving your ideas.
    Next the therapist explains the play activity:

Therapist: We're now going to make an animal/monster together as a
                group. First we will decide together what to make. Then we
                will discuss some ideas about what it might look like. Then
                we will make it. While we're doing this let's all think about
                the things we just figured out about cooperation and being
                helpful.

After this decision has been made and ideas discussed, the therapist
explains the rules of the game.

Therapist: I'm going to give each of you a can of Play Doh. I will start
                our animal/monster by putting down a part of him. Then

we will go around the circle and each take a turn adding a part until each of us has had three turns. The rule is, you can't change anything anyone else has put on our animal/ monster. You can give your ideas or ask other people for ideas if you want to.

The play then proceeds until each member has had three turns and the animal/monster is complete.

Therapist: Who noticed someone in our group being helpful?

Child: I saw Marcus help Josh open his Play Doh.

Therapist: All right! Everybody, thumbs up for Marcus! That was a helpful thing to do. Did anyone else notice a helpful thing?

Child: I saw Jenny show Lindsey how to make a curly-Q.

Therapist: Thumbs up for Jenny! Anyone else?

The therapist makes sure that each child receives positive feedback on a cooperative behavior.

If the group is still attentive, the therapist may want to engage them in the process of naming their animal/monster. If there is a polaroid camera available, the therapist can take a picture of the group with its creation to add to a group poster.

APPLICATION

This technique can be used in any type of group to build individual cooperation skills and/or group cohesiveness. Additional skills of self-control and communication are also practiced through this game. The making of a scary monster might be especially useful in a session focused on coping with fears. Children of ages 4 to 10 years can participate in this play activity.

A variation for children who are 11 years old or older is to eliminate the structure of the turn taking and to give a collection of odd materials (e.g., a shoe box, popsicle sticks, bottle caps, a length of string, sheets of construction paper, scissors, markers, and a roll of masking tape) with instructions to build something, anything they want to, in twenty minutes. The only rules are everyone helps in some way and the end product is one creation. Pre- and postdiscussions would be included, as above.

87

Abuse Buster—The Use of a Mascot in a Treatment Play Group for Sexually Abused Boys

Mark Berkowitz

INTRODUCTION

Treatment groups for sexually abused boys are an effective modality for helping boys work through their victimization experience(s). Creating a club-like atmosphere within the group setting enhances the experience by strengthening group cohesion and improving attendance.

A programmable robot purchased at Radio Shack was used as a mascot for a treatment group for preadolescent, sexually abused boys. The robot stood approximately thirty inches high and was manipulated through a wireless remote control. Utilizing features on the remote control including a microphone, the robot could move, make robot noises, and "talk." There was a built-in tape recorder in the body of the robot.

RATIONALE

There are several factors that explain the usefulness of group treatment as an effective modality for working with sexually abused boys. First, being part of a group breaks down the feeling of isolation. Second, there is an increased sense of safety. Third, the group process provides the boys with an opportunity to develop new interactive skills and a social support network.

A mascot is one technique utilized to help create safety, lessen defenses, and bring about change. While the mascot is not a specific therapeutic activity designed to meet a specific group goal, goals may be reached indirectly through its use.

DESCRIPTION

The mascot performs several tasks during group sessions:

1. Administrative tasks: The mascot can introduce new topics, review previous session accomplishments, and explain general housekeeping issues. This can be done through a prerecorded message in the tape recorder or by one of the facilitators using the remote control microphone.

2. Opportunities to feel special: Through the use of the built-in tape recorder and a prerecorded message, the robot is able to talk about the boys and focus on their uniqueness as well as commonalities. Based on information gathered during the screening process or as sessions progressed, messages were made that identified the boys and their individual differences, including hobbies, birthdays, interests, and special occasions. The goal was to develop both uniqueness and commonalities among the boys.

3. Group cohesion: A cohesive group can be built by incorporating the robot into therapeutic activities. Group projects like naming the robot or building a puzzle of the robot enable the boys to cooperate and work together. As the group becomes more cohesive, a greater sense of safety and loyalty is achieved.

4. Identification and expression of feelings: Through the use of prerecorded messages, the robot developed a personality and described its own feelings. For example, during the first session, the robot was anxious about being the only robot in the group

(isolation theme). The intent is to model the boys' own anxiety/ fear about their initial group experience. In later group sessions, the robot described feelings such as anger, helplessness, loneliness, sadness, excitement, surprise, and happiness. This was done through the use of the built-in tape recorder and prerecorded speeches.

5. Opportunities for empowerment and control: The loss of control is a consistent and predominant theme for sexually abused boys. Through the use of the remote control, the boys can manipulate the robot's movements and gain a sense of control.

6. Safety to disclose: Disclosing victimization experience(s) can be a difficult and anxiety-provoking experience. Through the use of the remote control, the boys were able to sit in one part of the room, speak through the remote microphone, and have the robot "tell" their story.

The use of the robot/mascot is one of several props used in a treatment play group for sexually abused boys. The intent is to develop a club-like atmosphere and remove any stigma attached to their victimization.

APPLICATION

A treatment group mascot need not be a programmable robot. Other mascots could be large stuffed animals or puppets. A mascot is beneficial with boys or girls of ages 6 to 11 in other treatment group programs that address grief, divorce, or anger management.

88

Treasure Time: A Journey in Communication and Understanding

Marcie Fields Yeager

INTRODUCTION

When a young person is a member of a group—whether a sports team, a group of students working together on a school project, or a family—good communication skills are an essential ingredient to success. Group members need to be able to tell one another about their ideas, opinions, and feelings. They need to be able to talk together in order to make plans and solve problems.

The Treasure Time board game uses the metaphor of a ship's crew on a quest for treasure to provide youths and their families with an opportunity to learn and practice essential communication skills.

RATIONALE

With cell phones, beepers, and the Internet, young people today are able to communicate in many ways. Yet a child's success and happiness are still determined largely by the old-fashioned ability to talk face-to-face with others. Good communication skills help young people to make and keep friends, get along with parents and teachers, and work with others to set goals and solve problems. The Treasure Time board game provides an opportunity for players to identify and practice essential communication skills. It also helps the therapist to assess skill levels and to identify problem issues.

In keeping with the game's basic metaphor and theme, the game includes a written code of conduct "for the crew of the good ship Treasure Time." The therapist can use the code to involve the players in identifying the essential attitudes, behaviors, and skills that contribute to working together as a team.

Answering questions on the cards gives players the opportunity to learn and practice four different types of communication skills: (1) formulating and expressing opinions on a given topic; (2) sharing one's feelings, experiences, dreams, and hopes; (3) expressing appreciation for the contributions of others; and (4) speaking up to resolve conflict in a respectful manner.

At the advanced level of play, players are challenged not only to answer questions, but also to initiate interactions/communications with one or more of the other group members.

The game includes a parents' guide that provides the therapist with a means to help parents reinforce the skills at home, through the use of family meetings.

Answers to the game's questions often reveal areas of concern; the therapist can note these issues and address them at a later time through other forms of therapy.

DESCRIPTION

The treasure theme of the game is carried out in all of the materials. It is recommended that the therapist begin by discussing the code of conduct with the players. This establishes the theme and purpose of the game, and helps to stimulate player imagination and interest.

The game board is a map of the Golden Path Coast, surrounded by a border that consists of thirty symbols. There are also thirty treasure coins in a bag, and the symbols on these treasure coins match the thirty symbols in the border of the map. Each player (or "member of the crew") has a job—to collect the coins corresponding to the symbols on his or her section of the border.

Players earn coins by answering questions in one of four categories: Voice Your Opinion (players express opinions on a number of different issues), Speak from the Heart (players share their experiences, feelings, hopes, values, and dreams), Express Your Appreciation (players make positive statements about the contribution of others), and Handle Conflict with Care (players give specific suggestions for handling problem situations in a fair and compassionate manner).

In the center of the board is the Travel Wheel—a path on which players travel north, south, east, and west. The spaces of the path correspond to the colors of the four sets of cards. A player rolls the die, lands on a space, and chooses a card that matches the color of that space. After answering the question, the player draws a coin from the treasure bag. If it matches one of her symbols, she places it on top of that symbol. Unmatched coins are placed in front of the player. (Not all cards have questions; Danger and Challenge and Adventure cards carry out the theme of a quest for treasure and also redistribute the extra coins by directing player to gain, lose, or exchange coins.)

The first player to complete his collection of coins is declared the winner, but if time allows, play can continue until all members of the crew complete their jobs.

APPLICATION

The Treasure Time board game is ideal for groups (including families), as the communication skills learned in the game are essential to any group. The code of conduct can be copied and given to the members of the group as a reminder of the skills learned in the game. In individual therapy, the therapist may want to play the game with the young person first, then allow him or her to help introduce and explain the game to other members of the family. The reproducible parents' guide is included so that the parents can reinforce the skills at home through the use of family meetings.

Resource

For more information about the Treasure Time board game, contact Golden Path Games, 219 West Brentwood Blvd., Lafayette, LA (phone: 337-993-7927, fax: 337-993-7929, email: danyeager@wornident.att.net).

89

Playback Theatre

Gregory Ford and Dottie Ward-Wimmer

INTRODUCTION

Playback theatre is a "form of theatrical improvisation in which people
tell real events from their lives, then watch them enacted on the spot"
(Salas 1993, p. 6). Playback fuses elements of improvisational theater
exercises, psychodrama, drama therapy, and an oral tradition of storytelling in which the values of a community are passed on from one
generation to another. It is practiced around the world in workshops,
performances, and clinical settings. We have used several playback
theater–related exercises with children and adolescents.

RATIONALE

Playback theatre, an improvisational technique developed by Jonathan
Fox in 1975, is a valuable therapeutic projective storytelling technique in
which participants verbalize personal stories and feelings and enact those
stories and feelings for each other. It allows the child to address his/her
own feelings, internal conflicts, joys, and stories without having to reex-

perience them. The interaction that follows the playing back, however, allows the therapist to provide an appropriate intervention. In essence, it is the three-dimensional reflection of feelings. Playback theatre allows participants to experience what it is like to be respected and heard. It encourages participants to think about their lives as stories and feelings that can be expressed, remembered, and cared for. By performing, the children often gain insights into their own feelings and develop empathy toward peers.

DESCRIPTION

A person who has a story or feeling that they want to see enacted will tell the story to the conductor (therapist). The conductor will help the teller choose actors to portray the characters in the story. Then the teller will watch the enactment. Unlike psychodrama, in which the protagonist becomes an actor in the enactment, in playback theatre the teller merely watches (Salas 1993). A feeling is enacted or made concrete as a fluid sculpture, similar to Virginia Satir's family sculpting (cited in Emunah 1994). The teller, by staying outside the story as witness, can then choose to integrate the event into his here-and-now life.

Playing Back Feelings in a Circle

Participants stand in a circle. The therapist explains that we are going to introduce ourselves in a different way. "One at a time, we will each step into the center of the circle and say our name. At the same moment that we say our name, we will show with some kind of movement of our body, how we feel about ourself right now. We won't use any words to describe the feeling. We will just *show* how we feel with our body while we are saying our name. After we say our name while showing how we feel, we will immediately rejoin the circle and just watch."

The first person steps into the circle and performs the actions outlined above. Everyone who is standing in the circle waits for the first partici-pant to return to her place in the circle. Then everyone, except the participant who initiated the action, takes one step into the circle and repeats the initiating participant's name and simultaneously repeats the same motions she used to show how she felt about herself. The initiating participant watches while her feelings are reenacted or played back. At the conclusion of the playing back of each experience, the group participants return to the perimeter of the circle and give eye contact to the person who initiated the experience. Each member of the circle would have an opportunity to do this and to see her feelings about herself played back.

The therapist should encourage participants to allow themselves to play back the initiator's action without judging it. She could say, "It may feel silly, naughty, or unruly. But this is the initiator's feeling, not anyone else's. Try to play it back accurately for her. Suspend your reluctance for a moment." (The therapist can step in to clarify, censor, and prevent abuse of the opportunity, if necessary.) At the conclusion of the process, or during it if desired, the therapist asks, "What was it like to show us how you were feeling? And what was it like to then see it played back?"

Fluid Sculptures

Participants stand in a circle. Therapist asks each participant to show how he/she feels about something (e.g., money, ice cream, etc.) by making a "sound and motion." Each person is told to remember the sound and motion they create. After everyone has had a chance to show his/her sound and motion, the therapist has three or four participants stand in a line in front of the others. The remaining participants become, for the moment, an audience and can sit. The therapist reminds the four actors of the sound and motion each created and explains that when she says, "Let's watch," one of the actors will take one large step forward and perform their own sound and motion over and over. After that sound and motion has been repeated two or three times, the next person in the line will step forward, join the first person, and repeat his own original sound and motion, making sure to physically connect with the person who first stepped out. By doing so the actors will create a fluid (i.e., moving) sculpture showing their individual and collective feelings. This continues until all four actors have joined the sculpture, at which point the therapist calls out "Freeze." The actors hold the pose for a moment. Then the therapist calls out "Relax." The therapist encourages the audience to applaud. The people who were the audience now get a chance to do their version of the fluid sculpture.

APPLICATION

We have used this with children and families dealing with grief, trauma, and chronic illness such as HIV/AIDS. The following example describes an interaction with a teen. We have, however, done playback with children as young as 5, and although usually practiced with groups, it is also possible to adapt the techniques for use with individual clients.

The therapist asks, "Sharon, what is one feeling you have about having to spend time with your mom in one place and having to spend time with your dad in another place?" Sharon replied that she felt sad. The therapist asked, "What is it about this that makes you feel sad?"

The therapist reflected Sharon's feelings back to her and said to the actors, "You have listened to what she just said and you have felt what she just said. Think about how that feeling would look if you could show it using only your body and a sound. Now, when I say, 'Let's watch,' one at a time, step out and show us that feeling using a sound and motion." To Sharon she added, "Sharon, this is the sadness you feel when you have to see people you love in separate places: Let's watch."

After the playing back, Sharon felt less alone as she realized that others could understand how she was feeling. Seeing the concrete image also helped her to feel more in control and less overwhelmed by the events and her feelings. Whole stories are especially useful for putting events in perspective, clarifying memories, confronting trauma without having to relive it, and putting closure on open-ended events. Whether metaphor or reality, stories can bring healing when they are heard, respected, and worked through. They can be as short as a singular feeling, or complex with many characters and actions. Playback theatre is a gentle way to reach into a child's pain and bring it close enough to hear without hurting.

References

Emunah, R. (1994). *Acting for Real: Drama Therapy, Process, Technique, and Performance.* New York: Brunner/Mazel.

Salas, J. (1993). *Improvising Real Life: Personal Story in Playback Theatre.* Dubuque, IA: Kendall/Hunt.

Resource

School of Playback Theatre, 137 Hasbrouk Road, NY 12561 (914) 255-8163. Fax (941) 255-1281. E-mail: jonathanfox@compuserve.com.

Section Seven

Other Techniques

90

Broadcast News

Heidi Gerard Kaduson

INTRODUCTION

This technique was created to enhance the child's verbalization and problem-solving skills. It has been seen that children can solve some of their own problems when there is a certain amount of distancing from the problem. Children play out their problems much more easily than they can talk about them. Even verbal children still cannot communicate their feelings or what is bothering them until the formal-operations period of development (11 or 12 years old). Therefore, this technique helps children play out the problems they may be experiencing and come up with solutions to those problems.

RATIONALE

Children often find it difficult to solve their own problems due to several factors. While it is easier to help others, and they might be very willing to do that, children find it threatening to answer "why" questions about their behavior. However, when Broadcast News is used, the children have enough distancing from the problem to view it objectively, and they find it easier to solve "other people's" problems. In effect, the children are working on their own problems but in the context of helping others who have certain situations similar to their own. The therapist facilitates the discussion on the Broadcast News and helps the child stay focused on the problems presented through the telephone callers.

DESCRIPTION

Materials Needed

> Video camera
>
> Telephone
>
> Paper
>
> Table and chairs

Process

The therapist introduces the Broadcast News as a news program starring the therapist and the "expert" (the child). The therapist talks about what news the two of them will be covering. The child may add any other news stories as well, as long as they are following the theme of the newscast. The therapist introduces the first news story, and states again that the child is the expert for the day. When the introduction of the story is complete, the therapist says that a caller is on the phone. The child picks up the phone, and the therapist changes his/her voice to pretend to be a caller. All of the calls that are to be received pertain to the client's own real problems. When the caller asks the question of the "expert," the client then responds to the caller on the telephone. The therapist directs the next newscast and the play follows until the therapist closes the newscast. If at any time the child cannot find an answer to the problem, the therapist may guide the child to get help from a puppet, the wizard, or any other possible source. Then the therapist can help the child with possibilities for solving the problem. A copy of the videotape can be made if the therapist deems it helpful to allow the family to see what the child has come up with.

APPLICATION

This technique is very useful with highly verbal children of ages 6 to 13 years. Extremely outgoing children find this very easy to do, while withdrawn or anxious children may find it more difficult. In a case where the child does not get into the play enough, puppets may be used to distance the child even further from the real problems that are being talked about in the newscast.

Michael, a 9-year-old, is diagnosed with bipolar disorder. He is extremely talkative, but has difficulty dealing with his own problems. He rarely takes responsibility for his actions, and therefore his parents are often angry with him. He has severe anxiety that is comorbid with the bipolar disorder, and his fears are difficult for him to manage. He was introduced to the Broadcast News and was eager to play. At first he wanted to do "news" about tornadoes and hurricanes, but the therapist had to introduce the theme of the play (taking control of oneself). He agreed to let her begin. She talked about how things get out of hand in the world and sometimes we have to take control of our own emotions. She then stated "We are lucky, ladies and gentlemen, to have an expert in the field of emotions—Mr. Michael." He took a bow and then the phone rang.

Michael picks up the phone and says, "Welcome to Broadcast News. May I help you?" The therapist changes her voice and says, "Mr. Michael, my son is 8 years old [caller's child should always be younger than the client], and he is having a lot of trouble controlling his emotions. He loses his temper and screams at everyone, but he won't tell us what is wrong." Michael continues, "Maybe your son is scared that he is not doing things right all the time, and maybe he wants someone to help him stop losing his temper all the time. Have you ever checked with him on that?" The therapist as the caller answers, "He doesn't want to talk about anything like that." Michael responds, "Give him some time to calm down and then tell him you want to help him deal with his problems. Let him have some of his favorite cookies and milk, and give him space to talk. I'm sure once he feels you won't get mad, he will tell you what is happening." The therapist as caller says, "Thank you, Mr. Michael. I will try that." Michael responds, "You're welcome, and thank you for calling."

The technique continues with talking about hurricanes and tornadoes but keeping the theme by the callers being the same (expression of emotions). This technique can take up an entire session if the child is really engaged, and the videotaping of his information would then be replayed to him in the next session so that he could see how he can problem solve all by himself.

A Mirror as Transitional Object

Berrell Mallery

INTRODUCTION

A mirror can serve as a transitional object. Mallery and Navas (1982) videotaped a series of group therapy sessions of boys ages 9 to 12, spanning a 10-month period. The camera and microphone were in separate locations and emerged as fixed boundaries, providing the boys with well-defined boundaries of communication. This was especially important because the psychological profiles of the boys included the diagnostic factor of weak boundaries.

In my current work with special education preschool children ages 2½ to 5 years, the use of a mirror facilitates engagement with the environment in ways similar to the use of videotaping. This population is accustomed to classrooms and related services that are highly structured, and in contrast client-centered therapy is not structured or less structured. Thus the presence of structure exists in a new form; that is, the mirror provides structure and feedback on the child's terms. In the small playroom the children need to test boundaries in their play or avoidance of play. The mirror has provided a fixed boundary that has encouraged more structured acting out (better controlled) in the expansive or aggressive children, fostered initiations in withdrawn and withholding children, and enabled reactions and overall engagement that is safe and comfortable.

RATIONALE

This population of special education preschool children presents limitations in engaging them. Their development of language, motor, emotional, and social skills is usually delayed or disordered. Clinician verbalizations and nonverbal initiations are usually not very helpful in sessions. Yet positive responses to mastery provide one of the most powerful tools in engaging the children, especially when they achieve a goal that pleases them. Thus the mirror has been used to aid in mastery with materials, and it has also been used in mastery of a safe and comfortable development of engagement between child and therapist.

DESCRIPTION

Place a mirror in the playroom at the level suitable for the size of the children. The mirror discussed in this chapter was fixed on the wall next to a small table placed against the wall. In classrooms, vertical or freestanding mirrors are suited to dress-up play and often foster expansive enactment. The mirror in the playroom was incidental to the activities chosen, and offered the therapist and children more options for gradations of engagement. The children who choose to turn their backs to the therapist can still see the therapist. The expansive aggressive children wanted to see themselves act out, and the mirror provided desired feedback simultaneously tempering follow-through of aggressive posturing. The children who situate themselves in conventional placements at the table may use the mirror to make visual contact with the therapist when direct visual contact is too threatening.

APPLICATION

This technique was used in the following cases: Mark, 3½ years old, was diagnosed with attention-deficit/hyperactivity disorder (ADHD) and aphasia. The mirror seemed to help him with mastery. The only activity he enjoyed enough to stay with, if even briefly, involved playing with Play Doh. Motor weakness and coordination difficulties made removing the lid a challenge for him. Easy frustration led to his quickly giving up or moving on to another toy. In the mirror he not only studied his work fostering sustained attention to one activity, but also benefited from seeing the lifted portion of the lid in the mirror not visible to him directly. That awareness gave him the extra moment of attention and effort to spur him on to success. Subsequently his attention to tasks of interest to him was extended enough by the feedback of the mirror to enable more rapid progress of mastery. His heightened interest in Play Doh, the mastery of cutting with scissors, and the feedback of the mirror fostered longer spans of attending and gratification with respect to his progress. He was very happy when those three elements worked together to help him.

Morgan, aged 4, initially presented as a selective mute. He withheld language. He also withheld socially and emotionally. He initially chose to play with a Fisher-Price house in a controlled manner. He reluctantly picked up a figure and leaned his head over the partially opened house to play with it, creating a private but very confined area. Over time his play area widened. In slow motion he lifted certain figures and pieces of furniture onto the roof of the house as he studied them in the mirror. Also in slow motion with great dexterity he negotiated sequences leading to key characters being pushed off the roof toward the mirror as he watched the image. As he became comfortable with these behaviors he expanded his play to more deliberate unfavorable outcomes. Eventually he used the car and stroller, which collided, leading to less of a Morgan/mirror engagement and more of a character to character engagement. Gradually he engaged the clinician in his themes.

The mirror was also useful to Morgan in his experiencing an apparent discrepancy between his internal perception of how he intended to appear to an observer, deriving from the feelings motivating his behaviors, the mirrored image of his actual behaviors, and subsequent more focused controlled depictions of his feelings. A more meaningful integration of his feelings and behaviors began to emerge as he studied his reacting images in the mirror.

The mirror proved to be useful to Chichi, a twin, age 3, in helping her regulate her disorganized behaviors. Initially she gave the impression of being the twin whose role it was to react, not initiate. In transit to and during sessions she stood in anticipation at all times. She continually engaged in gestures, facial expressions, statements, and behaviors attempting to provoke reactions. When this was not effective in gaining engagement that was comfortable for her, she began to engage in provocatively silly behaviors constantly seeking reactions of limit setting or retort. In sessions she primarily focused on getting a reaction from the clinician rather than initiating her own play.

Once the mirror appeared in the playroom, Chichi's primary interest in mastery was heightened, but this time her own reactions were central to her continued motivation. She began to spend more time at the table. Her poorly regulated efforts at mastery of tasks and interactions gradually emerged into awkwardly focused efforts. A spurt in her progress was seen in sessions when she used the mirror to watch herself trying to use scissors. Prior to that, her initiations at cutting were immediately interrupted by her looking up at the clinician and laughing in a silly overstimulated anxious fashion. However, when using the mirror, she studied the positioning of her arm, much like physical therapy patients using a mirror in aiding correct positioning. She watched her hand open and close the scissors. She seemed to be working on the learning process based on her observations of other people followed by what she believed was imitation of them. The serious sustained focus on her face as she looked at her movements offered the impression that the images provided comparisons for her experience of the sensation of using the scissors. She could get direct feedback of her efforts at altering hand and arm positioning.

The rapid onset of Chichi's actually cutting, first with the clinician holding the paper taut and then more independently, led to more appropriate and gratifying interactions with the clinician. Within a short period of time, Chichi greeted the clinician in her classroom in an unusually playful and related manner. This continued in transit to the playroom and throughout the session. She initiated verbalizations and expressed interesting thoughts despite her very impaired language skills. She appeared brighter than initially believed. Later her teacher reported a sharp contrast in Chichi's behavior that day and subsequently. She became outgoing, bold, engaging, and involved with others.

Thus, the clinical/empirical evidence strongly suggests that use of a mirror is quite helpful for these children, especially because of the very important nature of the mirror as transitional object.

Reference

Maller, B., and Navas, M. (1982). Engagement of preadolescent boys in group therapy: videotape as a tool. *International Journal of Group Psychotherapy* 32:453–467.

92

The Modification of Nondirective Play Therapy for Use as an Evaluation Tool

Terry Boyle

INTRODUCTION

A simple modification of traditional play therapy can provide information that enables a therapist to make impartial recommendations in custody cases. In traditional experiential play therapy, the therapist not only follows the child's themes but also simultaneously explores them. Thus the therapist may make interpretive comments as themes are manifest in the play. Modification of this method involves providing a setting of total acceptance while not actively exploring themes as they develop in the child's play. Observation of nondirected play provides the therapist with a clear description of a child's world.

RATIONALE

Play therapists are frequently asked to assist in determining the safety of a child in the middle of parental allegations of child abuse, especially in custody disputes. There are often several parties involved who have questioned/interviewed the child with inconclusive results, usually due to the child's loyalty to the parents or the young age of the child. Cases such as these pose a significant challenge for a therapist attempting to elicit an unbiased description of the child's experiences. The modification of nondirective play therapy allows the evaluator to assess the child's story by observing the interaction between the child and his/her physical and emotional environment in the language of play.

DESCRIPTION

The therapist's comments are limited to describing the play, which minimizes the chance of influencing the developing theme. The therapist encourages the activity of play throughout the session by simply putting into words what has occurred. No interpretive comments are made to the child during her play.

Case Study

A request was made by the Department of Social and Health Services (DSHS) to evaluate 5-year-old Mindy to assist in the determination of custody and living arrangements. The evaluation was necessary due to ongoing allegations by the mother regarding sexual abuse of Mindy by the father. There was no physical evidence to substantiate the claims. The father had physical custody for two-and-a-half years, during which time Mindy visited her mother every other weekend. The final allegation by the mother resulted in Mindy being removed from her father's home by DSHS and placed in foster care. Mindy returned to her father's home approximately seven weeks later due to unrelated problems in placement and the original parenting arrangement resumed.

Immediately after her return to her father, Mindy entered therapy for assistance in determining if the child was safe. The parents' conflict with each other continued to be extremely tense and accusations began within one week of the return. The utilization of a nondirective approach was chosen to help evaluate Mindy.

In her first three sessions, Mindy moved from painting to sand tray to doll house, repeating the same painting each time and the same theme in the sand tray and dollhouse. The therapist followed with simple acknowledgment of her activity.

Painting

Mindy: This is red and yellow blood.

Therapist: There's a lot of red and yellow blood on the picture.

Mindy: It's called a dying picture.

Therapist: The painting has a name, a dying picture.

Sandtray

Mindy: (Using two nuns) They're jumping up and down on Ariel (mermaid). They have guns.

Therapist: Ariel is under the sand and they're jumping on her.

Mindy: (Pounds harder with the nuns on Ariel.)

Therapist: They're jumping harder on Ariel.

Mindy: Ariel likes it.

Dollhouse

Mindy: (Peeking under the doll's skirt.)

Therapist: She's being looked at under her skirt.

Mindy: They're looking at her go to the bathroom.

Therapist: She's going to the bathroom and someone is looking.

Mindy: Shh, she doesn't know it.

Therapist: Oh, she doesn't know it.

I needed to determine if Mindy was being abused by her father or coached by her mother. After observing the patterns of behavior indicative of a child experiencing high anxiety and chaos, I requested a change in Mindy's living arrangement that would provide one less factor to this equation. I requested that Mindy remain with her father and have no contact with her mother for two months. This arrangement would maintain Mindy's daily routine and not cause a complete change in her environment, reducing the risk of affecting her behavior in therapy.

In the fourth session, following a two-week period of no contact (letters or telephone calls) with her mother, Mindy continued the same order of play as before but with a different theme. In this session Mindy removed the paint lids and got brown paint on her finger. She turned and smiled.

Painting

Therapist: You're going to paint a picture again.

Mindy: I don't want to paint THAT this time.

Therapist: Oh, you're painting something different.

Mindy: This is a rainbow.

Sandtray

Mindy: The fish are all swimming together.

Therapist: They're all in the water together.

Mindy: They're OK in there.

Dollhouse

Mindy: She's taking a bath (she holds another doll, which is giggling).

Therapist: She's laughing at her taking a bath.

Mindy: (Stands up and goes to the center of the room and looks all around her) Oh! You have other things in here.

Therapist: You can see a lot of other toys in here.

Mindy: (Picking up the telephone) What's this?

Therapist: You're wondering what you can use that for.

She continued to explore the toys for the remainder of the session. In the following six sessions, Mindy showed significant increase in imaginary play. Several play themes involved nurturing, which she stated she learned from her dad. On one occasion, Mindy brought up her mother.

Mindy: (On telephone) Mommy said not to talk to you.

Therapist: Oh, Mommy doesn't want you to talk to me.

Following her comment she briefly commenced aggressive behavior with sand and painting and then returned to creative play with age-appropriate inclusion of the therapist.

The mother was invited to join in the next session. The therapist observed through a two-way mirror. The mother brought a present consisting of many small pieces and removed each piece while Mindy watched. Mindy then asked to paint. Mother instead showed her several rolls of snapshots of family and friends, describing each picture and who was portrayed in them. Several times the mother lamented her poor picture-taking skills and Mindy comforted her and encouraged her to keep trying.

At the end of the session, the mother asked twice for a "mouth kiss" and picked Mindy up, with the mother's back to the viewing room window. The mother leaned in toward Mindy and quickly withdrew saying loudly, "No tongue, Mindy." Upon the mother leaving the therapist entered the room, stood still, and said, "I'll be in here for a while."

Mindy: I want to paint.

Therapist: You'd like to paint now.

Mindy: (Sitting and preparing the paints, she turns to therapist) This is going to be really scary.

Therapist: You want to show me a scary painting.

Mindy: (Stabbing overhand on to the paper with brushes) This is blood. (She stands up) I'm done. (Leaves the room.)

Evaluation through this modification of nondirective play therapy allows themes to emerge unencumbered by interpretation. In the case study, the themes changed as the context of Mindy's experiences changed. Her sudden awareness of the playroom surroundings coincided with a time when she was no longer immersed in a struggle between her parents and when she had been living solely with her father. Previous exposure to conflict and to her mother had seriously disrupted normal processes of engagement and exploration. This modified technique revealed other important themes. It was striking, for instance, that there were no themes of separation anxiety or loss following her mother's two-month absence. Also, in the session with mother, it was noteworthy that the mother was clearly unable to attend to her daughter's needs. The reintroduction of the mother had striking effects on the play that had evolved while Mindy was living with her father. Free exploration and themes of happiness came to an abrupt end. Her dramatic return to painting blood made it exquisitely clear that she did not experience her mother as a source of safety.

APPLICATION

This form of nondirective play is a powerful and successful assessment tool for serious custody cases requiring impartial recommendations. The evaluation of Mindy would not have been possible or credible if the evaluator had engaged in any interpretation of her play. At no time was the child "led" nor were any of her parents' conflicts discussed. When the evaluation was completed it was the child's play, standing entirely by itself, which provided the clearest description of her dilemma.

Bibliography

Axline, V. M. (1969). *Play Therapy*, rev. ed. New York: Ballantine.

Norton, B. E. and Carol, C. (1997). *Reaching Children through Play Therapy: An Experiential Approach*. Denver, CO: Publishing Cooperative.

93

Home Visiting and Play Therapists

Virginia Ryan

INTRODUCTION

Helping children relax and feel comfortable with their therapist in their initial sessions is an aim for all play therapists, regardless of their approach. Another common aim for play therapists is to help children link their play therapy sessions to their everyday lives, with progress generalizing from the therapy room to the children's school and home environments. In my own practice with children who are in foster care, and in my training of play therapists from a variety of professional backgrounds, I have adopted an essential component of social work practice, namely home visiting. This chapter discusses one kind of visit to children's homes, the introductory visit, and gives an illustration of the technique I use.

RATIONALE

Children who have impermanent care arrangements and extensive involvement from a variety of professionals must deal with strong anxieties without help from secure and supportive permanent attachment figures. With such children, therapists must first decide whether an individual play therapy intervention would benefit them and whether their current home circumstances would support such an intervention (see Ryan and Wilson 1996, Chapter 1, for a fuller discussion). After this decision is made, I embark on my work by visiting children in their current homes. This technique is based on several underlying rationales. First, following attachment concepts, all children in strange situations need additional support from their primary attachment figures. Children in impermanent care, who have been separated from their first caregivers, often need additional reassurance from their substitute attachment figures in anxiety-provoking situations. Viewed through children's eyes, the play therapy room, regardless of its interesting and enticing toys, is a strange environment, and the therapist is a stranger to children beginning therapy.

DESCRIPTION

To reduce unfamiliarity, therapists often have an introductory visit to the playroom for the child and caregiver prior to individual therapy sessions beginning. A disadvantage, however, is that the therapist is then primarily associated with the playroom, rather than with the child's wider environment. Home visits, on the other hand, provide children with concrete, action-based memories of the therapist in their home environment. (And an introduction to the playroom can easily be incorporated into children's first play therapy session.) A second reason for home visits, therefore, is based on child development theory and research on children's memory. Links between play therapy and home environments can be made more easily for young children and children who are under emotional stress when concrete actions and real settings provide them with action based memories. A third reason for a home visit at the outset is to enhance the therapist's understanding of the child more quickly. Therapists can become acquainted with the members of the household (including pets) and the general atmosphere of the child's home directly, rather than indirectly through the child's and other adults' eyes.

Susan and her two brothers were in a foster home and the local authority had been granted a Care Order. The children had been subjected to serious and lengthy neglect by their parents, and Susan's older brother had been physically abused. All three children were referred to me for play therapy. Their distress after contact visits and their emotional development were of concern; they seemed to require therapy as well as the warm and appropriate parenting provided to them by their foster caregivers. The local authority also wished me to provide an opinion on the children's needs, wishes, and feelings regarding contact with their parents, which would be based on my play therapy sessions with the children over several months.

I had an introductory meeting with Susan, aged 6, and her brothers, Gerry, aged 8, and Mark, aged 4 (see Ryan and Wilson 1996 for a more complete case presentation). My meeting with Susan and her brothers took place in the playroom at their foster home. After Cath, the foster caregiver, introduced them to me, Gerry continued to play on his hand-held computer game and Susan rushed around the room with a doll's pram. Mark sat very close to me on the couch and talked rapidly to me about his morning's activities, trying to have my exclusive attention. When Mark paused, I said that maybe Cath had told them that their social worker, John, had asked me to see them in my playroom. My job was to try to help children who were worried and unhappy or afraid of things. I had already talked with John and Cath. "They said that maybe I can help you."

None of the children looked at me or responded when I paused, but their unnatural stillness was an indication to me that they were listening intently: "Maybe you don't know what to think about what I said." Pause. "When you come to see me, you can play with things or talk, or just sit with me. You'll each have a turn by yourself in the playroom. It will be time for you to choose what you want to do there." Pause. "Cath will wait for you in another room and you can be with her when you're waiting for your turn. Maybe I can tell you about my playroom. It's in a building near the park. I can draw the building for you now and then you'd know what it looks like."

As I found a piece of paper and a pen in my bag, Susan and Gerry moved closer to Mark, and Mark said he wanted to draw. I got more paper and pens out of my bag, and talked about the building and the park. As Mark and I drew, Susan and Gerry watched closely and listened to me as I described the playroom and what was in it. I then talked about when they would come to see me, and about other court-related and practical issues (Ryan and Wilson 1996).

This example is a composite one, based on my own play therapy referrals with troubled children. These children seemed more comfortable as a sibling group with their caregiver, rather than on their own with their foster caregiver at our initial meeting. Their foster caregiver and the setting of the playroom in their foster home also seemed to provide conditions that lessened their anxiety when meeting a stranger who spoke about their worries. Concrete representations of the playroom (e.g., my drawings) were used as aids for them in linking the playroom and their new experience with their more relaxed feelings associated with their foster home. (Play therapists may decide to bring photos of the playroom with them, rather than drawing.) Another important concrete aid therapists may consider is bringing a few small toys from the playroom on the initial visit. This use of playroom toys as transitional objects works well with young and highly anxious children. Finally, this example illustrates how my meeting with the children together at home gave me important information on their individual presentations and on their relationships with one another and with their caregiver.

APPLICATION

A home visit for an introduction of children to their therapist is helpful for all children referred for play therapy, but especially useful for children who are in temporary care arrangements. It is also very important with young children and children with serious anxiety problems, who will have more anxiety over staying in a strange room with a stranger. In addition, it is very useful to speed up the process of therapy for children. Finally, it also enables play therapists to work systemically within children's wider environments. This technique is used successfully by trainees in our nondirective play therapy program at the University of York, England, in their play therapy interventions with troubled children and their families (Ryan 1992).

Reference

Ryan, V., and Wilson, K. (1996). *Case Studies in Non-Directive Play Therapy.* London: Bailliere Tindall. Reissued by Jessica Kingsley Publishers, London, 2000.

94

The Wall

Mary L. Hammond-Newman

INTRODUCTION

I do play therapy from a strictly child-centered and environment-centered point of view. Thus, rather than introducing an activity to a child, teen, or adult directly, the activity will be added to the playroom for the client to choose. The playroom was designed to create a place that would elicit both spontaneous verbal expression and large motor expression with generally messy play and art materials. My caseload consists largely of children, teens, and adults from addictive or other dysfunctional families. They learned that child-like spontaneity and the expression of feelings and opinions are not tolerated while addiction, illness, or abuse is occurring in the family.

RATIONALE

For many play therapy clients, a point of change occurs when they are given permission to explore the edges and extremes of their behavior safely. For clients who have never yelled in anger, or who have always muffled screams of terror in silence, it is important to have the opportunity to venture into this unexplored territory in the emotional realm. If one has never laughed boisterously or giggled with delight, the playroom and the therapist ought to offer this opportunity. A wall was added to the playroom to explicitly encourage unexplored levels of the extremes of one's behavior.

DESCRIPTION

The wall is a 4-foot by 8-foot piece of clear Plexiglas bolted vertically on the room's wall. A piece of plastic cloth is taped to the floor directly underneath the Plexiglas, and is changed periodically. Adjacent to the wall are beanbags, foam balls, and stuffed animals. Next to the wall on the opposite side are cups of paint, medium-size and large paint brushes, a tub of clay, and a tub of Play Doh. The wall is easy to clean using a scraper and/or window cleaner. Sometimes it is appropriate for the client to assist in cleaning up the mess and sometimes the mess is best left, depending on the therapeutic needs of the client.

Play therapy clients of all ages are intrigued by this wall. It is often avoided and not mentioned in the first few sessions as the client's psyche prepares for its possibilities. Because of the intensity it evokes it is generally chosen both mid-therapy and mid-session for the client to express difficult feelings or issues. Young children tend to use it to experiment with free expression or to show the therapist the limits of expression in the family. Older children tend to use it aggressively to express their outrage or their parents' outrageous behavior. Teens and adults tend to focus on an emotion that gets targeted on the wall, or on a person to whom they have aggressive energy to express. Because it is both large and yet contained, the wall holds the duality for the client of being safely out of control.

The wall allows many rules learned in unhealthy families to be broken, such as "Don't express feelings openly," "Don't be angry at adults," "Don't be loud," "Don't be happier than your parents." There is a gain of personal power when one breaks these rules in a safe environment with a supportive play therapist.

R., an 8-year-old boy, was referred to me because he is the child of an absent alcoholic father whom he is mandated to visit every other weekend and on some vacations. R. has attention-deficit/hyperactivity disorder (ADHD) and is stable on medication. Mother and son report typical addictive overly controlling, unpredictable behavior from the father. In play therapy R. has worked on expressions of hurt and grief at both the separation from and treatment by his father. Additionally, he is addressing the emotional underpinnings of ADHD, the confusion regarding his perceptions of the world and differing parental messages, and his hurt and anger at others' responses to his behaviors and immaturity. Initially he used other materials in the room to express his hurt and grief.

He walked around the playroom in his sixth session, glanced sideways at the Plexiglas on the wall, and said "What's that for?" I replied, "Some kids use it for painting, some throw balls at it, some throw clay or Play Doh at it, or you may think of something else to do with it." He said, "I want to throw Play Doh at it." The following therapy segment ensued:

Child: (Digs out a wad of Play Doh from the tub, which he throws at the wall. It splats and sticks to the wall.)

Therapist: Splat! It's on the wall.

Child: I'm strong. I can make it stick.

Therapist: You ARE strong. You are making it stick.

Child: (Grits his teeth and grunts as he throws.)

Therapist: That's a mad ball of Play Doh.

Child: Yup! (Throws three balls in a row rapidly.)

Therapist: Mad! Mad! Mad!

Child: (Winds arm and throws ball very hard.)

Therapist: That Play Doh is furious!

Child: (Throws balls erratically to the sides and corners of the Plexiglas; some stick and some don't.)

Therapist: That Play Doh is out of control. You don't know which way it's going or where it is going to land, or whether it will stay or not.

Child: (Continues throwing until he is exhausted physically and emotionally.)

APPLICATION

The above example is typical of how children from 3 to 11 years of age, teens, and adults have used the wall. Children, like R., who have frustration and anger expressed heretofore inappropriately finally have an outlet for aggression that incorporates their need and adeptness for large motor play.

Anxious, fearful clients are at first afraid to approach the wall because it demands from them that which has gone unexpressed or has been forbidden. Their first attempts at throwing things at the wall are timid and weak. They may giggle self-consciously. The therapist's role then is to encourage the next throw to be stronger and the next expression to be louder, and the next to be yet stronger and louder. The therapist may sometimes join the activity, modeling overt expression.

Depressed clients find power and renewed energy when encouraged to paint the wall. Painting out their darkness in wide swipes or discovering their brightness in large strokes assists the emergence from the depressed state. When working with images one may be tentative about expressing, it is particularly helpful to have them be removable and temporary.

Sometimes something so outrageous is perpetrated on a client that, even in this era of controversy about fostering violence in the playroom, it is essential the client have full permission to metaphorically strike back in order for full recovery and healing to be possible. Thus, a child, teen, or adult may paint a specific figure on the wall, name that figure, and blast it with balls, balls of clay, or Play Doh. The younger the clients, the less likely they will be to name the figure. The therapist must hold the space for the client's outrage. There is an essential exchange here when victim acts as perpetrator in retrieving lost dignity and power.

The wall, a plain, nondescript addition to the playroom, adds a dimension of expression to the playroom. It allows the timid to become bold, the depressed to become energized, and the outraged to become outrageous. It allows clients to push and stretch their limits and boundaries to that magical place where resolution and healing occur.

Acknowledgment

The wall is an adaptation of the Plexiglas art walls in the Infant-Toddler Center at Pacific Oaks College in Pasadena, CA, where the author received her master's degree.

95

Video Replay

Jeanine Austin

INTRODUCTION

Many children have difficulty recognizing the underlying causes of their negative feelings and behaviors, and they do not realize that there are a number of different options available to them in responding to stressful life events.

RATIONALE

Video replay is a dramatic play activity that helps the child recognize the causes of negative behavior through observation, and concretizes the concept of behavioral choice. It empowers the child by pointing out ways to successfully resolve personal problems.

DESCRIPTION

Materials Needed

Video recorder

One video tape (for therapist)

VCR and TV for play back

"Academy Award" certificate for "best choice"

Signed release for videotaping

Optional Materials

One video tape (for child to take home)

Sunglasses

Costume

Puppet (and) puppet theater

Real or pretend microphone (for acceptance speech)

Process

The child is encouraged to act out a specific, problematic incident, including its antecedents, accompanying feelings, and the resulting maladaptive response by the child. This problem can be acted out with puppets, in a costume, or from behind sunglasses. Sometimes a problem is still too threatening for a child to re-create in fantasy. In such a case, a similar or fictional problem may be used, or the therapist may act out the scenario first if the child is still reluctant.

After the vignette is videotaped, the therapist and child view the video. Together, they brainstorm how the child could choose a more positive outcome for the problem. The goal is to think of (and write down) a number of better ways to respond to the problem. For younger, delayed, or challenged children, pictures can be drawn to depict each option.

The next step is for the child to act out several positive choices. The "best choice" is selected by the therapist and/or child (who represents "The Motion Picture Academy"). The tape is then rewound to the precipitating event. This point is agreed upon by the therapist and the child who both briefly comment on emotional and behavioral precipitators.

The previously negative outcome is taped over by the best choice (leaving the originally taped beginning circumstances intact). The tape is viewed again so the child can view herself acting more appropriately. The therapist briefly presents the child, puppet, or character with the Academy Award certificate for best choice. During the acceptance speech, the child is encouraged to explain the differences observed between the two tapes in regard to thought processes, body language, and felt emotions. This award speech is taped following the best choice segment. A copy of the tape is given to the child along with the "Academy Award" certificate. (Be sure to obtain a signed release for videotaping prior to this activity.)

APPLICATION

This technique is appropriate for use with children and adolescents, ages 4 to 18+ years. I have found it effective with anxious, impulsive, and hyperactive children, as well as with children with social difficulties, such as making friends or dealing with bullies. This activity can be used effectively with children and teens working on value clarification. It is also effective as a group exercise.

Case Example

Janet, an 8-year-old, was residing at the time of the session in a residential treatment setting, and was reportedly having difficulty making appropriate behavioral choices. Janet told me that she really wanted to make better decisions because she wanted to earn special privileges and rewards. She was taking medication to address attention-deficit/hyperactivity disorder (ADHD) and had some success, but still had trouble with incidents of aggression. She described these incidents as happening "way too fast." She described one incident during which she was taunted by a 5-year-old boy at school, who said, "You're stupid" and "You're ugly." The second time she was taunted, Janet physically attacked the boy and was suspended.

Janet was excited about using this technique. First, she acted out and taped the scene as it occurred. (She chose to do it without a costume or puppets, but wore sunglasses.) Second, we briefly discussed at which point she had a chance to make a different choice. Third, we came up with two possible choices and their resulting outcomes. We chose our favorite option. Next we rewound the tape to the point from which she would make a different choice. We taped and acted out the drama together. Finally, I ("The Motion Picture Academy") presented her with a best choice award. She took a "microphone" and made her acceptance speech, which we also taped. She frequently asks to review the tape, which we do together.

96

Joining the Resistance

Sophie L. Lovinger

INTRODUCTION

Many years ago one of my supervisors suggested that the use of a technique, in treatment, is the therapist's problem. As I have thought about this statement I have come to realize that he was talking about gimmicks. I believe that a gimmick ignores the needs of the individual. The techniques I do are tailored to meet the needs of the patients and to address their issues. This chapter presents three ways of joining the resistance exhibited by children in treatment.

RATIONALE

A direct assault on the resistance usually results in the increase and hardening of the resistance. This is especially so with children who can deliberately resist the attempts of the therapist to help. Thus I join it.

426

DESCRIPTION

The following cases demonstrate the technique. Twelve-year-old Kent left a message that his session was being canceled. My secretary said the message had come from the child. Since this was quite unusual for this child, I called his home, reaching his mother. She told me that Kent had informed her that I had called canceling the session. When it became clear I had not done so, she asked what to do. As they lived not too far from my office and there was still session time, I asked his mother to bring him in.

He came in in a huff and seated himself in my chair with arms crossed and an angry look on his face. I knew I could not reach him by confronting him directly so I said, "That was a great trick you played on your mother and myself." He visibly relaxed and began to smile. I then said, "Now you have a problem. You can't try that one any more since your mother and I both know about it." He just continued to smile broadly and then we were able to talk about what was behind his canceling of the session.

I did not confront him about his behavior, in fact I supported and praised him for his ingenuity. Providing him with an unexpected response was helpful in beginning to understand what was underneath the behaviors and to gain a greater understanding of what was motivating the child.

I received a phone call from the parents of 10-year-old George, who had urinated into a paper bag and left the remains in his bedroom closet. When George came to the session I informed him that his parents had called. He was seated on the playroom table with his back against the wall. When I told him about the call, he blanched and flattened his body against the wall. The child was so terrified, I knew that I could not hope to understand the behavior of this seriously disturbed youngster if I did not reduce the affect. I leaned over and said that I had to ask him a question. I said, "How did you prevent it from leaking out of the bag?" The color flooded back into the child's face, once again he looked three dimensional, and he became animated. He told me he had urinated two times and stuffed the bag with lots of tissues to absorb the fluid. I said that his father had told me he had to clean the bathroom for a week.

George wrinkled his nose and nodded. We were then able to discuss what was behind the incident and tease out the child's anger and other ways of expressing it.

Nine-year-old Jenny took twenty-five minutes to inch her way from the waiting room to the playroom, a distance of about 20 feet. Not only behaviorally, but verbally as well, she told me how much she did not want to see me. That evening I received a call from her mother, who was distressed that the child did not want to see me. I arranged for the mother to come in and talk to me about the situation.

When she came to the session she told me that Jenny's father did not support her efforts to obtain help for the child. She felt Jenny was tapping into the conflict between the parents in her refusal. She also mentioned that the behavior she was most concerned about was slowly clearing up as the child's resistance to treatment increased. After much processing with the mother, she was able to accept the recommendation that the child not continue. She was also prepared to tell the child she did not need to come back to see me as long as the changes Jenny had shown continued, but if the old behaviors returned she would be taken back to talk with me. I have not seen her since.

APPLICATION

In each of the vignettes presented above, the needs of each child were responded to in a way that allowed the child to grow and change. I use this approach with most issues of resistance. This approach cuts across all types of problems children present in the treatment setting as well as all types of diagnostic categories. I did not use a particular way of dealing with the problem that had presented itself in treatment, but rather responded to each child in the moment in a way that freed up the child to do further work on just those areas the child was reluctant to deal with initially. I became the ally of the child, which was enabling.

97

Using Magic Therapeutically with Children

Brian D. Gilroy

INTRODUCTION

For many counselors, psychologists, and clinical social workers, a major challenge in working with children and adolescents is achieving rapport and gaining trust. Young children may initially come to counseling in a lot of emotional pain and be fearful of talking or expressing their feelings. Teens often resist counseling and view it as a threat to their independence. Teens pigeonhole counselors as busybodies who will analyze them and reveal their innermost secrets to parents.

To meet these challenges, one of the finest additions to my private practice and school counseling toolbox has been the careful use of high-quality magic tricks. I came to understand why magic has therapeutic value several years ago when assisting as a chaperone for 125 about-to-graduate eighth graders on their overnight class trip to Boston. Hoping only to allay some boredom on the six-hour bus ride, I brought along some magic tricks and brain teasers, and their impact greatly exceeded my expectations. Magic gave me a highly nonthreatening way to interact with greater numbers of children. It provided an easy opportunity to approach shy and withdrawn students and others who didn't normally open up to adults. Often I was able to use magic to redirect misbehaving children and maintain their attention.

RATIONALE

The mystery, excitement, and challenge of magic captivate children. Magic provides a quick and easy way to engage children in their natural language of play. There have been many therapeutic benefits of magic in my work with children.

DESCRIPTION

Rapport Builder

Magic is a highly engaging activity that can get the attention of children quickly. It can help counselors appear more playful and approachable. Magic is a very effective distraction from tension/anxiety.

Strengthening Groups

Magic can be a highly effective tool for breaking the ice in children's support groups. It can also be used to promote positive group norms and cooperation.

Teaching Tool

Magic can be used metaphorically to teach life skills. For example, magic tricks that include "break-out" or "escape" can represent overcoming obstacles and achieving goals.

Diagnostic Aid

Magic can be a useful and commonsense tool for detecting depression in children.

Behavior Management

For interested younger children, magic can work well as positive reinforcement. Children can earn magic tricks for good behavior.

Therapeutic Alliance

When used properly in long-term individual counseling, magic can provide a shared activity, common ground, and something for the child to look forward to.

Social Skills

You can teach children to perform magic and in the process they can learn presentation skills, assertiveness, and confidence. (For details, see *Counseling Kids* in Resources.)

APPLICATION

Using Magic in One-to-One Counseling

Magic can be highly effective in one-to-one counseling with children and teens. It can reduce tension and serve as a rapid rapport builder. For two brothers, ages 6 and 9, our school was their third in eighteen months. These boys and their mother had recently moved out of a battered-women's shelter. When they initially came into my school office, it seemed that the last thing that they wanted to do was talk with another stranger. However, after carefully weaving some well-chosen magic into the session, the boys reported to their mother that they liked their new counselor, enjoyed talking, and wanted to return to see more magic. They even accepted a referral to our cross-age peer-helping program.

Guidelines for Using Magic with Children

- Before doing a trick, always obtain the children's consent. This will prevent them from feeling manipulated or "tricked" into self-disclosure. In my experience, the majority of children/teens will happily agree to see a magic effect. Express it as an invitation: "Want to see a great magic effect?"

- When working with children, who are highly suspicious or guarded, you may want to show them the secret to the trick after you perform it. This can build trust and a sense of sharing.

- Use magic that the children can touch, examine, and try for themselves.

- Use magic that facilitates interaction between you and the child (as opposed to the kind of magic that is performed on a stage). It is ideal when the child feels part of the magic.

- Be cautious about using magic with children who have poor reality testing or psychosis.

Using Magic in Groups

Magic can be an outstanding energizer for your group, classroom, or any activity where children gather regularly. It can facilitate interaction, participation, and learning in delightful ways. Groups are naturally drawn to the fun and skill of magic and generally love the challenge of figuring out the secret to a fine effect. Magic is a great attention getter.

Guidelines

1. To help promote good group behavior, you may announce the possibility of doing some magic toward the end of the session. Emphasize that in order for the magic to take place, the group members must abide by the rules (respect, listening, cooperation, etc.). Much positive peer pressure can result from this.

2. Set parameters prior to doing magic in groups. They can have an overall positive impact.

   a. "When I'm doing a trick, no calling out, no getting out of your chairs, no talking, no disruptions."

b. "If you think you know the secret to the trick, don't tell anyone because it could spoil it for the rest of the group. If you have any questions about how the trick was done, see me privately."

c. "Any serious infractions of the rules could result in a cancellation of the trick." I've repeatedly seen many of my groups have a burning desire to participate in these end-of-session magic tricks and I've rarely had to cancel one.

3. Use magic that requires participation from all of the group members. Magic that generates interaction and teamwork is ideal. Tricks that involve "mentalism" can be particularly entertaining and effective for groups. Some of the very finest effects that I have used are Die-cipher II, D'Lite, and Mental Prediction Board.

Magic and Conflict Mediation

Magic can be a great way to conclude conflict-mediation meetings. The people in conflict walk out with a smile, having already shared a positive experience together.

Magic as a Teaching Tool

Because magic is such a strong "hook" for children, it gets their attention very quickly, creating many of those coveted teachable moments. Thus, it is often a great idea to use it metaphorically to teach and promote social/emotional development and health/wellness in children. For example, the Half and Centavo magic trick, which changes a Mexican coin into an American coin, is a fascinating effect that occurs right in the palm of the child's hand. It provides the opportunity to teach about "the power for change in all of us" and "transforming negatives into positives." When used metaphorically, magic can be an effective segue into classroom or group discussions on a variety of life skills. For an example, see the D'Lite routine described in this article. Magic can easily be used with your existing prevention programs such as "Here's Looking At You

2000," "Quest," and many other life skills curricula (see Resources). Magic can augment these efforts, helping to maximize the learning. It can make a powerful impression, so why not attach a positive message to it, one that is therapeutic or growth oriented.

I am not suggesting that one use metaphor with all magic, but it is most appropriate in many situations, particularly with groups. I recommend not overdoing it. Keep it light, simple, and specific to the needs of the population with whom you are working. An example of magic as metaphor is provided, but there are limitless opportunities to develop your own and be as creative as you want.

Aristotle recognized the value of metaphor long ago and considered it to be the richest form of verbal communication. Shakespeare was a master at it and Milton Erickson, a famous Phoenix psychiatrist, was a genius at using it to deal with client resistance. Here are the major areas in which you can use magic as a metaphor:

Self-confidence

Interpersonal skills

Body image

Problem solving

Alcohol/drug prevention

Appreciating differences

Conflict resolution

Responsibility

Career awareness

Tolerance

Safety/health

School success

Friendship

Coping with loss

Decision making

The following routine using D'Lite is a good example of how magic can be used metaphorically as a teaching tool.

D'Lite

D'Lite is available in most magic stores. The cost is $25 to $35. It requires no skill. An instructional video is also available for $10.

General Effects

Show your hand empty, reach anywhere, and produce a bright red light out of thin air, pass it from hand to hand, vanish it, and make it reappear time and time again. Elegant, glittery, and very magical (ages 5 to adult).

Metaphor

This effect is a metaphor for respect, tolerance, and resolving interpersonal conflict. A special routine with D'Lite can generate enthusiastic class/group discussion on these topics by delightfully illuminating the uselessness of put-downs.

Routine

For this effect you will need two lights, one for each hand. Start off getting audience attention by pulling the light from your pocket, ear, etc. (See instructions that come with the lights.) Present both lights illuminated next to each other, one in each hand. Raise the right hand light and say: "This is your candle." Raise the left hand light and say: "This is my candle." Hold both lights up close together and say: "As you can see, your candle and mine are glowing at the same brightness, don't you agree?" Ask the group to focus attention to the candle on the left (your candle). Blow out the candle on the right hand and say, "I've just blown out your candle and you didn't see my candle glow any brighter, did you?" Light up the right hand candle again. Ask the group to now focus on the right hand candle (theirs). Blow out the candle in the left hand (your candle) and say, "My candle has just been blown out; you didn't see yours glow any brighter either, did you?"

Conclusion

"We don't have to blow out each other's candles to make our own glow more brightly. What does this mean to you? Let's discuss this." Continue group/class lesson on tolerance, respect, and put downs.

Getting Started

What to Look for When Selecting Magic

The following criteria are important when selecting magic for use in counseling with children:

> User-friendly/uncomplicated
>
> Magic that is examinable
>
> Quick preparation/setup
>
> Capacity to astonish
>
> Pocket-sized/portable
>
> Facilitates interaction
>
> Few pieces/parts
>
> Suitable for repeated use
>
> Close-up magic (not stage magic)
>
> Helps children interact as a team
>
> Durable/high quality materials

The Top Ten Best Magic Tricks for Counselors

The following is a list of counselor-tested magic that meets the above criteria. They are available in most magic stores and cost from $5 to $25.

They are categorized by their appropriateness for individual counseling, group counseling, and age range.

Dice Bomb,** for ages 6 to adult.

Magic Coloring Book,** for ages 5 to 9.

Die-cipher II,** for ages 12 to adult.

Shrinking Die,* for ages 6 to 9.

Crystal Cleaver,* for ages 10 to adult.

Mental Prediction Board,** for ages 12 to adult.

Floating Dollar,** for ages 5 to adult.

Puff the Magic Dragon,* for ages 5 to 9.

D'Lite,** for ages 5 to adult.

Vanishing Dollar,** for ages 5 to adult.

*Individual Counseling.

**Group counseling.

Making Your Own Magic

If one has plenty of time and some of patience, and doesn't mind deciphering instructional manuals, the best book is *Mark Wilson's Cyclopedia of Magic* by Mark Wilson, Running Press Book Stores, Philadelphia, PA 1995, ISBN-1-56138-613-8. This comprehensive manual is over 625 pages, is available in bookstores, and is inexpensively priced between $10 and $15.

Instructional Video

If you think you may enjoy using homemade materials to make your own magic (and also economize), a fine way to do it is through videos. Videos are a fast and effective way to learn. They can also be used to teach magic to children. I highly recommend *Beginner's Magic* by Tony Hassini.

This video is also reasonably priced between $10 and $15 and is available in most magic stores.

Resources

For more information on a catalogue of mail order magic tricks for counselors and the book *Counseling Kids: It's Magic, Therapeutic Uses of Magic with Children and Teens*, 1998, by B. D. Gilroy, ISBN 0-9670054-0-X, which includes a social skills program, call/write Therapist Organizer Publishing, 1926 Inverness Drive, Scotch Plains, NJ 07076, 908-233-4290, $29.95.

"Here's Looking At You 2000," Comprehensive Health Ed. Found., 22323 Pacific Highway South, Seattle, WA 98198, 800-321-3007.

Quest International, 537 Jones Road, Granville, OH 43023, 800-446-2700.

98

The Three-Step
Emotional Change Trick

John Sommers-Flanagan and
Rita Sommers-Flanagan

INTRODUCTION

Alfred Adler (1969) described an approach to emotional change that was later referred to as the pushbutton technique (Mosak 1985). It was designed to help adult clients have greater control over their emotional states. Early research indicated that the pushbutton technique was effective in alleviating depressive states among adult clients (Brewer 1976). Following Adler's lead, we have modified the pushbutton technique for child therapy purposes. We refer to the technique as the three-step emotional change trick (TSECT).

RATIONALE

The TSECT can be used directly with children who are experiencing a negative mood, didactically with children who may want greater control over a future mood, or symbolically through traditional play therapy formats, for example, by having the therapist or client teach the technique to a puppet or doll (Sommers-Flanagan and Sommers-Flanagan 1997).

The TSECT provides clients with emotional education and emotional empowerment experiences. The rationale is based on several research and clinical findings: (1) depressed or irritable mood is often the reason a child is referred for therapy (Achenbach 1991a,b); (2) when young clients are moody, they are difficult to engage in treatment (Sommers-Flanagan and Sommers-Flanagan 1995a); and (3) children who come to therapy often lack emotional education and feel emotionally disempowered.

Description

Although the TSECT includes three primary stages, there is also a fourth step. The rationale for adding a fourth step, which often surprises young clients, is to illustrate that when dealing with emotions there are sometimes surprises and to deepen client learning.

Introducing the Emotional Change Trick

Depending upon the child's age, therapists can introduce this strategy as a trick, magic trick, or simply as "a good way to get out of a bad mood when you want to."

Before teaching the four steps, the concept of emotional change is introduced. Whether working with an individual or a group, this can be done by inquiring, "Have you ever been in a bad mood?" Alternatively, when working with a child who is currently irritable, a reflective comment may be adequate: "Hey, I noticed you seem like you're in kind of a bad (lousy, rotten, etc.) mood." In this second circumstance, care must be taken to validate and give the client permission to be in a bad mood (e.g., "It's okay for you to be in a bad mood here"). If the client's bad mood is not validated, he or she may remain in the negative mood for oppositional purposes.

After acknowledging that bad moods are natural, formal emotional education continues: "Bad moods are weird. Even though they don't feel good, lots of times people don't *want* to change out of a bad mood and into a better mood. Do you know what I mean? It's like you don't want anybody forcing you out of a bad mood."

Another way to generate empathy and provide emotional education is to state (with feeling), "Don't you hate it when someone say, 'Cheer up!' or 'Smile!' Man, that makes me want to say, 'Hey, I'm staying in a bad mood just as long as I feel like it!'"

Therapists should acknowledge the client's personal control over his or her mood: "One thing for sure, I'm not gonna try to get you to cheer up . . . no way. But if you want to get in a better mood, I can show you a trick to help you change your mood whenever you want to."

Step 1

The first step is to give young clients permission and skills for feeling and expressing whatever they're feeling: "Sometimes you need to let yourself be in a bad mood. Once you've felt your feelings, you might express them, too. By getting feelings out and expressing them, you are in control. If you don't feel and express your feelings, especially icky ones, you could get stuck in a bad mood."

Brainstorming with clients about specific methods for expressing feelings can be helpful. The client and therapist should work together (perhaps with a chalk/grease board or large drawing pad), identifying expressive strategies, such as (1) scribbling on a note pad; (2) punching a pillow; (3) writing a nasty note (but not delivering it); (4) making angry faces into a mirror; and (5) using words, perhaps even yelling, to express specific feelings.

Therapists should actively model affective expression or assist clients in affective expression. We have had particular success making facial grimaces into a mirror. (Young clients often become entertained when engaging in this task with their therapist.) The optimal time for shifting to step 2 in the TSECT is when clients have shown a slight change in overall demeanor and affect. Often this occurs when the therapist and client join in expressing various emotions.

If a young client is unresponsive to step 1 of the TSECT, do not move to step 2. Instead, consider an alternative mood changing strategy (see Sommers-Flanagan and Sommers-Flanagan 1995b). Reflect what you see: "Seems like you aren't feeling like expressing those yucky feelings right now. Hey, that's okay. I can show you this trick some other day."

Step 2

This step involves helping clients select and focus on a pleasant memory, a humorous event, or emotionally distracting thought. The following statements and questions are used to help clients shift from negative thoughts to positive thoughts: "Did you know you can change your mood just by thinking different thoughts?" "Thinking new thoughts is like pushing a button in your brain. It can change your emotional channel." "Tell me the funniest thing that happened to you this week."

What young people consider funny may not seem particularly funny to adult therapists. For example, one girl said that she liked to change her mood by having her cat sit on her head while she watched her pregnant gerbil. This difference in humor is a cultural-developmental difference between children and adults that must be overcome by the therapist.

Young clients may be unable to generate a funny story or a funny memory. This may be an indicator of depression (Forgas 1991). Although it may be necessary for the therapist to tell a joke or humorous story, the goal is to have the client generate a funny story. If he or she cannot, you can stop teaching and say, "There are some days when I can't think of any funny stories either. I'm sure you'll be able to tell me something funny next time. Today I was able to think of some funny stuff. Next time we can both give it a try again."

Step 3

This step involves teaching young clients about the contagion quality of mood states and reinforces the new good mood achieved by step 2. Teaching clients about contagious moods provides further emotional education and emotional empowerment opportunities: "Moods are contagious. Do you know what contagious means? It means that you can catch them from being around other people who are in bad moods or good moods. Like when you got here. I noticed your dad was in a pretty bad mood, too. It made me wonder, did you catch the bad mood from him or did he catch it from you? Anyway, now you seem to be in a much better mood. And so I was wondering, do you think you can make you dad catch your good mood?"

Young clients may need assistance in coming up with how to spread the good mood, because spreading a good mood to someone else requires a certain amount of empathic perspective-taking. Depending on your client's age and temperament, it is sometimes helpful to introduce the idea of changing other people's moods as a challenge (Erikson 1968). "I bet you don't have this idea down well enough to actually change your mom's mood." When working with highly oppositional youth, we use this type of challenge statement fairly often (e.g., "You're probably just stuck in a bad mood for today. I have this emotional change trick that I could teach you, but I don't know if you'd be the kind of person who'd want to know how to do that.")

Step 4

When using the TSECT procedure, we have found it useful to request that clients teach this procedure to another person after they have learned it in therapy.

APPLICATION

As Mosak (1985) stated: "The pushbutton technique, like other techniques, is selectively effective. It . . . adds to the repertoire of the clinician" (p. 213).

The TSECT is especially useful in three circumstances. First, it can be an essential teaching/learning strategy when working with children who are regularly troubled by depressive, angry, or anxious emotional states. Second, it can be helpful in cases where children are stuck in a particular emotional state during a therapy session. Third, it can be used as a playful technique for teaching emotional education to small or large groups of children.

References

Achenbach, T. M. (1991a). *Manual for the Child Behavior Checklist and 1991 Profile.* Burlington: University of Vermont, Department of Psychiatry.

————. (1991b). *Manual for the Youth Self-Report and 1991 Profile*. Burlington: University of Vermont, Department of Psychiatry.

Adler, A. (1969). *The Practice and Theory of Individual Psychology*. Paterson, NJ: Littlefield.

Brewer, D. H. (1976). *The induction and alteration of state depression*. Unpublished doctoral dissertation, University of Houston.

Erikson, E. (1968). *Identity: Youth and Crisis*. New York: Norton.

Forgas, J. P. (1991). Affect and social perception: research evidence and an integrative theory. In *European Review of Social Psychology*, ed. W. Stroebe and M. Newstone, pp. 183–223. New York: Wiley.

Mosak, H. H. (1985). Interrupting a depression: the pushbutton technique. *Individual Psychology* 41:210–214.

Sommers-Flanagan, J. and Sommers-Flanagan, R. (1995a). Psychotherapeutic techniques with treatment-resistant adolescents. *Psychotherapy* 32:131–140.

————. (1995b). Rapid emotional change strategies with difficult youth. *Child and Family Behavior Therapy* 17:11–22.

————. (1997). *Tough Kids, Cool Counseling: User-Friendly Approaches with Challenging Youth*. Alexandria, VA: American Counseling Association.

99

The Child's Creation: Guided Imagery Combined with Music Tapes

Janet Logan Schieffer

INTRODUCTION

Play therapists know the importance of actively involving a child in the change process. The more engaged the child is in the change process, the greater the likelihood for positive outcome. When the child has an opportunity to establish her own goal in play therapy and use her innate creativity, a ripple effect may occur. For example, imagine a child given the diagnosis of attention-deficit/hyperactivity disorder (ADHD) who wants to, and has the opportunity to, record her own guided imagery combined with music (GICM) tape with assistance from the play therapist. The child becomes calmer, more peaceful. The consequent outcomes for the child may include improved peer relationships, greater completion of tasks at school and home, and a sense of agency as someone who *can*. Thus, utilizing the child's imaginative powers combined with her particular interests may enhance positive therapeutic outcomes for a child. The child's imaginative powers are expressed through metaphor or symbols.

These symbols serve as a child's metaphor for change. One of the most productive ways to use children's metaphors is for the play therapist to communicate through them instead of directly interpreting them. The GICM script serves as a metaphor. When the child relaxes, she is in a suggestible state. Listening to a tape is an ideal time for the child to remind herself of important coping strategies and new attitudes that she is striving to remember. The secret of success in creating and listening to a GICM script for the child is to enter deeply into her own emotional life with all its rich symbols, thus becoming an active change agent within her own metaphoric story.

RATIONALE

There are many advantages to the play therapist assisting a child in recording a GICM tape: (1) the script is individualized based on what the play therapist knows about the child, the child's presenting issue, the child's interest, and play; (2) The child's assistance with the recording deepens the learning experience; (3) the child learns to speak clearly, slowly, and soothingly, thus learning to calm and soothe the self; (4) the child learns how to communicate to herself trust, comfort, and relaxation as her words come out at a measured, even pace; (5) the child can be creative, developing her own unique approach and creating special relaxation or coping scripts, or visualizing images that the child finds uniquely peaceful or calming; (6) the child may use any accompanying music or sound effects that she wishes or leave the background entirely quiet; (7) the child can hear her own voice, which may be uniquely peaceful and calming; (8) the child may listen to the tape at various times throughout the day to remind herself of coping strategies, important affirmations, and new attitudes that she is striving to remember; (9) other family members may participate in listening and making the tape as appropriate; and (10) the process of making a GICM tape is easy.

DESCRIPTION

The therapist needs two tape recorders. If the therapist wishes for the child to have the option of including music in her GICM tape, the therapist will need to have an assortment of relaxing percussion instruments, such as wind chimes, rain sticks, and bells (Oaklander 1990) and/ or suggested tape recordings that aid the effectiveness of the GICM script (Allen and Klein 1996, Bonny and Savary 1990, Campbell 1997, Early 1990). Music, such as Baroque or New Age, has been found to be effective in enhancing relaxation and learning, reducing heart rate, and aiding the effectiveness of the GICM script (Bonny and Savary 1990, Campbell 1997).

Steps for making a GICM tape are as follows: (1) The therapist asks the child if she is interested in making her own GICM tape to use when the child is outside the playroom. The therapist explains the goal and usefulness of GICM to the child: "GICM helps kids to learn how to feel happy, calm, and relaxed with having some fun." (2) The therapist explains to the child that the GICM tape will have three parts that they will make together: (a) a short relaxation piece; (b) a story, journey, or fantasy piece; and (c) a return to "this place" piece. (3) The child and the therapist make up a story together that is related to the child's presenting issue, or the therapist creates a story based on metaphors the child has presented during play therapy, or the child and therapist use a story from a previous session. Another option is for the therapist and child to select a script that has already been written (Davis et al. 1988, Oaklander 1988, Ziegler and Ziegler 1992). (4) The therapist assists the child in working on her voice, so it is at normal volume, but in a flat, almost monotonous tone. The therapist encourages the child to take time to actually imagine that she is taking a deep, happy breath and seeing the story in her mind. (5) If the child wishes to include music in the GICM tape, the child selects percussion instruments, such as wind chimes or rain sticks, or already recorded musical selections. (6) The child records the GICM piece. (7) The child and therapist listen to it together. (8) The child thinks about where and when it may be useful for her to listen to the tape outside of the session. The completed GICM tape should be approximately 5 to 10 minutes in length.

A variation in this play therapy technique is for the child to make a homemade book with the child's own drawings to accompany the GICM script. Sometimes it is useful for the child to make the book before making the GICM tape recording. As the child experiments by including or omitting different parts, she will discover what procedures work best for her. The only rule to follow is: Do what works.

APPLICATION

Since over 250 therapies make use of relaxation and imagery, the research base on the therapeutic benefits of relaxation and imagery interventions is substantial (Sheik and Jordan 1983). Most children who are interested in learning how to calm themselves can benefit from creating their own GICM tapes. The author has used this technique with children who have been diagnosed with cancer, learning disabilities, conduct disorders, and anger management, as well as children who have siblings or parents diagnosed with chronic mental illness. GICM is not recommended for children who have been diagnosed as having difficulty separating fantasy from reality.

The following illustration shows how GICM can create positive therapeutic outcome for a child and single parent with whom the author worked.

The 8-year-old child had a diagnosis of attention-deficit/hyperactivity disorder (ADHD). During the history intake, the child indicated interested in dolphins, stress-reducing techniques, and computers. Needless to say, stress-reducing techniques were also of interest to the mother. She was seeking a method of positive interaction for her son and herself. At their request, I wrote and recorded a relaxation script with dolphin music in the background for the two of them to listen to together. This strategy proved quite successful for each of them individually and their relationship. They went on to record their own scripts using their voices and had fun doing it together. The son would take the audiotape to school and listen to it as needed. His teacher reported improved behavior.

Sample GICM Script Used in Case Illustration

Music Selection (by Child)

Various artists. (1998). Celebration of the Hawaiian Spinner Dolphin (CD). Magical Sound Studio: Hawaii.

Relaxation Script (Read by the Child)

I would like for you to get as comfortable as you can, [child's name]. Close your eyes and take three long, deep happy breaths (pause). A happy breath is a big breath that helps you relax . . . and feel calm. . . . Let the music calm you. . . . Feel your muscles relax and your heart relax and breathe slowly and deeply. Say to yourself, "I am calm and relaxed." [Child's name], you are going to take a make-believe trip. See if you can follow along. Imagine what I tell you, and see how you feel while you are doing it.

Imagery Script (Written by the Child with Assistance from the Therapist)

In your imagination, let yourself become a dolphin. Feel the great size of you gliding effortlessly through the ocean. Feel very large and at the same time very light, held up by the water. See yourself breaking through the surface of the water and then diving deep. You are having fun, swimming with your other dolphin friends. See yourself, [child's name], moving effortlessly through the ocean. As you break through the surface of the water, you look up at the sky and see the clouds quietly floating by you. The clouds change shapes. See what shapes are hidden in the clouds (allow time). Notice that one of the clouds is dark, and it is a special cloud. You can put things that you get angry about in that cloud. Put what you get angry about in that cloud. Now breathe deeply, imagining yourself blowing away the cloud that has the things you get angry about. See the dark, angry cloud disappearing or maybe changing into a happy shape . . . whatever you want . . . because what you put in that cloud you no longer need to feel angry about. Wave good-bye to the cloud. You feel good inside. You feel peaceful and calm. Now make a big dive to the bottom of the ocean. . . . There you find a treasure chest with your name on it. . . . You use your powerful nose to open it. Inside the treasure chest is a secret message just for you. You open the secret message. It tells you everything you feel happy about and tells you that you are well loved. You say good-bye to the treasure chest, taking with you the things that you feel happy about. The treasure chest tells you to come back soon. Now because you are a dolphin, imagine that you are with your other dolphin friends. . . . See yourself having fun with your other dolphin friends. . . . What are you doing together? What heroic adventure have you been on? What good deeds have you accomplished?

Coming Out of the Fantasy

And now just relax for a while. Breathe quietly and dream of yourself floating on the ocean. Feel the sun warming you. Drift with the breeze. Feel totally relaxed from you day's adventure as a dolphin. You feel refreshed, calm, and peaceful. Now take a deep breath and return to this room. Open your eyes and stretch. (If the child is in the playroom, the child may draw about his experience, and he may tell the therapist about the drawing.)

References

Allen, J., and Klein, R. (1996). *Ready, Set, Relax: A Research Based Program of Relaxation, Learning, and Self-Esteem for Children*. Watertown, WI: Inner Coaching.

Bonny, H., and Savary, L. (1990). *Music and Your Mind*. Barrytown, NY: Station Hill.

Campbell, D. (1997). *The Mozart Effect: Tapping the Power of Music to Heal the Body, Strengthen the Mind, and Unlock the Creative Spirit*. New York: Avon.

Davis, M., Robbins Eshelman, E., and McKay, M. (1988). *The Relaxation and Stress Reduction Workbook*, 3rd ed. Oakland, CA: New Harbinger.

Early, J. (1990). *Inner Journeys*. York Beach, MI: Samuel Weiser.

Oaklander, V. (1988). *Windows to Our Children: A Gestalt Therapy Approach to Children and Adolescents*. Highland, NY: Gestalt Journal Press.

———. (1990). Music as therapy (audiotape). Seattle, WA: Max Sound.

Sheik, A., and Jordan, C. (1983). Clinical uses of mental imagery. In *Imagery: Current Theory, Research, and Application*, ed. A. Sheik, pp. 391–435. New York: Wiley.

Ziegler, R., and Ziegler, P. (1992). *Homemade Books to Help Kids Cope: An Easy to Learn Technique for Parents and Professionals*. New York: Magination.

100

The Power Animal Technique: Internalizing a Positive Symbol of Strength

Deborah Armstrong Hickey

INTRODUCTION

Children who are referred to play therapy are often under the influences of low self-esteem, ineffective problem-solving skill, and difficulties in their relationships with peers and adults. These children may also have difficulty controlling and influencing their impulses, and may resort to aggression to get their feelings expressed and their needs met (albeit unsuccessfully). Additionally, children generally do not have the self-knowledge or affective skills necessary to cope with these challenges in ways that make them feel more confident and positive about themselves and others.

Techniques that increase children's positive sense of self and increase their coping skills in challenging situations can be powerful catalysts for change. Still, any technique that is grounded in the world of language can work against their best interests developmentally and therapeutically.

Children find it difficult to articulate the strengths they would like to have or what kinds of attributes might serve them better in challenging situations. However, children can usually identify the animals that exhibit and have the kind of power they would like to have. I often invite

451

children to choose an animal (or occasionally two animals) that they emulate or would like to be like in some way.

This technique is based on Native American practices that invite individuals to call upon a nature totem in service of integrating a specific type of energy or attribute that they may want to manifest in their waking life. A totem is any natural object, being, or animal whose phenomena and energy an individual might exhibit or desire over the course of a lifetime (Andrews 1997). Each animal carries in it certain ways of being that can be viewed as strength and can be used by adults and children alike to deal more effectively with life situations.

RATIONALE

Communication for children is best accomplished through the language of play, symbol, and imagination. Children will generally be very reticent to talk about the strengths they would like to have or their intense yearnings for feeling more confident and successful. Still they almost always hold a natural interest and fascination with animals who hold these attributes. This can be used to a great advantage in play therapy.

Playing with these symbols can facilitate their internalization of the strengths they project onto these animals. When children play with the animals, they imaginatively move from one solution to another when problems surface, allowing development and creativity to open space for the most satisfying solutions, and comfort in expressing their deepest feelings, fears, and hopes.

DESCRIPTION

The therapist can begin by reading or telling a story about how the Native Americans often require that children go off into the wilderness and dream a dream of an animal who will bring the strengths of that particular animal to them as they grow and develop. However, this preparation may not be necessary, and simply bringing out a box of pictures of animals is usually enough of an invitation for children to pick an animal that is of interest to them. The pictures should not have words on them and there should be a wide variety of animals of all species.

The therapist can invite the children to make this animal in clay or plasticene or to construct a mask with the animal face on it. Then, depending on what the children do or need to do, the therapist can follow their lead. Eventually the therapist may want to invite the children to imagine what the animal might do if such and such happened and how they might solve a problem. Consulting regularly with the power animal in play therapy sessions can move the child deeper into an internalization of the strengths and attributes of the animal.

I would recommend that the therapist invest in at least one or two books about Native American beliefs about animal attributes (e.g., Andrews 1997, Casler and Begay 1994, Sams and Carson 1988). These references can be used if children are inclined toward having an animal resort to aggression perseveratively to solve problems. It can also be very helpful for the therapist (with the children's permission or invitation) to take on the voice of the animal in play, offering advice to the children as they play.

I suggest that the animal symbol (picture/clay or plasticene figure) remain in the therapy office for the children's personal play each time they return. However, parents can be counseled about securing a small plastic animal figure for the children to have at home and/or to carry with them if desired.

APPLICATION

The power animal technique can be used with any child who might benefit from a positive introject. It can be used with any age group of children, ranging from very young children to teenagers.

It can be particularly helpful when working with children who have the following symptoms:

Poor impulse control

Depression

Low self-esteem

Peer and sibling conflict

Separation anxiety

Anxiety and fear

Social phobia or shyness

Learning difficulties

ADD/ADHD.

References

Andrews, T. (1997). *Animal Speak: The Spiritual and Magical Powers of Creatures Great and Small*. St. Paul, MN: Llewellyn.

Casler, L., and Begay, S. (1994). *The Boy Who Dreamed of an Acorn*. New York: Philomel.

Sams, J., and Carson, D. (1988). *Medicine Cards: The Discovery of Power through the Ways of Animals*. Santa Fe, NM: Bear.

101

Shazam

Donna Cangelosi

INTRODUCTION

Shazam is an imaginary, transitional object created by the child, which serves to remind him about lessons learned in therapy. The technique was developed for children with impulse control difficulties to assist them with the concept of thinking before acting, thus reducing their behavioral problems and leaving them with a sense of personal control and empowerment.

RATIONALE

Impulsive children often have difficulty holding onto information they may know and even understand cognitively because they tend to act prior to thinking through their options. "Shazam" (a title coined by one of my young patients who successfully used this technique) is a fun, imaginative activity that provides the child with a personal "messenger" who reminds him to think about options before acting. With practice and reinforcement during play sessions, this technique helps young children to internalize, not only the messenger Shazam (who is actually a symbolic representative of the therapist) but the messages Shazam has to offer.

DESCRIPTION

Materials

This technique is best used with a wide assortment of art supplies. These might include various colors of construction paper, colored pencils, crayons, markers, buttons, glue sticks, fabric pieces, yarn, and some form of soft clay.

Process

The child is given a variety of art supplies and asked to create a "messenger" friend, small enough to fit on his shoulder, which will help him to solve problems. The therapist explains that the friend is just for the child and can therefore be whatever the child likes: a fun creature; an animal; cartoon character; alien; guardian angel; miniature parent, teacher, or therapist. While the child works on creating the figure (over one or two sessions) the therapist can discuss with him what problems the friend will help with. The child is given the option of naming the creature or calling it Shazam, after a magic wizard.

When the child is done creating his messenger, the therapist asks the child to close his eyes and imagine the creature. The therapist then explains that Shazam will now become invisible to everyone but the child and therapist, but will nonetheless remain with the child at all times. It is explained that Shazam will remind the child about options for dealing with the problem at hand (e.g., not calling out in class, not hitting, not name calling, etc.).

The child can decide to take Shazam home or to leave it with the therapist. If the child chooses to take it, the ideal situation is to have a Polaroid picture of Shazam in the playroom so that it can be referred to in subsequent sessions. During subsequent sessions, the therapist inquires if Shazam is doing a good job of helping the child with his problems. Problems can be reviewed and revised as necessary from session to session.

APPLICATION

This is a fun, imaginative activity that is especially well suited for elementary-school children who need assistance in stopping to think before reacting. I have used this technique successfully with children with difficulties related to impulse control, conduct disorders, attention-deficit/hyperactivity disorder (ADHD), as well as with children with low self-esteem. The latter population has benefited from thinking about their positive attributes before acting (e.g., thinking through a response before reacting to being ostracized by peers).

When given the opportunity to create their own imaginary messenger, children tend to become more enthusiastic and open to hearing reminders about changing behaviors and thought patterns. Through the process of internalization, they eventually learn to incorporate new behaviors into their everyday lives, and achieve a sense of accomplishment and personal control.

ABOUT THE EDITORS

Heidi Gerard Kaduson, Ph.D., RPT-S, specializes in evaluation and intervention services for children with a variety of behavioral, emotional, and learning problems. She is Past President of the Association for Play Therapy and Co-Director of the Play Therapy Training Institute. She has lectured internationally on play therapy, attention deficit/hyperactivity disorder, and learning disabilities. Dr. Kaduson co-edited *The Quotable Play Therapist*, *The Playing Cure*, and *Short-Term Play Therapy*, as well as *101 Favorite Play Therapy Techniques*. She maintains a private practice in child psychotherapy in Monroe Township, New Jersey.

Charles E. Schaefer, Ph.D., RPT-S, a nationally renowned child psychologist, is Professor of Psychology at Fairleigh Dickinson University and Director of its Center for Psychological Services in Hackensack, New Jersey. He is co-founder and Director Emeritus of the Association for Play Therapy. He has authored or edited more than forty books on parenting, child psychology, and play therapy, including *The Therapeutic Use of Child's Play*, *The Therapeutic Powers of Play*, *Family Play Therapy*, and *101 Favorite Play Therapy Techniques*. Dr. Schaefer maintains a private practice in child psychotherapy in Hackensack.